Pan Africanism

To: D.R
& Tuckey and family from Joseph Oladosu a gift of love and appreciation October 1998.

Pan Africanism

**Politics, Economy and Social Change
in the Twenty-First Century**

Edited by
Tajudeen Abdul-Raheem

Pluto Press

First published 1996 by Pluto Press
345 Archway Road, London N6 5AA

Copyright © Tajudeen Abdul-Raheem 1996

The right of the individual contributors to be identified as the authors of this work has been asserted by them in accordance with the Copyright, Designs and Patents Act 1988 (UK).

British Library Cataloguing in Publication Data
A catalogue record for this book is available from the British Library

ISBN 0 7453 1148 2 hbk

Designed and produced for Pluto Press by
Chase Production Services, Chipping Norton, OX7 5QR
Typeset from disk by Stanford DTP Services, Milton Keynes
Printed in the EC by J.W. Arrowsmith, Bristol

Dedication

This book is dedicated to the memory of four people who worked tirelessly for the 7th Pan African Congress but sadly died before or after the Congress; Victor Sebelo-Phama, former Commander of PAC of Azania's African People's Liberation Army (APLA) a 'historical' member of the original International Preparatory Committee (IPC) of the Congress, was killed in a mysterious road accident along Dar-es-Salaam–Morogoro Road in Tanzania before the Congress; Lt. Col. Serwanga Lwanga and Major Ondoga ori Amaza, respectively Publicity Secretary and Deputy Publicity Secretary at the 7th Pan African Congress Secretariat, died after the Congress; and Warren Bantariza, a dedicated young Pan Africanist at the Documentation Unit of the Pan African Movement lost his life in November 1994 to mindless killers – a grim reminder that our society needs to be reborn.

Contents

Acknowledgements — viii
List of Acronyms — x
Notes on Contributors — xiii
Introduction: Reclaiming Africa for Africans — 1

Part I
The Politics and Economics of African Unity

1. Conditions of Africans at Home
   Chango Machyo w'Obanda — 33

2. The African Woman on the Continent:
   Her Present State, Prospects and Strategy
   Victoria Sekitoleko — 67

Part II
Africa and the World

3. The New World Disorder – Which Way Africa?
   A.M. Babu — 89

4. Global Africa: From Abolitionists to Reparationists
   Ali A. Mazrui — 123

Part III
Continental and Regional Unity

5. Creating an African Common Market
   Sam Tulya-Muhika — 145

6. Improving Access to Natural Resource Potentials
   and Regional Cooperation in Southern Africa
   Sam Moyo — 167

7. Towards a New Political Map of Africa
   Arthur S. Gakwandi — 181

Part IV
Facing the Future

8   Science and Technology as a Solution to Africa's Underdevelopment
    Yoweri K. Museveni — 193

9   Pan Africanism, Democracy, Social Movements and Mass Struggles
    Ernest Wamba-dia-Wamba — 198

10 Pan Africanism in the Twenty-First Century
    Horace Campbell — 212

11 The OAU and the Future
    Salim A. Salim — 229

12 Building a Pan African Women's Movement
    Fatima B. Mahmoud — 237

List of Tables

2.1 Schools by Level: Selected Years (up to 1987) — 73
2.2 Total Education Enrolment by Level, 1987 — 74
2.3 Gross Primary School Enrolment by Region, 1980 — 74
2.4 Progress of Female Enrolment in Secondary Schools, Uganda, 1976–1983 — 75
2.5 Household Population by Industry and Sex (urban) — 78
2.6 Household Population by Occupation and Sex (urban) — 78
2.7 Some Indicators of Health Situation, Uganda — 79

Map

7.1 Proposed New Political Map of Africa — 188

Acknowledgements

Who should I name? Can I even remember everybody? It is not possible because too many people were involved in bringing this first volume of the proceedings of the 7th Pan African Congress to fruition.

However I wish to place on record my deep gratitude to the secretarial staff of the Pan African Movement who have been involved in the preparation of this book: Vivian Ndumu, Betty Tomusange, Bernadette Kakooza, Carolyn Muruiki, Jane Mbabazi, Ruth Babirye, Grace Akello, the late Warren Bantariza, John Musinguzi, Alex Bigombe, Kyadze Hannington, Odrek Rwabwoogo and other members of the staff who all provided technical and administrative support for the book.

My thanks also go to my executive colleagues for their constant camaraderie and support: Lt Noble Mayombo, Chief of Staff, and Imoro Alhassan Abdulai, ex officio member of the secretariat, for his Napoleonic pressures and encouragement without which this book will have remained 'a project'. Our Chairman, Colonel Kahinda Otafiire, must be thanked for everything he has done and continues to do to ensure that we rebuild the Pan African Movement. Kampala was just one end of the sacrifices, support and encouragement for the book, my colleagues at the Africa Research and Information Bureau (ARIB) in London helped to provide a secretarial and administrative base whenever I was in the UK that facilitated my work. In particular Ama Biney (PPPC!) was indeed a sister in deed, always obliging with my numerous last-minute 'urgent tasks'; Felicity Ayisi for 'typing these few pages' that always end up being a whole chapter (!) and Zaya Yeebo.

I would also like to thank our co-publishers, Pluto Press, for risking to take on this highly elusive editor, chasing him across the globe with faxes, telephones, and email for clarifications and editorial queries. In particular I thank Roger van Zwanenburg, Pluto Press's Managing Director for refusing to be defeated by my elusiveness since he first saw the outline of this book.

My greatest thanks is to all the contributors to the book, sons and daughters of Africa, for honouring the Congress with their presentation – all prepared in advance without the usual conference inducements of per diem, advance fees, etc. They acted in the true spirit of Pan Africanism: service to the people and the duty to share knowledge to empower our people. Dr Makini-Roy Campbell was most helpful in allowing me to hijack Dr Fatima Mahmoud's presentation which she had edited for use in a different publication. Horace Campbell, Thomas Deve, Dr Koso Mandaza and the Pan African family in Harare have all been most supportive in selfless sacrifice for all our post-Congress work including this book. So has been Comrade Karrim Essack in Tanzania and his network of 'horses'.

My partner, Mounira Chaieb, has been a tower of strength, understanding and unalloyed encouragement since that Sunday morning in the summer of 1992 when brother Bankie Foster Bankie and Mzee Babu called me from Entebbe, Uganda, informing me of their suggestion to the International Preparatory Committee (IPC) that I be appointed Secretary-General for the 7th Pan African Congress. Effectively Mounira became a widow to Pan Africanism that day but continues to provide me with the space and support to do my duty in spite of the objective and subjective pressures on our family life.

Finally, I neither wish nor could I claim or disclaim a collection of papers written by twelve different people. However, putting them together has been a personal honour for me. They are not meant to be definitive statements on Pan Africanism but an attempt to light some candles in our march for true Liberation and Unity.

Tajudeen Abdul-Raheem
Kampala, Uganda
1 May 1996

List of Acronyms

AAPC	All African Peoples' Conference
AAPRP	All African People's Revolutionary Party
ACBF	African Capability Building Foundation
ADB	African Development Bank
ADF	African Development Fund
AEC	African Economic Community
AFRAND	African Foundation for Research and Development
ANC	African National Congress
ARC	aid retention coefficient
ARIC	African Regional Integration Commission
BACAS	Bank of Central African States
CBC	Congressional Black Caucus
CD & W	Colonial Development & Welfare Acts
CEAO	*La Communate Economique de l'Afrique de l'Ouest*
CPP	Convention People's Party
CODESRIA	Council for Social Science Research in Africa
COMECON	Council for Mutual Economic Aid, or Assistance (Communist Nations)
COMESA	Common Market of East and Southern Africa
DESSA	Distressed and Expatriate Scientists and Scholars from Africa
EAC	East African Community
EADB	East Africa Development Bank
ECCAS	Economic Community of Central African States
ECGLC	Economic Community of Great Lakes Countries
ECOWAS	Economic Community of West African States
EEC	European Economic Community
ERP	economic recovery programme
EZLN	*Ejercito Zapatista de Liberation Nacional*
forex	foreign currency earnings from exports
GATT	General Agreement on Tariffs and Trade
GDP	gross domestic product
GNP	gross national product

IBRD	International Bank for Reconstruction and Development (World Bank)
IPC	International Preparatory Committee
IMF	International Monetary Fund
LIMA	League of the Independent Women of Angola
MNC	multinational corporations
MRU	The Mano River Union
NAFTA	North American Free Trade Agreement
NATO	North Atlantic Treaty Organization
NGO	non-governmental organization
NIC	newly industrializing country
NKG	New Kenya Group
NRA	National Resistance Army
NRM	National Resistance Movement
OAU	Organization of African Unity
ODA	official development assistance
OECD	Organization for Economic Co-operation and Development
PAC	Pan African Congress
PAEC	Pan African Economic Community
PAFO	Pan African Forum
PAM	Pan African Movement
PAWLO	Pan African Women's Liberation Organization
PTA	preferential trade area
SACU	Southern African Customs Union
SADC	Southern African Development Coordination
SADCC	Southern Africa Development Cooperation Council
SAP	structural adjustment programme
SAPEM	Southern Africa Political Economy Monthly
SATCC	Southern African Transport and Communication Coordination
SPLA/M	Sudan People's Liberation Army/Movement
TANU	Tanzania African National Union
TNC	transnational corporation
UDEAC	*Union Dovaniere et Economique de l'Afrique Central*
UNC	Uganda National Congress
UNECA	United Nations Economic Commission for Africa
UNESCO	United Nations Educational, Scientific and Cultural Organization
UNICEF	United Nations Children's Fund

UNITA	*Uniao Nacional por Independência Total de Angola*, National Union for the Total Liberation of Angola
USAID	United States Agency for International Development
WAEC	West African Economic Community
WADB	West African Development Bank
WASU	West African Students Union
WHO	World Health Organization
WID	Women in Development
WPA	Working Peoples Alliance

Notes on Contributors

A.M. Babu A Leading Pan Africanist scholar and activist. He was one of the leaders of the Umma Party, in Zanzibar, that led the revolution in that country heralding the union of Zanzibar and Tanganyika to form the United Republic of Tanzania. He held many cabinet posts under the Nyerere government including Trade and Economic Planning before he was detained without trial in 1972. Since his release in 1978, he has lived in England where he is a freelance development journalist and lectures both in Europe and America. He is the author of *African Socialism or Socialist Africa* (Zed Books, London, 1981).

Horace Campbell Professor of Pan African Studies at Syracuse University, New York, USA. He is currently Head of the Syracuse Africa Programme in Harare, Zimbabwe. He has published widely on Pan African topics (including his book on *Rasta and Resistance*) and taught at a number of African universities including Makerere and Dar-es-Salaam.

Arthur Gakwandi Has been a senior lecturer in African literature in universities in Africa, including Bayero University, Kano, Nigeria and Reader at the Department of English Language and Literature at Makerere University, Kampala, Uganda, before his current appointment as Deputy Ambassador of Uganda to Ethiopia with responsibility for the OAU.

Chango Machyo w'Obanda A veteran Pan Africanist who studied at the London School of Economics and was very active in the African Students Union and University of London Students Union (ULU). He is now a Deputy National Political Commissar at the National Resistance Movement Secretariat in Kampala and an elected Constituent Assembly Delegate for Bugweri South.

Fatima B. Mahmoud A well-known Sudanese scholar, political activist and feminist. She published the seminal work *The Sudanese*

Bourgeoisie and was a senior lecturer in political science at the University of Khartoum before she was forced into exile in London in the late 1980s. She teaches development studies and offers consultancy services to many international agencies for development. At the Pre-Congress Meeting of African Women during the 7th PAC in April 1994, she was elected the first chairperson of the Pan African Women's Liberation Organization (PAWLO).

Ali A. Mazrui A well-known academic who has taught and continues to teach in universities in America and Africa. He is currently Director, Institute of Global Cultural Studies; Albert Schweitzer Professor in the Humanities, State University of New York at Binghamton, New York, USA; Albert Luthuli Professor-at-large, University of Jos, Jos, Nigeria; and Senior Scholar and Andrew D. White Professor-at-large Emeritus, Cornell University, Ithaca, New York, USA. He is also a member of the Organisation of African Unity (OAU) Eminent Persons Group on Reparations.

Sam Moyo Has published widely on the environment and technology in Zimbabwe and Southern Africa in general. He was Director of the Institute for Development Studies, University of Zimbabwe, Harare and is now a founding professor at the Southern African Institute for Policy Studies in Harare.

Yoweri Kaguta Museveni The President of the Republic of Uganda since the National Resistance Movement (NRM) and its allied army, National Resistance Army (NRA) captured power in 1986, after a five-year armed struggle against the Obote II regime (1980–1985) and the military rule of Generals Bazilio Tito Okello and Lutwa Okello (1985–1986). Museveni studied at the University of Dar-es-Salaam in the late 1960s and was in exile in Tanzania throughout the 1970s where he became involved with African liberation movements, in particular FRELIMO in Mozambique and different exiled military/political groups who were planning to overthrow the brutal dictatorship of Idi Amin (1972–79). After several failed military incursions the Ugandan opposition's efforts were boosted in a combined counter-attack with Tanzanian troops on Amin's force in 1979. After Idi Amin was defeated a transitional government was set up by the Uganda National Liberation Front in which Museveni was both Minister for Defence and Deputy Chairman of the Military Commission. The Military Commission organized an election in which former President Milton Obote's party, UPC, was able to manipulate its way back to power. Subsequently Museveni and his group went to the bush in 1981 under the banner of NRA/M which came to power in 1986.

Salim A. Salim   Current Secretary-General of the OAU. Before that he has been Ambassador to India/Cairo, Foreign Minister and Permanent Representative of the Republic of Tanzania at the UN. But for the Cold War rivalry between the West/USA and the Soviet Union, Salim could have been the first African Secretary-General of the UN in the early 1980s, but his nomination was vetoed several times by the USA.

Victoria Sekitoleko   Formerly Minister for Agriculture, Animal Industry and Fisheries in Uganda and now UN Food Programme Regional Representative in Harare, Zimbabwe.

Tajudeen Abdul-Raheem   Was Secretary-General for the Secretariat for the 7th PAC and now heads the permanent Secretariat for the Pan African Movement in Kampala.

Sam Tulya-Muhika   Professor of Statistics and Applied Economics at Makerere University, Kampala, Uganda. Formerly, Director of the Institute of Statistics and Applied Economics (Regional Project), Makerere University (1972–89), Kampala. He is currently Chairman on a number of Boards: East African Cooperation Forum; Uganda Revenue Authority; Federation of Ugandan Consultants (FUCO); and Chairman and Development Consultant of International Development Consultants (a PTA-Wide Consultancy Forum).

Ernest Wamba-dia-Wamba   One of the very few Zairois scholars known in the English language. He is Professor of African History at the University of Dar-es-Salaam. He has published widely in the areas of mass struggles, popular democracy and social transformation. He is currently President of the Pan African Research Network of Academics, CODESTRIA, based in Dakar, Senegal.

Introduction: Reclaiming Africa for Africans – Pan Africanism: 1900–1994

Tajudeen Abdul-Raheem

The 7th Pan African Congress (7th PAC), held in Kampala, Uganda, from 3–8 April 1994 was organized to keep alive a tradition that has been around for about a century. The word 'Pan Africanism' first entered the political lexicon in 1900, when the Trinidadian barrister, Henry Sylvester Williams, then based in London called a conference of black people to '... protest stealing of lands in the colonies, racial discrimination and deal with all other issues of interest to blacks'.[1] It was, however, in 1919 when the African-American scholar and political activist, Dr William Edward Burghardt Du Bois, convened what he called the first Pan African Congress in Paris that the Pan African Congress series, of which the 7th Pan African Congress was a continuation, came into being.

However, while the years 1900 and 1919 can confidently be cited as important reference points for the Pan African movement, the movement stretches much farther into the distant history of our people. Indeed, the roots of the Pan African Movement can be traced right back to the ravages of the first European slave ships to touch the African coast, some five hundred years back. In this connection, it is not at all surprising that the founders of Pan Africanism, as well as some of its leading warriors, have been Africans from the diaspora, who are descendants of the millions of Africans captured in the transatlantic slave trade. Explaining the diasporan origins of Pan Africanism as a movement, W.E.B. Du Bois has noted, 'Africans in the Diaspora tend to look to Africa as one united continent, one unit, mainly because they cannot trace their particular roots.'[2] Moreover, the desire to cease being slaves was necessarily accompanied by the desire to go back home – to Africa. The precursors of Pan Africanism as we know it today are all the Back to Africa movements that sprung up in the US, Brazil and the Caribbean during the early nineteenth century. It was the 'Back to Africa' movement that for the first time conceived of Africa as a 'nation' having socioeconomic and political problems that needed to be confronted on the basis of a Pan African strategy. At the same time, the Back to Africa movement made it imperative for the diasporan Africans to focus their attention on the problems of the continent. Apart from protesting the conditions of slavery under which they were living, the Back to Africa movement also called for the abolition of colonialism in Africa. The legendary Marcus Garvey is the most famous of the pioneers of the return to Africa movement.[3] Pan Africanism can thus be said to have its origin in the struggles of the African people against the enslavement and colonization of their people by extra-African forces. Under the unrelenting onslaught of Pan Africanism, especially since the 1945 5th Pan African Congress of Manchester, most countries on the African continent ultimately regained their independence. However, the regaining of independence did not end colonialism but only transformed it into neocolonialism: political independence without economic independence. We held the 7th Pan African Congress at a time when neocolonialism was threatening to give way to recolonization. More than ever in the past, Pan Africanism as a counter-force to imperialism is a necessary tool of analysis and organizational format for the whole Pan African world. That is why its general declaration, the Kampala Declaration, called on Africans to resist recolonization by organizing instead of agonizing, on the many fronts in which we are struggling to make true the libertarian and freedom-loving spirit that made our forebears to proclaim 'Africa for Africans'.

The early Pan African gatherings 1900–1927

The Pan African Conference of 1900
The 1st Pan African Conference 'to protest stealing of lands in the colonies, racial discrimination and other issues of interest to Blacks' took place from 23–25 July 1900 at London's Westminster Central Hall. It was called by a Trinidadian barrister then based in London, Henry Sylvester Williams. Dr W.E.B. Du Bois who played a leading role during the conference drafted a letter to the Queen of England and other rulers of Europe which contained 'an appeal to struggle against racism, to grant the Black colonies in Africa and the West Indies the right to responsible government; and demanded political and other rights for the Blacks in the United States'.[4] The document asserted: 'The problem of the 20th century is the problem of the colour bar.'

The 1st Pan African Congress of 1919
What we now know as the Pan African Congress series was first organized by Dr Du Bois from 17–21 February 1919. The meeting which took place in Paris, France, demanded: 'The land (in the colonies) must be reserved, with its natural resources, for the natives; their working conditions must be regarded by the law, and slavery and corporal punishment abolished, as well as forced labour, except for criminals ... the natives of Africa must have the right to participate in government as rapidly as their development will permit ... with the goal that in due time, Africa will be governed with the consent of Africans.'[5]

The 2nd Pan African Congress of 1921
The 2nd Pan African Congress of 1921 was held in September 1921, with successive sessions in London, Brussels and Paris. The London session, which was the most radical of all, ended with a resolution known as 'Declaration to the World' or simply the 'London Manifesto'. In several aspects this statement was similar to Marcus Garvey's 'Declaration of the Rights of the Negro Peoples of the World' which had been issued in 1920.

The 3rd Pan African Congress of 1923
The 3rd Pan African Congress was held in November and December, 1923. The first session which took place in London lasted from 7–8 November 1923. The second session was held in Lisbon from 1–2 December 1923. As with the previous Congresses its main demands were 'The Right of Black Peoples to speak for themselves to their respective Governments; and the Right to Land and its Produce'.[6]

The 4th Pan African Congress of 1927
The 4th Pan African Congress was held in August 1927 in New York. Earlier attempts to hold it in either Tunis or the West Indies could not take off owing to opposition from the French and British governments who were the colonial powers. It has been reported of the 4th Congress that:

> The Resolutions adopted were similar to those passed by the third Congress. Notwithstanding, there were two remarkable developments: the presence of radical Black personalities and the tribute paid by Dr. Du Bois to the Soviet Union regarding the policy followed with its various nationalities in sharp contrast with imperialism's colonial policy.[7]

The 5th Pan African Congress of 1945

The 5th Pan African Congress took place in the Charlton Town Hall, Manchester, from 15–19 October 1945. For Africans on the continent it remains the most important Congress ever, considering the manner in which it addressed the question of colonialism and set the independence movement in first gear. For the first time a large number of Africans from the African continent were in attendance, among them leading personalities like Wallace Johnson (Sierra Leone), Obafemi Awolowo and Nnamdi Azikiwe (Nigeria), Jomo Kenyatta (Kenya), Hastings Banda (Malawi), Peter Abrahams (South Africa), Ako Adjei (Ghana), Jaja Wachukwu (Nigeria), and of course, Kwame Nkrumah of Ghana. African political parties fighting for independence were for the first time represented at the Congress, and there was strong representation by trade unions and student organizations such as the West African Students Union (WASU). The Congress resolutions put emphasis on the need for speedy decolonization on the African continent. The Congress document entitled 'The Challenge to the colonial powers' stated:

> The delegates to the Fifth Pan African Congress believe in peace ... nevertheless, if the western world continues determined to rule humanity by force, then the Africans, as their last resort, may have to resort to force, in the effort to achieve liberty, even if that force destroys them, themselves and the world.[8]

This was a radical departure from the benign petitions of the past that appealed to the reasonableness of the colonialists instead of proffering a direct political challenge. The result is that a little over a decade after the Manchester Congress, Africa was on the way to regaining its independence. The Congress unanimously approved and adopted the Declaration to Colonial Peoples of the World which was written by Dr Kwame Nkrumah:

> We believe in the rights of all peoples to govern themselves. We affirm the right of all colonial peoples to control their own destiny. All colonies must be free from foreign imperialist control, whether political or economic. The peoples of the colonies must have a right to elect their own government without restrictions from a foreign power. We say to the peoples of the colonies that they must strive for these ends by all means at their disposal. The object of imperialist powers is to exploit. By granting the right to the colonial peoples

to govern themselves, they are defeating that objective. Therefore the struggle for political power by colonial peoples is a first attempt towards, and the necessary pre-requisite to complete social, economic and political emancipation. The fifth Pan African Congress, therefore, calls on the workers and farmers of the colonies to organise effectively. Colonial workers must be in the front lines of the battle against imperialism.

The fifth Pan African Congress calls on the intellectual and professional classes of the colonies to awaken to their responsibilities. The long, long night is over. By fight-operatives, freedom to print and read literature which is necessary for education of the masses, you will be using the only means by which your liberties will be won and maintained. Today there is only one road to effective action – the organisation of the masses.

The All African Peoples' Conferences

The Du Bois led series ended with the 5th Congress in 1945. Key figures who participated in that Congress were to later play a prominent role in the decolonization process in Africa. They included Kwame Nkrumah who became Ghana's first president; president Jomo Kenyatta of Kenya 1963–78; the prominent political leader Obafemi Awolowo in Nigeria's first and second republics; Jaja Wachukwu, Nigeria's first African Foreign Minister; Hastings Kamuzu Banda, Malawi's first president, and others. With the sweeping force of African nationalism blazed by the independence of Ghana in 1957, Pan Africanism began to acquire greater political clout backed by state power.

Nkrumah and the Convention People's Party (CPP) declared to the world at Independence that the independence of Ghana is meaningless if it is not linked to the total liberation and continental union of the whole of Africa. Thus in April 1958, Nkrumah called a meeting in Accra of all the then independent states of Africa, namely Egypt, Sudan, Libya, Tunisia, Liberia, Morocco and Ethiopia. This became the first Pan African conference to be held on the continent. This made Nkrumah to observe then that 'Pan Africanism has finally returned home', that is, it ceased to be a diaspora-inspired and led movement. The resolution at this conference reclaimed the central demands of the 1945 Congress in relation to self-determination for all African peoples with the added boost that there are now independent states that could offer support.

To buttress the strong and militant resolutions of April 1958, later in December 1958 another conference was called this time comprised of both independent states and nationalist movements. At this meeting, 62 nationalist and liberation movements/groups were represented. Prominent individuals like Frantz Fanon, Patrice Lumumba, Abdul-Rahman Babu, T.B. Makonen, Tom Mboya, Ahmed Ben Bella, Modibo Keita, Joshua Nkomo, Oliver Tambo, Sekou Toure, Kenneth Kaunda and a host of others were present. The conference pledged political, moral and diplomatic support for all liberation movements and endorsed the principle of 'freedom by any means necessary, including armed struggle'. It also sensitized the groups to the need for continental union as the goal of national independence. Similar conferences were held in Tunis (1961) and Cairo (1962).

The formation of the OAU
The 1960s saw the formal decolonization of many of the African states such that by 1963 there were 31 independent states. Increasingly there appeared divisions both of emphasis and ideology between the nationalist leaders about the kind of unity desired and achievable. The divisions became popularized around two blocs: the Casablanca (radical) group and the Monrovia (moderate) group. One was for the immediate political union of the continent while the other argued for slow steps gradually leading up to unity.

In May 1963 both camps represented by the 31 independent states met in Addis Ababa and formed the Organization of African Unity (OAU), whose charter and governing principles were a compromise between the aspirations of the two groups. Critics have described the OAU as a 'toothless bull-dog' while others counsel a more sympathetic understanding emphasizing the modest success of the organization in the early years in the area of diplomatic and political and even material support for African countries still under colonialism and settler minority rule. If we put the OAU in the same dialectical evolution and progression as the Pan African Movement from 1900 when the Congress merely 'draw attention to the suffering of the natives' to 1945 when they demanded self-determination and independence without equivocation, maybe we can be more sympathetic about the OAU, that is, understand it as an organization which was possible in the 1960s, but needs to be radically transformed to respond to our contemporary requirements.

The 6th Pan African Congress
The limitation of the OAU has been clear to many militants and Pan Africanists ever since its inception. For Pan Africanists its main preoccupation almost exclusively with the continent without equal

participation for the diasporic Africans has always been a source of disappointment. To others some provisions in the agreed charter tied the hands of the OAU and prevents it from usefully offering solidarity to other Africans and solving some of the problems faced by Africans both on the continent and in the diaspora.

Thus it was not surprising that in the 1970s efforts were being made to revive the Pan African Movement and the PAC series. According to a key participant[9] and organizer for the 6th PAC: 'The initiative for organising the sixth Pan African Congress came from a small group of Afro-Americans and Afro-Caribbeans who met in Bermuda and the United States in 1971 and 1972'. The ideological orientation of the group ranged from 'African Liberationists' – those whose primary aim is the political, economic, social and cultural liberation of people of African descent all over the world, to 'African Avengers' – those who are consumed by anger against and hatred for white people even though they try to concentrate on black pride and development. A number of the former were independent leftists in the tradition of the organizers of the earlier Pan African Congresses while the latter came from some spin-off groups from the Garvey and student non-violent co-ordinating committee movements. Personalities dropped in and out of the preparatory groups in the early stages but a hard core gradually hammered out a consensus on the following points:

1. The 6th Pan African Congress should have as its theme self-reliance, self-determination and unity of black people throughout the world.
2. Central to the theme of self-reliance and self-determination in today's world is the command of science and technology.
3. Tanzania as the principal example of self-reliance in the African world should be asked to host the 6th Pan African Congress.

The objectives of the organizers were that there was to be a progressive thrust to the Congress and emphasis would be placed on people's organizations as opposed to governments. The early 1970s represented the decade of a renewed onslaught by liberation movements in Angola, Mozambique, Guinea-Bissau, Zimbabwe and South Africa against colonization and settler minority racist rule. Therefore the organizers wanted to provide concrete support for the liberation efforts. The organizers met with sympathetic response from the Tanzania African National Union (TANU) government of President Julius Nyerere and from their first meeting in May 1972 the government and the ruling party of Tanzania threw their weight behind the initiative. This political support had both negative and positive elements in it. One of the negative side-effects was that some of the initial mobilizers for the effort, such as the late C.L.R. James who wrote 'The Call' for the Congress and other Pan Africanists in the Caribbean, could not attend the Congress due to the participation of governments they were fighting against from the Caribbean. However, individuals from the Caribbean who were then based in Africa, such as the late Walter Rodney, Horace Campbell and others, played crucial roles in the Congress.

The 6th Pan African Congress was held in June 1974 at the University of Dar-es-Salaam and was attended by 52 delegations from African and Caribbean states, liberation movements, communities of Africans in North America, South America, Britain and the Pacific. As to be expected the Congress mirrored the global ideological and political struggles of the period and their manifestation within the Pan African world. Issues of the right to self-determination through armed struggle, and questions of imperialism and neo-colonialism, underdevelopment, Third Worldism, self-reliance in education and culture, continuing colonialism in the Caribbean, and the role of African women were addressed and analysed; resolutions were adopted in spite of the different views and perspectives of the participants. Thus the official book on the congress could declare that

> The documents ... resolutions ... record both the disparity of views under played at the 6th Pan African Congress and the relative strength which came to be exercised – despite predictions to the contrary – by the progressive forces. The lead, in many cases, was fittingly taken by the liberation movements.[10]

Perhaps the greatest weakness of the 6th Pan African Congress was the inability to transform all the good resolutions into a concrete organizational and institutional framework of action. Subsequently, its impact was not as decisive as it could have been, than if it had had an institutional base after the Congress. It is a mistake which the 7th Pan African Congress sought to rectify by agreeing to set up a permanent secretariat in order to reverse the spasmodic initiatives of the past.

The road to and from the 7th Pan African Congress

The 7th Pan African Congress took place in Kampala, Uganda, 3–8 April 1994. It was originally scheduled to take place in December 1993 but had to be rescheduled, at the last minute, due not only to logistical problems of travel but also because certain objective and subjective obstacles surfaced in the first week of December when the decision was taken by the International Preparatory Committee (IPC) for the Congress.[11]

Though there was understandable disappointment and demoralization in certain organizing committees, the delay was quickly converted into an opportunity to carry the message to places and people we had not yet reached. The rescheduling also gave us the opportunity to clarify further our objectives to some African governments who were suspicious of the congress. Some of them had feared that the Congress, because of the prominent participation of opposition activists, was going to be yet another government-bashing event. Though a majority of them stayed away from the Congress, at least they did not prevent a majority of our people who wanted to attend from doing so.[12]

It was not altogether unexpected that the role, status and participation of governments should again be a bone of contention as we began preparing for the 7th PAC in 1992. In this instance it was not so much the participation of Caribbean governments but that of African governments. This opposition came from a number of angles,[13] but the most pertinent is a group allied to the Lagos 7th PAC group.

The Lagos group, led by Brother Naiwu Osahon, had been the first group to start organizing for a 7th PAC in response to C.L.R. James's influential paper, 'Towards the 7th PAC'. In that paper James sought to correct the political and ideological errors committed in giving too prominent a role to governments at the 6th PAC. His view was that Pan Africanism must be built as a vanguard of the oppressed masses allied to global revolution and socialism. However the Lagos group, while taking up James's challenge for a Congress, did not share his revolutionary ambitions and proceeded in its efforts as a black-only initiative with a bias towards a black nationalist bourgeois position.[14] The Kampala 7th PAC initiative was in a sense both an ideological and practical response to the Lagos initiative. Indeed many of the people who were to play an important role in it were formerly with the Lagos group. The idea of breaking with the indecisive Lagos group took shape in 1990.[15] At a conference on the impact of the collapse of the Eastern European Bloc on global progressive forces, in the Libyan capital, Tripoli, a number of Africans representing liberation movements and progressive governments or progressive parties both from Africa and the diaspora met and decided that a direct political intervention was necessary by Pan Africanists. A small group of them was tasked with the responsibility of finding an African country that could facilitate the hosting of a 7th PAC in an all-inclusive manner and with a guarantee of independence for the organizers. As to be expected a number of African countries were interested but were unable to guarantee the kind of autonomy that was needed.[16] Col. Kahinda Otafiire,[17] a leading member of the National Resistance Army/Movement in Uganda was a member of the working group and he was able to secure the backing of the government of Uganda for the Congress. Subsequently in August the Libya group met in Uganda and accepted the offer from Uganda and transformed itself into an International Preparatory Committee for the 7th PAC.[18] It decided that a secretariat needed to be constituted to organize the Congress. That was the stage where I was appointed Secretary-General for the secretariat with Honourable Miriam Matembe as Deputy with responsibility for the mobilization of women and two other appointments (Serwanga Lwanga and Ondoga ori Amaza) as Publicity and Deputy Publicity Secretary respectively.[19]

Our brief was very clear from the start: the Congress was to be convened in the shortest possible time to respond to and intervene in the rapidly unfolding global events; it was to be an all-inclusive gathering, on the basis of 'Come one, come all',[20] including the Lagos initiative and other opponents of the initiative; all African and Caribbean governments were to be invited but on the basis of equality with non-governmental groups, and finally, all delegates were to be equal and limited to a maximum of two per organization (governments were considered as individual organizations).

These guidelines were meant to assuage the fears of many that governments would dominate the Congress. In the end, that fear was proven unfounded: a majority of governments did not feel comfortable with coming to Kampala on an equal footing with their opponents or those they regarded as political dissidents, and they stayed away.[21] The government of Sudan, which sought to directly influence the proceedings by sponsoring many organizations, could not be said to have achieved much because all its opponents, including the various factions of the Sudanese People's Liberation Army/Movement (SPLA/M), Umma Party, Communist Party, etc. were present in great numbers too.[22] The government of Ghana, which was one of three countries (the other two being Uganda and Libya) that provided the biggest support for the Congress was seriously censored at the Congress, by participants led by some of its political opponents both in exile and from Accra itself. In truth only 17 African governments were represented either by their diplomats accredited to Uganda or official ministerial delegations. Yet more than 30 African countries were represented by different political forces and groups, especially opposition and pro-democracy groups and youth and women activists. The other point of disagreement with the Lagos group was about the place of North Africa in the Pan African Movement. The Lagos group holds the view that Africa is black, which is not a new current in the movement but is as old as the movement itself. However, we in Kampala rejected as reactionary blackism this attempt to balkanize Africa behind the so-called Saharan and Sub-Saharan divide. We accepted as African any citizen (by whatever means acquired) of any of the countries of Africa, from Cape Town to Cairo and all our islands (Madagascar, Mauritius, Cape Verde, etc.) and also recognize anybody of African descent in the diaspora. While a majority of Africans are of Negroid origin, it is not true historically, factually or even politically that blackness is the only condition of Africanness. We also reasoned that every government or organization that was invited had asked and answered for themselves the question 'Who is a citizen?' Therefore it was not our responsibility to decide who was more African than who. If the ANC for instance had sent the late Joe Slovo to the Congress it would have been proper. If he could represent the country, and even headed Umkhonto we Sizwe what other proof of Africanness was needed? In fact the Pan Africanist Congress of Azania delegation to the 7th PAC included Gora Ibrahim, its foreign relations spokesperson, and now Member of Parliament who is of Indian origin. In fact being African alone (including being black) does not make one a Pan Africanist. The Buthelezis, Mobutus, Abachas, Bokassas, Idi Amins, are as black as you can get but can we truly infer any Pan African commitment from their ignominious acts? It is one's commitment and willingness to sacrifice for the unity and progress of Africa at home and abroad that is crucial; it is a question of consciousness and action. This is a progressive line within the movement that had been illuminated by Du Bois, James, George Padmore, Kwame Nkrumah, Walter Rodney and many others. We believed that is the correct position but did not shut the door to others who believed otherwise and they were represented adequately at the Congress. The clash between the two currents briefly reared its head during the debate on reparation but the Congress took a principled position that recognized the role of Arab slave traders but demanded reparation not from Morocco or Algeria but from the perpetrators of the Atlantic slave trade that is responsible for our underdevelopment today.[23]

The above were the substance of the Kampala and Lagos divide. The Lagos initiative seems to have collapsed completely since the Congress was held and we are happy to state that many of the people in it are working closely with us to rejuvenate the movement.[24]

Many have come to realize that the issue is not whether governments should be part of the movement or not but the potential governments have to hijack the goals and objectives of the movement. Between 1900 and 1945 when the first conference and five congresses were held we were all subject peoples with the exception of Ethiopia and Liberia; therefore, the question of involving governments did not arise. But since the late 1950s, there has emerged a proliferation of states which Pan Africanists may not recognize as they epitomize our lack of unity and we must get rid of them. Our not agreeing with their existence, however, does not remove the fact that they are there and we have been up to now unable to do anything about them. The fact that most of them are illegitimate if judged against the goal of satisfying the greatest interest of the greatest number of our peoples is not the issue. Even the various state elites recognize this and that is why they have to pay regular lip-service to the OAU and Pan Africanism. Realism therefore dictated that we find a way of accommodating them without derailing the movement. If we had said we did not want them there all they needed to do was not permit our delegates from travelling out to the Congress or refuse them entry in the host country. In fact in 1993, I was denationalized by the government of Nigeria which confiscated my passport (and has not returned it up till now) while I was in the country to canvass for support for the 7th PAC. Also some of the Nigerian delegates who attended the Congress in 1994 were temporarily prevented from travelling out.[25] Therefore concrete reality dictated that governments be involved. The anti-government posture is also influenced by the current fad for NGOism which is disempowering African people and shifting focus away from the contest for political power. Thus there were people who argued that the movement needs to be non-governmental; our position is that the movement, though it has its cultural and social components, has always had as its primary goal the seizure of political power by Pan Africanists in order to unify politically our divided peoples, without which democracy, social progress and economic development will continue to elude us. Thus we cannot leave governments, even the unwilling ones, out of it. Also there is no Chinese wall that separates Pan Africanists from government figures. Just as everyone who is an NGO member is not necessarily progressive or Pan Africanist so it is that not everyone in government is opposed to Pan Africanism.[26] It is a duty of Pan Africanists to attract into the fold all those who express interest or are committed to the movement. That was the main argument in favour of 'Come one, come all' by the International Preparatory Committee for the 7th PAC.

Apart from the above operational, political, ideological and definitional differences with the Lagos 7th PAC there were other criticisms emanating from a vocal minority, the UK in particular, who were opposed to the Congress taking place in Uganda because they feared that it would bolster the image of the government.[27] Their opposition rested on two political positions: that the government of Uganda was dictatorial and therefore could not be trusted with a PAC, and that the government was IMF/World Bank controlled. On the first charge the IPC was clear that the holding of the Congress in Kampala was not tantamount to endorsing the policies of the government of Uganda. We went to Kampala because the government agreed to the principle of independence for the organizers and it had no opposition to anybody, including its political opponents, participating. The second charge was really rhetorical because there is no single African country (excepting maybe Libya) that is not under the stranglehold of the Bretton Woods institutions. There was nothing in all the resolutions or the Kampala Declaration that can remotely suggest that the 7th PAC took a pro-IMF/World Bank position. In fact the Congress has been receiving criticisms that it was dominated by 'Marxist-Leninists ... enemies of Pan Africanism ...'.[28] The IPC felt that the Congress had to hold on to the African territory. Wherever it was held we were not going to have unanimity from local political actors as to the nature of the local regime. From the narrow sectarian concerns of some of the critics, anywhere else was acceptable except their own countries! Yet we could not host such a Congress in Europe again! The essence of Pan Africanism demanded a willingness to surrender petty nationalism for the greater unity of Africa.

The success of the Congress in April 1994 answered some of the issues raised while some other issues are continuing points of discussion, debate and confrontation in the movement as it gropes for a renewed relevance and clarity in these times.

This book is part of the continuing struggle to give clarity to the movement. It is the first of three volumes that are planned as output of the 7th Pan African Congress. The second and third volumes will focus on conflicts in Africa, and the important speeches and messages with a full list of participants and the resolutions and declaration.

The present volume is a collection of twelve chapters of varying scope, content and perspective. The only binding interest in them, apart from being specifically written for and/or delivered at the 7th PAC is their Pan Africanist vision. They offer both analysis and practical solutions on how Africa can get out of its current rut, reclaim the march of its history so rudely interrupted by slavery, colonialism, neocolonialism and the contemporary threat of recolonization through IMF/World Bank structural adjustment policies imposed on our peoples, the debt crisis and the domination of our civil society by northern NGOs to whom our hapless governments have only been too happy to surrender social welfare activities like education, health and even rural development.

The book is divided into four parts: The Politics and economics of African Unity, Africa and the World, Continental and Regional Unity and finally, Facing the future. The first part consists of two chapters – 'Conditions of Africans at Home' by Chango Machyo and 'The African Woman on the Continent' by Mrs Victoria Sekitoleko. It had been hoped originally to include a chapter in this section on the condition of Africans in the diaspora to complete the Pan African picture but this became impossible due to logistical reasons. Chango Machyo's chapter presents the historical background to the heritage of neocolonial political economy by the post-colonial African states. He puts the blame for the current crisis in the African political economy on the twin shoulders of both the imperialist forces and the local petty-bourgeois leadership that inherited the post-colonial state without altering its purpose and vision. Consequently a majority of African countries are characterized by sham independence without development. Even when many of them during the first decade of independence witnessed fantastic growth they were not accompanied by the development of the people. This led to opposed expectations between the rulers and the ruled. Just as the unequal socioeconomic system under colonialism was responsible for the rebellion and mass struggles against the once-awesome oppressive machine of the colonial powers, neocolonialism has also provoked mass resistance. The struggle against colonialism was eventually won, in spite of all the distortions by the nationalist elites. It is that victory and the heritage of struggle and resistance of African peoples from slavery through colonialism/neocolonialism to the current real threat of recolonization that convinces Machyo, himself a veteran of the radical wing of the nationalist movement that 'The stage is ... set for the struggle for the second liberation.' Victory in this struggle he puts squarely at the feet of an organized, popularly based Pan African Movement that is internationalist, anti-imperialist, and socialist-oriented ideologically.

Sekitoleko looks at the condition of the African woman and makes suggestions about how African women, who constitute more than 50 per cent of the population, can be made to contribute fully in the development process. She argues that the marginalization of women through structures of patriarchy, colonial racism and sexism and neocolonialism have combined against the advancement of women in areas of education, economic progress and political leadership. However she does not see women as mere victims but also as agents of change together with democratic-minded men in order to reorder the social relations that continue to block women's progress. She identifies areas where progress has been made through a combination of political will both at the national and international levels but concludes that more needs to be done and specifies how. Discussions and presentations during the 7th PAC by delegates from North America, Europe and the Caribbean agreed broadly (although there are varied specificities brought about by post-industrialism and the chronic racism in these societies) with the pictures painted by both Machyo in the area of economic progress for Africans in the diaspora and also the conditions of African women in the diaspora. Like settler colonialist states in Africa, African women in the diaspora face the triple oppression of race, class and gender.

The second section – Africa and the World – contains two chapters; from different ideological stand points and political focus, they locate the position of Africa in the present global geopolitical and economic relationship and provide concrete ways by which Africa and Africans can realign their sociopolitical and economic forces to avoid marginalization by the dominant forces in the international system. In the first chapter ('The New World Disorder – Which Way Africa?') Abdul-Rahman Mohammed Babu, a veteran nationalist and socialist radical takes stock of the global situation since the collapse of the bipolar hegemony between the USSR and the US observing that

> Old political assumptions and economic certainties are crumbling one by one. Old alliances are rapidly being replaced by new ones. Old contradictions: ideological, north/south, economic, environmental, have not gone away; but new ones: economic, religious, territorial, have emerged with a vengeance, threatening the stability of the world.

Contrary to the widespread notion of declaring this conjucture as a unipolar world under the hegemony of the Yankees, Babu looks at the position of Africa not in any unipolar world but in an 'unsettled multipolar world' where Africa is '… embroiled in dramatic changes of her own…' with new political forces of different persuasions emerging everywhere both in Africa and in her diaspora (confronting the new realities of rising racism and Neofascism in Europe and North America demanding new solutions) but with a clear message:

'We want change in this changing world!' He argues for a serious understanding of the situation without demagoguery and confused thinking, if we are to arrive at a realistic 'African position'. In spite of the different manifestations of this crisis (cultural, social, political, etc., which must be taken into consideration) Babu strongly insists that '... the economic base ... must be our starting point'. Thus he enunciates the economic foundation of the African crisis brought about by a number of factors both internal and external such as the historical legacy of economic backwardness inherited from a primitive colonial economy, failure of the nationalist elites to restructure the economy, proliferation of weak states and leadership vulnerable to political instability that disrupt the development process and are too unbalanced structurally to participate profitably in the international political economy thereby becoming victims instead of being agents. Consequently we have not only a disunited continent and people but unstable individual polities. We have economies that are not complementary but competitive 'producing what we do not consume and consuming what we do not produce'. This is the context in which the new political and social ferment on the continent is brewing. In order for it to yield meaningful fruits for the mass of our peoples, Babu suggests a fundamental shift in vision, thought, action and philosophy, planning and approach, that abandons the top-down statist, narrow nationalist, framework in favour of a genuinely Pan Africanist socioeconomic and political strategy. He provides a detailed alternative economic programme and also political principles for the new democracy in Africa.

In the second chapter of this section ('Global Africa: From Abolitionists to Reparationists'), Professor Ali Mazrui, a difficult friend for both the radical and liberal wings of the Pan African Movement, takes on the issue of reparation and how it can be a practical programme in the overall restructuring of the African economy and socio-political and economic regeneration. Perhaps there is no other issue at the moment that generates such tremendous passion and emotion within the movement, especially in the diaspora as the question of reparation. Reparation from whom by whom? Why claim from Europe alone when the Arabs preceded them in the slave trade? What about the indigenous slave trade? We already mentioned briefly at the beginning how this issue was potentially disruptive during the 7th PAC. Ali Mazrui argues that the agenda for the reparations crusade must '... begin with the horrendous consequences of the transatlantic slave trade' because in his view both the indigenous slave trade that preceded the Arab trade and the Arab slave trade were intra-racial and multiracial respectively, needing calculations of 'a different kind' whereas the transatlantic slave trade is the one that has had the most impact on our current situation and its beneficiaries, the best placed to pay. This is not a unanimous position in the Pan African Movement but Mazrui's position is in broad agreement with the 7th PAC resolution (Workshop No. 9) on the issue.[29] He sees the reparations movement as a development from abolitionism with the moral and political proposition that '...the injustices of enslavement and bondage could not have ended with formal emancipation. They can only truly end with the atonement of reparations.' He identifies many areas in which reparations can help ameliorate the current conditions of Africa and Africans everywhere in the world through cancellation of debts, capital transfer, comparable in scale and effect to the Marshall Plan, skills transfer, 'power-sharing' and a greater say in global institutions such as the IMF/World Bank, the UN Security Council, etc. For the diaspora he argues for a transition from affirmative action to a more comprehensive reactivation:

> Conservatives believe that the next step after affirmative action should be a free play of the market forces. But the bondage of history denies the market autonomy. Residual racism is an impediment to the market. We have to move beyond affirmative action to the affirmative reactivation of the black peoples the world over.

If the above section provided a programmatic approach, the third section, in three chapters, provides the institutional mechanism through which the unity project can be accomplished. A persistent, often unjustified, criticism against the Pan African Movement is that we are strong in theory and ideology but weak on the practicalities, the demands of governance, the intricacies of state institutions and the international system and its institutions. While it is true that inexperience and the overwhelming optimism that characterized the decolonization process in a large part of the Third World after the Second World War meant that the leadership underestimated the resilience of the colonialist forces and exaggerated its own capacity to influence things, too many events have happened to disabuse all of us of our naivety. Since the collapse of the Pan Africanist regime of Nkrumah in 1966, Pan Africanists including Nkrumah himself (in all his writings in Conakry, 1966–72) have been rethinking the project within a changing global situation. Even if Pan Africanism did not exist before, it would have been invented in these times when every region of the world is busy reorganizing its economic relations within its backyard in order to be effective participants in the new realities of globalization.

There are three chapters in Part III – Continental and Regional Unity. In Chapter 5, Professor Sam Tulya-Muhika reviews the global situation in economic integration and provides a very detailed analysis of all attempts at regional and continental integration in Africa, their weaknesses and what can be done to make them work. His chapter makes clear that if Africa is not united it has not been due to lack of trying. The weakness has been largely political: the lack of political will to break down the borders (mental, political, ideological, economic, etc.) that continue to stand in the way of the desired unity. Tulya-Muhika believes that part of the problem could be the fact that most of the negotiations, agreements and discussions in the last four decades have been dominated by the state elites and their bureaucracies and legalistic cultures, which are thought necessary to provide the framework but cannot on their own bring about unity. Therefore in this epoch of liberalization, it is important for other segments of our societies to be fully involved and integrated in the unity efforts. These must include the vibrant private sectors (especially those in the so-called informal economy which actually carries out the bulk of the intra-African trade and the subsistence economy), professional groups and popular forces and political groups. The liberalization of the economies must also be accompanied by free movement for people because we cannot operate a free economy with an imprisoned people behind our inherited political borders. He suggests a new framework of consultative regional planning, private-sector empowerment and a restructuring of the OAU to make it an effective African supranational institution. This kind of fundamental shift, he argues, needs '... an economic liberation ... a mass movement for economic liberation of the African person just as was the case for political liberation'.

If Tulya-Muhika gave us the continental dynamics of unity, Professor Sam Moyo's chapter – 'Improving Access to Natural Resource Potentials and Regional Cooperation in Southern Africa' – looks at the regional components of the unity project within the context of Southern Africa. This is very important because of the historical hostility of many Pan Africanists to regionalism which is seen as compromising the all-Africa unity agenda. However the reality is that there is an undeniable regional push and pull continentally just as there are similar forces within the various countries. The challenge for Pan Africanists is to evolve all-embracing practical institutions and programmes that can carry along all sectors of our people. Yes there are dangers of regionalist chauvinism that can imperil our progress just the way narrow nationalism has done until now. This is especially true of the new post-apartheid Southern Africa whose big business interests both in the region and globally are treated (because of South Africa) as part of the First World. There is a very great risk of South Africa, which has been the greatest beneficiary of Pan African solidarity, becoming the most self-absorbed petty nationalist state because of the dominant economic powers of the pre-apartheid bourgeoisie and its allied bureaucracy, financial establishment and the creation of a black neocolonial elite. At best the South African bourgeoisie sees Africa as just an expanded market, not people. Thus there is a danger of Pan Africanization of apartheid! Moyo develops '... a framework for improving the efficient use of natural resources in the Southern African region and improving access by the majority to those resources to improve their livelihoods and productivity'. He outlines the resources available, their current utilization, how they can be improved and their relation to power and poverty in the states, between the states and in the region as a whole. He argues that the issue of the environment and sustainable development cannot be removed from the central question of participatory democracy, concluding that

> The Pan African agenda has to focus on ways to achieve more equitable access to the use and benefits of nature, to improving the productivity and livelihoods of the African people and invoking the participation of the majority of the region's poor people in an African strategy for sustainable development.

The last chapter in this section, Arthur Gakwandi's 'Towards a New Political Map of Africa', is probably the most revolutionary contribution in the whole Congress. It concerns the great untouchable issue of African inter-state relations. The colonial borders which the founding fathers (and they were all fathers!) of the OAU tactically agreed in 1963 had to be respected as bequeathed by colonialism. So many dictators, killers and genocidists on the continent have hidden behind the principle of non-interference contained in the OAU charter to prevent Africans from censuring their illegitimate governments. However a majority of African peoples have never really respected the colonial borders that turn us into Francophone, Lusophone, Anglophone and all the phoney phones that hinder our march towards unity. On the whole even the African states who preach inviolability have obeyed the principle mostly by default especially from the onset of the economic crisis of the 1970s. The legacy of civil wars, wars of liberation, refugeeism, and mass displacement of our peoples in the last decades have really proven that there is no such thing as purely national issues. How much of national sovereignty can be exercised when all your neighbours are in crisis or when you have peoples across the border who share culture, religion and other affinities? The African state which has been weak historically has been further overwhelmed by the current threat of recolonization through the IMF/World Bank and the structural adjustment policies imposed on our peoples. The states are not even able to reproduce themselves as neocolonies, which is why the imperialists have to step in directly through the Bretton Woods institutions. Some of the states even have armies and police maintained by 'aid' from their colonial masters or transnational corporations! Imperialism is trying to impose its own form of rationalization on these states by streamlining its activities on the one hand through joint European Union positions and diplomacy, while, on the other hand, the US is increasingly focusing on a few strategic states as cornerstones of its activities. The old Cold War diplomacy of counting the number of states under your control is collapsing very fast. Thus many of the artificial states are withering into absolute insignificance. In fact Liberia and Somalia have more or less disappeared! When last did we hear anything about Chad? The renewed interest of Africa's leaders in regionalism and resuscitation of regional blocs such as the East African Community (EAC) or the revival of the Economic Community of West African States (ECOWAS), is an attempt to make their weak states relevant again. But this type of tactical rather than strategic Pan Africanism cannot succeed because it will not serve the interest of the people. The neocolonial states cannot fix it this time when recolonization is at the door. What is needed is the genuine and courageous political will to smash the borders and free our peoples.

In his chapter, Dr Arthur S. Gakwandi seizes the bull by the horns by suggesting a new boundary adjustment in Africa that will wipe out the current 53-odd states on the continent and replace them with six regions that take into consideration shared history, culture, economic viability and political stability. These regions will be able to take advantage of economies of scale, an expanded internal market, physical size and human and material endowments to satisfy the yearning of their peoples for real economic and social progress. They will wipe out refugeeism from the continent in one go since most of the fleeing refugees and displaced people often flee to neighbouring countries of which they will now be legal citizens. The prospects for liberalization and open economies in these enlarged areas will improve and with committed leadership the people can better participate in the political processes. Gakwandi's submission may not be the final word on the adjustments but it is important that this much-needed discussion start seriously. He has thus belled the cat.

The final section of the book – Facing the Future – contains five chapters that look at the building blocks of the Pan African Movement for the future. The first, by President Yoweri Museveni ('Science and Technology as a Solution to Africa's Backwardness'), argues that the acquisition of scientific knowledge and available technology is indispensable for Africa to develop its vast human, natural and material resources. He observes that our ancestors made their own tools and weapons, clothed themselves, housed and fed themselves whereas the Africa of today in spite of its vast potential is not able to do these. One of the reasons responsible for this is the slave trade which robbed us of our early scientists, technicians and most of our active population, at the same time as the greatest industrial development was taking place. He argues that 'Societies that do not master science and technology will either be slaves, survive at the mercy and sufferance of others or will perish...'. Therefore he calls for the incorporation of scientific and technological development in the national development plans of African countries, and for the cooperation among African countries in research and development as well as in the commercialization of the results of research. Development also requires the conquest of illiteracy if we are to create a scientifically and technologically conscious population. He draws attention to positive signs that Africans have woken up to the challenge and are embarking on various initiatives to combat technological backwardness. They include the Presidential Forum on Science and Technology, the Gaborone Forum, the African Capability Building Foundation (ACBF) based in Harare, the Distressed and Expatriate Scientists and Scholars from Africa (DESSA) and other groups that need to be supported and facilitated by African governments and people in order to develop our own capacity. Museveni believes that while it is true that scientists and engineers need peace and stability to do their work:

> ... it is also true that most of the discoveries, especially in the military field, are made during periods of turbulence and war. So our skilled people cannot continuously cry wolf and stay away from their continent on account of instability. They must combat instability. At the same time the instability should stimulate them to invent or learn techniques that can help their communities during the instability and afterwards.

The difference between Africa and the developed countries is not one of superior intellectual endowment but organization. For instance, some statistics show that there are about 100,000 highly skilled African scientists, managers, engineers, doctors, etc. who have been drained from Africa yet there is a similar number of expatriate 'experts' from Europe and America in Africa! The challenge is for us to create the enabling environment for our people to return for us to build Africa together. It is said that Rome was not built in a day but at least the Romans were there to build it! We must organize and tap our own human resources on the continent and the concentrated skills and financial resources of our people in the diaspora.

Both Professors Wamba dia Wamba ('Pan Africanism, Democracy, Social Movements and Mass Struggles') and Horace Campbell ('Pan Africanism in the Twenty-First Century'), in looking to the future for the Pan African Movement, restate its historical vision of liberation and emancipatory politics from the anti-slavery movement through the anti-colonial struggles and the struggles against neocolonial dictators and the current resistance against IMF/World Bank recolonization projects. If Pan Africanism is to have any future it must connect itself with the various struggles of today: the deepening of the democratization processes, participatory development, women and gender, youth, students, workers, the poor, peasants, patriotic intelligentsia and other manifestations of social and other mass struggles and also the global anti-imperialist and popular struggles. For Wamba, 'Pan Africanism must root itself in that process so that its vision can become enriched and popular' because

> The post-colonial state has continued to make it very difficult for African people to constantly interact and relate to themselves. Pan Africanism must bring together those forces, inside each country of Africa, which are active in making political pluralism a reality. It will be one way of contending with the pro-imperialist NGOs aiming at dominating civil society in African countries.

Campbell broadens the call for a resurgent democratic Pan Africanism by asking

> Which class is leading the present definition of the movement? What steps are being taken to end the historic silencing of women in the ranks of the Pan African Movement? What steps are being taken to end the demobilization and depoliticization of the youth? How capable are the leading forces in carrying out the present tasks of resisting and rolling back the looming recolonization?

Some of these questions were answered by the Congress in its resolutions on the creation of a permanent secretariat for the Pan African Movement. Gender balance and inter-generational representation were agreed upon. The bigger challenge is in ensuring that in our actions and activities these principles are given effective expression. As we will see in Dr Fatima Mahmoud's chapter on the formation of the Pan African Women's Liberation Organization (PAWLO) at the pre-Congress meeting of African women, the issue of marginalization of women is already being addressed concretely. In addition to correcting some of the historic anomalies in the movement that are militating against its liberation agenda, Campbell sets out three tasks for the movement in the twenty-first century:

> First, to make an impact on the African people in the process of transforming the nationalist consciousness of the twentieth century. Second, to make a decisive impact on world opinion with respect to the Africans at home and abroad. And third, to be able to realize the spirit of dignity for the renewal of the human spirit.

Western European narratives of both the modern and postmodern variants devalued the spiritual dimension of humanity with an artificial distinction between the material and the spiritual. One of the principal challenges of the Pan African Movement is 'to offer spiritual leadership to a world corrupted by worship of market forces'.

From this perspective therefore

> Pan Africanism is not only linked to the quest for a new social system, but also one in which the development of productive forces is not simply linked to the production of goods but also the creation of new human beings. This perspective of the transformation of gender relations, free men, women and children, of cultural freedom, of harnessing the positive knowledge of the African past now forms part of the conception of the struggle for Pan African liberation in the twenty-first century.

This struggle, all the participants at the Congress agreed must involve all sectors of our peoples, their institutions, governmental and peoples' organizations. Unity must and has to be all-embracing. It was in that context that Dr Salim Ahmed Salim, the Secretary-General of the Organization of African Unity (OAU) made his contribution, 'The OAU and the Future'. The OAU is still very relevant for the unity project in spite of all its weaknesses. These weaknesses themselves have a lot to do with its structure and its composition. Even though it developed as part of the Pan African Movement, its focus is continentalist thereby breaking the historical key link between Africa and its diaspora which is the essence of Pan Africanism. Even on the continent itself the non-interference principle encouraged narrow nationalism and weakened its effectiveness. Despite them, the OAU remains the single most important diplomatic and political forum for Africa, therefore Pan Africanists must rise up to the challenge thrown at the 7th PAC by Salim by seeking to influence it:

> Africans should stop treating the OAU as some distant body located in Addis Ababa where heads of State, Ministers, Ambassadors and officials frequently meet to deliberate on the destiny of our continent. Instead, the organization should properly be viewed as our own Pan African Organization and indeed, where necessary, even pressured to live up to the aspirations and expectations of our peoples in all domains. We must endeavour to strengthen it.

This is very important if we are to reverse the endemic process of systematic alienation of Africans from African institutions and Africa. We have no qualms about pressurizing so-called international institutions, be they the UN, the British Commonwealth of Nations, the Francophone group, the Franco-African Summit, etc., but are dismissive of African initiatives. Granted this dismissive attitude could be due to frustration at their little achievements, if any, or lack of them so far but the challenge is to change them (including the OAU) to make them respond to our needs. It is true that we cannot have Pan Africanism without Pan Africanists. Africans cannot unite if there is irredentism, regional and ethnic chauvinism across the countries but we Pan Africanists must claim Africa as ours, warts and all. Nobody is going to build it for us which means we have to act as suggested by Salim: '... think together, to cooperate and to work together' to strengthen our institutions. To do this Salim, like all other participants at the Congress and contributors in this book, needs the remaking of '... a new African, freed from the limiting interpretation of sovereignty and non-interference and imbued with a new sense of mission and purpose that transcends ethnic and national irredentism...'. The new Africans Salim called for are not exactly new because they have existed and continue to exist and fight in many fronts for our common struggle for unity and social progress from one epoch to the other. Our challenge now is to make the necessary connections, linkages and forge the fighting organizational framework to realize our long dream of unity.

The final chapter by Dr Fatima Mahmoud – 'Building a Pan African Women's Movement' – provides a way forward. If one must summarize in a few words what was significant about the 7th PAC and state what makes it distinct from all previous congresses, they must be: African women participated fully in the Congress but more than participating they formed PAWLO. From now onwards it will no longer be possible to write women out of the history of Pan Africanism. Attendance lists of previous congresses read too much like a register of an old boys' school where if there is a mention of women they would have been there as subordinates (wives, lovers, secretaries, ushers, hostesses, etc.) but the 7th PAC changed this. We can now talk of a movement that is reflective of all sectors of our society. To ensure that this is permanent the women formed PAWLO, not as a rival to the global movement but as an equal partner, fighting together, striking separately, in our joint struggle.

Notes

1. W.E.B. Du Bois in 'Origins of the Pan African Movement', *7th PAC News*, May 1993. For other accounts of the origins of the Pan African Movement, see V.B. Thomson, *Africa and Unity*, London: Longmans, 1969; Kwame Nkrumah, 'Towards African Unity' in *Africa Must Unite*, London: Panaf, 1963; George Padmore, *Pan Africanism or Communism*, London: Denis Dobson, 1956.
2. Du Bois, 'Origins of the Pan African Movement'.
3. For a summary of Marcus Garvey's writings and his role in the Pan African Movement see Amy Jacques Garvey with E.V. Essien-Udom, *Philosophy and Opinions of Marcus Garvey* Vol. 2, London: Frank Cass, 1977; T. Vincent, *Black Power and the Garvey Movement*, Ramparts Press, 1971; Tony Martin, *Race First: The organisational struggles of Marcus Garvey and the United Negro Improvement Association*, Greenwood Press, 1976.
4. Du Bois, 'Origins'.
5. Ibid.
6. Ibid.
7. Ibid.
8. Ibid. For a more recent appraisal of the 5th PAC see Hakim Hadi and Marika Sherwood, *5th Pan African Congress Revisited*, London: New Beacon, 1995.

9. Bill Sutherland was the Coordinator for the 6th Pan African Congress. He wrote a confidential memoranda about his experiences. All quotations except where stated are from this memo. Also there is an excellent thesis on the various ideological currents that shaped the movement between 1945 and 1974 by Armando Entralgo Gonzalez, *Pan Africanism from the V Congress of Manchester to the VI of Dar Es Salaam*, Havana, Cuba: Centre of Studies on Africa and the Middle East, 1987.
10. *Resolutions & Collected Speeches from the Sixth Pan African Congress*, Dar-es-Salaam: Tanzania Publishing House, 1976.
11. The Secretariat for the Congress (consisting of the late Major Ondoga ori Amaza, Deputy Publicity Secretary, Napoleon Abdulai, Executive Assistant to the Secretary-General, Lt. Noble Mayombo, Chief of Staff, Thomas Deve, IPC member for Zimbabwe and myself) was opposed to postponement and advised the IPC against the decision.

    Our arguments were three-fold. First, we believed then that a postponement was going to be demoralizing to the core of volunteers, activists, and committed Pan Africanists who had been working tirelessly for the Congress since the Kampala initiative took off in 1992. Second, we did not share the view that enough work had not been done and therefore the Congress was not going to be representative of the various fighting brigades of our people. Our optimism was based on our being in touch with various national committees and individuals, across the world who, in spite of very bad communication have expressed interest in the Congress and were mobilizing to come. We were in touch with people from as far afield as Martinique, Brazil and even remote places in Africa like Mauritius and Cape Verde. Even people from UNITA-controlled parts of Angola had been in touch. We also felt that while a representative Congress was desirable, it could not be used as an excuse to keep postponing. We could not have waited until everybody was ready. Were this the case, Henry Sylvester Williams, who called the first conference in 1900 in London could not have gone ahead. Even the famous 1945 Congress which was the biggest of the first five was attended by less than 200 people. Finally, Global events were continually unfolding regardless of whether we were prepared or not. The world would not wait for us therefore we felt that the Pan African Movement needed to lead events rather than react to or follow them.

    In the end we were overruled by the majority of the IPC members. The fact that most of our delegates expected from the

Caribbean and the Americas could not, due to last minute plane schedule cancellations, arrive in time for the Congress was the deciding factor. In retrospect we were glad to have been overruled because the 7th PAC was more successful than it could have been in many respects. Over 50 countries from Africa, Latin America, Europe, Asia, the Caribbean and North America were represented at the Congress.

12. There were so many pressures both direct and indirect from governmental quarters in Africa. Some of them who did not trust the National Resistance Movement (NRM) government of Uganda believed that the Congress was going to be a rebel meeting to destabilize them or even encourage armed resistance, since the NRA/M of President Yoweri Museveni had come to power in 1986 after a five-year armed struggle. The pressures were strongest from Uganda's neighbours. On one occasion a delegation of the IPC led by the Chairman and consisting of Mzee Abdul-Rahman Babu, Prof. Abdul Alkalimat, the late Lt. Col. Serwanga Lwanga, Noble Mayombo and myself, had to go meet the President in his home village of Rwakitura to discuss some of these problems. At the meeting he explained to us again the necessity of assuring the governments that the Congress was all-inclusive and undertook to speak to some of the governments for us.

    When the Congress finally took place, it was a few months more than 20 years after the 6th PAC, which was held in Dar-es-Salaam, Tanzania in June 1974. That Congress was convened by the late Walter Rodney who was unfortunately too sick at the time to participate in most of the proceedings. The call to that Congress was issued by another Caribbean luminary, the late C.L.R. James, who eventually refused to attend because of the invitation extended by the host government of Tanzania to governments in the Caribbean that C.L.R. and some of his colleagues considered to be reactionary and dictatorial and unworthy of being participants at such an assembly of progressive and revolutionary Pan African activists.

13. See 'Arguments for and against the 7th PAC' in *7th PAC News*, July 1993. The main disagreement between the Kampala initiative and the Lagos one is around the issues of Who is an African?, sponsorship by African governments, timing of the Congress, and ideological, political and organizational differences.

14. *The Black agenda up to the year 2000* (Lagos, 1992) published by Naiwu Osahon summarizes the black bourgeois perspective of the Lagos group.

15. 'Background to the 7th PAC' in *Programme of the 7th PAC* (Kampala, 1994).
16. The conditions include complete independence for the IPC and the secreteriat in organizing for the Congress and all opposition groups including political groups that are opposed to the host government must be free to participate.
17. The fact that Col. Kahinda Otafiire, the chairman of the IPC was a senior member of the NRM government of Uganda and also a serving military officer in its army (NRA) was used by some of the critics to impugn the integrity of the initiative. However the IPC was very broad and the majority of the members were very independent and thus there was no danger of the chairman commandeering the committee. His role was merely as a facilitator. Also the invitation to participate went to all Africans regardless of their status. Therefore the participation of soldiers was not an issue. Otafiire is an African patriot who abandoned a promising diplomatic career (in the Ugandan embassy to China) to join the bush war to liberate his country from dictatorship. The fact that the neocolonial army in Africa is very brutal made many people wary of soldiers, especially one who is convening a PAC. Many people bought the anti-Otafiire propaganda because of the mass ignorance by even progressive forces both in Africa and outside about the nature and direction of the NRA/M war of liberation and its leadership. It is only this year, ten years after they captured power and fifteen years since they went to the bush, that an authoritative book has been published: Ondoga ori Amaza, *Museveni's Long March* (London: Pluto Press, 1996).
18. The IPC consisted of Col. Kahinda Otafiire, chairman; A.M. Babu, former minister in Zanzibar and Tanzania; Abdul Alkalimat, a leading radical activist and scholar and founder of the 21st Century bookshop in Chicago; Akidi Ocan, a British lawyer born of Ugandan and Guyanese parents; Bankie Foster Bankie, another lawyer and former diplomat and an active Pan Africanist who is also a grandson of a veteran Pan Africanist; David Du Bois, son of W.E.B. Du Bois but a Pan Africanist in his own right; Eusi Kwayana, the veteran radical political ideologist and theoretician from Guyana; Falilou Diallo, a history professor from Dakar, Senegal and also president of the Pan African Observatory in Senegal; Gorkeh Nkrumah, Nkrumah's son active in his own right and now the Africa editor of the English language edition of *Al Ahram* newspaper in Cairo, Egypt; Horace Campbell, a professor of Pan African Studies at Syracuse University but based in Harare,

Zimbabwe. He was a participant at the 6th PAC and a colleague and comrade of the late Walter Rodney; Jean-Claude Njem, a leader of the UPC of Cameroon based in Sweden; Jose Van Dunen, a trade union leader from Angola; Karrim Essack, another veteran strugglist from Tanzania; Kwame Ture (also known as Stokeley Carmichael) formerly of the Black Panthers and leader of the All Africa Peoples' Revolutionary Party (AAPRP); Mohammed Akbar, Nation of Islam's chief representative in Africa; Perezi Kamunanwire, Uganda's Ambassador to the UN and Professor of Political Science at Columbia University; the late Victor Sabelo-Phama, commander of the APLA (PAC of Azania's liberation Army); a representative of the ANC; and Dr Yvonne King, African-American academic based in Nigeria.

As the initiative for the Congress gathered momentum the IPC was broadened to include more women and representatives of active national committees like Pan African Forum, PAFO of Kenya (Irungu Houghton and Berewa Jomo); UK National Committee (Ahmed Sheikh); Germany (Dr Moses Mensah and Marianne Balle); Zimbabwe (Thomas Deve); Ghana (Kwesi Pratt Jr); South Africa (Prof. Kwesi Prah and Prof. Vuyisile Dlova); Mauritius (Hon. L.L. Dega); Nigeria (Dr Attahir Jega); The Caribbean (Hon. Rosie Douglas, Leader of the Dominican Labor Party) and others.

Unfortunately both Eusi Kwayana and David Du Bois could not participate in the IPC and the Congress. Also a few of the members became active only in the last stages of the process when it was clear to the doubting Thomases that the Congress was really taking place.

19. Minutes of IPC August 1992 meeting.
20. See Invitation to 7th PAC, 'Come One Come All' in *Programme for the 7th PAC*, Kampala, 1994.
21. The governments who sent delegates or were represented by their ambassadors included Algeria, Egypt, Eritrea, Ethiopia, Ghana, Kenya, Libya, Mauritius, Nigeria, Rwanda, Sudan, Tanzania, Uganda, Zaire and Zimbabwe.
22. The number of Sudanese at the Congress was 100 with 54 representing the government and/or its allied institutions. 46 delegates came from SPLA/M, its two factions, the Umma Party and the Communist Party, and allied groups including the National Democratic Alliance.
23. The Crusade for Reparations, Workshop No. 9 in *Resolutions of the Seventh Pan African Congress*, Kampala: Pan African Publishers, 1994, pp. 42–4.

24. It seems that Naiwu Osahon's opposition to government funding and sponsorship was just a short-term manoeuvre. He wrote after the 7th PAC in 1994 to President Robert Mugabe of Zimbabwe requesting him to host another PAC. The government, whose Foreign Minister was then Dr Nathan Shamuyarira, led its delegation to the 7th PAC and was elected on to the Interim Management Committee, declined the request and advised him to work with Kampala towards the next PAC.
25. Dr Akilu Sani Indabawa, Dr Attahir Jega and Gloria Kilanko were initially prevented by Nigeria's security forces from travelling out for the Congress but changed their minds after political uproar.
26. Our experience in organizing the Congress gave me invaluable lessons in the working of the African establishments. While governments may be reactionary and unpredictable there are still many principled individual's who subscribe to Pan Africanism and go out of their way to facilitate us.
27. 'Arguments For and Against', *7th PAC News*.
28. 'Kwame Ture's Leaked Report' and 'Response to Kwame Ture's Leaked Report' by AWR participants at the 7th PAC in *SPARKS*, a publication of the Pan African Movement Secretariat, Kampala, October 1995.
29. Resolution No. 9 of the 7th PAC.

Part I

The Politics and Economics of African Unity

1

Conditions of Africans at Home

Chango Machyo w'Obanda

Introduction

The political independence that the people of Africa achieved over thirty years ago was not a grant or a gift from the European colonial powers. It was the result of a struggle for liberation and independence from foreign domination and exploitation that goes back to ancient times. From ancient times right up to the present, African peoples have never surrendered to foreign rule. Even when they suffered defeat at the hands of different foreign invaders, Africans never surrendered completely. The desire for freedom and independence kept on burning in their hearts until they regrouped and rose up again. The anti-colonial struggle was therefore not a new thing. It was rooted in the ancient struggle against the colonization of Egypt by various Asian nations and Europeans (Williams, 1987); the struggle of the peoples of North Africa against Greek, Roman and Vandal colonization (DeGraft-Johnson, 1955); and then the resistance against the European slave trade, followed by the resistance against nineteenth-century European colonialism.

But as the Egyptian *Charter* declared:

> The masses do not call for change or endeavour to realise or impose it merely for its own sake, that is, for sheer boredom. They only do so in order to attain a better life and in an attempt to raise the level of their reality to that of their aspirations (1962, p. 31).

Accordingly, when the people of Africa rose up against formal colonial rule, the imperialists tried to resist by the use of different levels of force. In Ghana and Uganda, for example, it was a limited force; but in Kenya, Algeria, Cameroon, Zimbabwe, Angola, Mozambique, Namibia and South Africa, fully-fledged brutal wars suppressed the movement for independence. However, the international power relations after the Second World War and the anti-imperialist consciousness that developed after that war, did not favour the European colonial powers that dominated Africa.

It is therefore wrong for the apologists of colonialism, and their African agents among us, to try to distort historical reality by presenting formal decolonization as a grant or a gift from the European colonial powers.

Those powers were forced to relinquish direct political control by forces beyond their ability to contain. They even made great efforts to bribe African nationalists in particular and the masses in general, by improving welfare services and allowing limited development projects. In the words of Professor D.K. Fieldhouse:

> There was a strong belief, particularly on the moderate left in Britain and French politics, that extended colonial acquiesence in alien rule could best be bought by providing dramatic evidence of social and economic development; hence the great increase in the flow of grants and soft loans under the British C.D. & W. Acts and the French FIDES programme (1986, pp. 22–3).

He then points out how these colonial powers 'though on different time scales, also believed that a controlled devolution of political functions to colonial elites' – those who led the anti-colonial struggle as well as those who held minor executive positions as assistants to the white officials – 'would assuage their hunger for the fruits of politics and sustain their belief in democracy as their own ultimate objective'. But as time went on, the colonial powers realized that such a course of action was too expensive for them to sustain. They therefore changed the method. The new method was to substitute the expensive 'postwar reformist empire for empire on the cheap', because those in Britain and France who would otherwise have 'clung indefinitely to established belief in the imperial mission and the rewards of empire' found it no longer attractive.

The 'empire on the cheap' meant giving up direct political control but retaining economic control as the most effective means of enjoying the benefits of the empire without being blamed for what happens in the former colony, which is merely reformed into a neo-colony. Thus, since economic independence was not achieved, political independence became meaningless. What actually happened was a reformed colonial system that soon manifested itself as a new form of colonial rule.

This new form of colonial domination was defined by the All African Peoples' Conference (AAPC) which took place in Cairo in 1962 as 'the survival of the colonial system in spite of formal recognition of political independence in emerging countries which become the victims of an indirect and subtle form of domination by political, economic, social, military or technical means'. It was then pointed out that the new form of foreign domination was 'the greatest threat to African countries' because those powers who practice neo-colonialism resort to 'economic and political intervention in order to prevent African states from directing their political, social and economic policies towards the exploitation of their natural wealth for the benefit of their peoples' (Machyo, 1973, pp. 23).

So-called independence was therefore meaningless. It meant more economic dependence on the former colonial powers in particular, and on the imperialist powers in general. And so-called *aid* became the most effective means of neocolonial rule. It is within this context that the 'state and conditions of Africans on the continent' must be seen.

This chapter discusses three main points: first, that sham independence could not lead to genuine development as a transformation of the ideological, technical and cultural conditions in the former colonies; second, that the state and conditions of the Africans on the continent flow from this failure to achieve genuine development; and third, to change the wretched state and conditions the African people have been forced into as a result of neocolonial domination and now the threat of recolonization, a second liberation struggle is required.

Sham independence and lack of development

The present state and conditions of the African people on the continent are rooted in three main problems: the different expectations from independence by the political and bureaucratic African elites on the one hand and, on the other, that of the popular masses; the wrong concept of development, and the designs of the imperialist powers on Africa.

Opposed expectations
Everywhere on the African continent, the root cause of the rebellion against colonial rule was neither racism nor communist influence. Africans have never been racists: they accommodated and safeguarded the interests of other races who proved to be genuine in dealing with Africans. For example, one of the 'admirable qualities' the Moroccan traveller Ibn Battuta (1929/57, pp. 329–30) found among the people of the ancient empire of Mali which he visited during the fourteenth

century was that 'they do not confiscate the property of any white man who dies in their country, even if it be uncounted wealth'. Students of ancient African history like Chancellor Williams (1987, p. 184–5) tell us that Africans welcomed honest non-African traders. It was the alien visitors who usually took advantage of, abused African hospitality, sincerity and honesty, and turned around to conquer, dominate and exploit their African hosts.

The root cause of the African struggle against colonial rule must therefore be sought in the adverse socioeconomic conditions that were imposed upon Africans by the colonial rulers. For example, in Uganda, the origin of anti-colonialism that developed into nationalism, was the land question in Buganda, started by the peasants' demand for the restoration of the pre-colonial land tenure system. According to H.W. West:

> So it transpired that the discontent of the *bataka* and of the peasantry, caused them to join forces in pressing for a return to the old customary forms of tenure. This dissatisfaction found expression in the establishment in 1921, of an association usually referred to as the 'Federation of Bataka' (n.d, p. 202).

The Federation consisted of 'The articulate elements ... young educated but landless Baganda; but behind them was a strong body of older peasant opinion which compared the exactions of its present landlords with the benevolent despotism of earlier days.' Not only them, but also even 'Certain landowners, acting from various motives, and a number of minor chiefs allied themselves with the movement, which was, however, essentially *the party of the "have nots" banded against the "haves"*' (emphasis added). In other words, it was a *class struggle*.

Later, the 'Federation of Bataka' developed into the Uganda Farmers' Union, which demanded the right to buy and process their own cotton and coffee crops and the formation of cooperatives for the purpose. The union spread to all parts of the country. In 1952, Uganda Farmers' Union changed into Uganda National Congress (UNC) which was the first genuine nationalist political party in Uganda. Its demands were in line with the demands of other African anti-colonial movements, for '*Self-government*' and '*Independence Now!*'.

The point being stressed is that everywhere in Africa, the demands expressed by the anti-colonial nationalist movements reflected the real demands, concerns and aspirations of the popular masses to get rid of foreign domination and exploitation. Indeed, the nationalist leaders strengthened this demand and raised the people's hopes when they made it clear that once the white man was removed and replaced by the African leaders, poverty, disease and ignorance would be wiped out, hence Nkrumah's famous statement: *'Seek ye first the political kingdom!'*

Accordingly, the people understood *Uhuru* to be complete freedom from all forms of colonial domination, oppression, exploitation and humiliation. It meant total liberation and emancipation from colonial ideological, technical and cultural domination. It meant removing colonial ideological shackles, carefully hidden under religious teachings, that the African found incompatible with his or her own genuine beliefs and very often in contradiction to what he or she understood the Bible to say. This led the Africans to break away from colonial churches and establish their own independent churches or religious sects, for example, *Dini ya Musambwa* or *Legio Maria* both in Kenya.

Technically, the popular masses aspired for control over their own economic structure which therefore would serve their interests. As we have noted, in Uganda they wanted to buy and process their own commercial crops; they wanted effectively to be involved in commercial and manufacturing sectors which were controlled by foreign comprador capitalists. That is why one of the aspects of the anti-colonial struggle was the implementation of trade boycotts and labour strikes. In terms of land, the popular masses demanded the return of their land which had been expropriated by the colonial rulers and either used to bribe the native ruling elite to make it side with the colonial government, as happened in Buganda in Uganda, or was declared Crown land and allocated to white settlers, as happened in Kenya and Zimbabwe; or was declared 'national' park or merely a reserved area.

Culturally, the people aspired to see the end of cultural alienation. They understood *Uhuru* as being free to reinstate their cultural values and practices; the redevelopment of their creative artistic works which had been condemned by the missionaries in the name of God. For example, Boris de Rwachewiltz, an expert on African art, tells us that 'colonization and the struggle against *paganism* waged by various missionaries, have for most part resulted in the decline of indigenous art forms and in the systematic destruction of so-called "idols"' (1966, p. 86). For example, a French Catholic missionary in Gabon boasted of having 'succeeded in burning more than 6,000 such pieces'. The African masses expected an end to regarding their song, dance and drama as evil and therefore a manifestation of the 'spirit of Satan'! They expected dignity to be restored to their own names instead of being labelled *'erinya ly'ekikafiiri'* (pagan name); they expected a restoration of respect for their marriage customs and practices, family ties and relationships and community collective spirit. This would in turn lead to the restoration of social harmony, mutual respect and trust as well as the spirit of mutual help. In terms of justice, they expected *Uhuru* to put an end to unjust colonial laws, to humiliating and degrading police harrassment and sub-human police cells and prison conditions which were deliberately meant to humiliate, degrade and deny the African a feeling of personal social value, respect and dignity. And not least, they expected an end to the education system which was not only meant to alienate African youth through the deliberate system of acculturation by the colonial missionary teachers, but what Walter Rodney described as 'education for subordination, exploitation, the creation of mental confusion and the development of underdevelopment' (1976, p. 264). The people expected an education system which would restore the dignity of their cultural values and their languages – to raise them from the status of *'vernacular'* ('the language of slaves') to that of an independent dignified status.

Needless to point out that *Uhuru* brought none of these things. It did not meet the expectations of the people: the expectations and aspirations of the black petty bourgeoisie who were now posed to replace the white officials were different. The point which is usually never mentioned when people discuss why independence has proved a mere sham in Africa is precisely the one important and therefore the root cause of what has happened to the African people since independence.

The anti-colonial struggle was not directed at changing the colonially established socioeconomic system. The sole objective of those who marched ahead of the movement was to replace the white officials and run the system themselves. In other words, the leaders of the anti-colonial struggle, were anti-imperialists, but they were not anti-imperialism. What they really wanted to see happen was therefore well-presented by Frantz Fanon when he wrote:

> The native town is a hungry town, starved of bread, of meat, of shoes, of coal, of light. The native town is a crouching village, a town on its knees, a town wallowing in the mire. It is a town of niggers and dirty Arabs. *The look that the native turns on the settlers' town is a look of lust, a look of envy. It expresses his dreams of possession – all manner of possession: to sit at the settler's table, to sleep in the settler's bed, with his wife if possible* (author's emphasis) (1963, p. 32).

Accordingly, when the so-called independence was achieved the black nationalists who stepped into the shoes of the white officials were quick to assure their former colonial masters that there would be no change. Things would continue to work as they had been under the formal colonial rule. The statement made by M'ba the President of Gabon on his official visit to Paris, quoted by Fanon, is very representative of what the black petty bourgeoisie wanted to do following independence. M'ba said to the President of France: 'Gabon is independent; but between Gabon and France, nothing has changed; everything goes on as before.'

Therefore, as Fanon comments, 'In fact the only change is that Monsieur M'ba is President of the Gabonese Republic and that he is received by the President of the French Republic' (p. 53). The change was in name only, not in the essence of the colonial relationship. The former African French empire became the French Community, as the former British empire became the British Commonwealth. In terms of the burning land issue, Kenyatta's statement is a classical example. Colin Leys tells us how 'From the moment of his release from detention in 1961 [Kenyatta] was completely consistent in his position' over the land issue:

> The Government of an independent Kenya will not be a gangster Government. Those who have been panicky about their property – whether land or buildings or houses – can now rest assured that the future African Government, the Kenya Government, will not deprive them of their property or rights of ownerships. We will encourage investors in various projects to come to Kenya and carry on their business peacefully, in order to bring prosperity to this country (1975, p. 62).

Addressing his fellow Kikuyu whose participation in the Mau Mau armed struggle was based on the land issue, Kenyatta boldly told them, and without any sense of shame that 'now the time had come to forget the past. People might have been Home Guards or Chiefs, they might have been detainees or in the forests, but they were all brothers and sisters and there should be no revenge.' In 1963, Kenyatta, addressing a meeting at Nakuru, the heart of diehard settlers, requested them 'to stay and farm in the country'. He also requested them to 'learn to forgive one another'. Kenyatta himself had 'no intention of retaliation or looking backwards', instead they were 'going to forget the past and look forward'. It is, however, important to mention that Kenyatta had acquired a huge farm in the Nakuru area. In Uganda, the peasants' land expropriated by the British in Buganda was now defended by the Buganda aristocrats as part and parcel of 'Buganda's culture'.

On what was to happen to education and culture after independence, the Director of Primary School Education in Antananarivo, Madagascar, could have been speaking for all Africa, when Professor Rene Dumont asked him about 'what modification would follow from the fact that education in the villages was ... concerned primarily with peasant children destined to become farmers themselves'. The Director's answer was brief and sharp: 'No lowering of standards, we'll give them exactly what they would get in France' (1966, p. 90). For the African post-colonial leaders, the belief was that 'everything that does not absolutely conform to the French (or British) educational norms can only be a "lowering of standards"'. Dumont naturally saw this as being 'ridiculous', but for the African elite it was 'normal' and therefore 'natural'. That is why Professor Germa Amare noted how there was a 'misconception widespread in Africa to regard the education that has been imported intact and unchanged from abroad *as the best education*'. Because of that misconception, post-colonial education in Africa was 'a replica of some European system of education' (1970, p. 196). In terms of language, former colonial masters' language became the 'official' and therefore 'national' language. The teaching of African languages at primary school level and even up to school certificate level was abolished in Uganda; Tanzania was the only exception where Swahili was elevated to a national status. The result is that today people cannot write and read their mother tongues! Yet they are 'educated'.

Wrong concept of development
In terms of the concept of development, what Fanon wrote is what actually happened. The African successors to the colonial rule turned their backs 'more and more on the interior and on the real facts of [their] underdeveloped country'. They turned their backs to the aspirations of the prime movers of the anti-colonial struggle – the popular masses – and looked towards 'the former mother-country and the foreign capitalists' who now counted much more than the people. Because these foreign capitalists, or 'investors' as Kenyatta referred to them, were seen to be more valuable in terms of personal gains – i.e. were profitable – by the emerging black national bourgeoisie, than the popular masses. We shall see this as the real reason behind the emergence of one-man dictatorship in Africa.

However, the new leaders' dismissal of 'the interior and on the real facts of ... under development', led to the wrong concept of development. To the African post-colonial leader, development was conceived as *modernization* and this was seen as being synonymous with Europeanization or Americanization. The aim of development was therefore to 'catch up' with the advanced industrial capitalist countries of the West.

The aspirations of the black bourgeoisie to catch up with Europe and North America were reinforced by the development model that was peddled by the World Bank, based on the theory of 'growth' and 'trickle down'. According to this theory, what mattered most in the development process was how much wealth was created first, then at a certain point it would 'trickle down' to the rest of society, in otherwords, 'wealth first, distribution later'. And an ex-colony could easily achieve such growth by relying on foreign investors and foreign economic and technical aid. Development was therefore conceived as the work of outside forces acting on the country's human and non-human resources to produce wealth.

The growth theory of development therefore means to produce more for export. Fundamental structural changes are not permitted. The colonially imposed vertical division of labour supported by the theory of 'comparative advantages' must be adhered to. In that model, the people are treated as a *means* not as the *object* and *agent* of development. Accordingly, the aim of development is not to meet people's basic needs: food, clothing, shelter, education, health and cultural requirements. These are not *primary*. The result is that wealth accumulated by foreign investors is superimposed on the people; it becomes not only superficial, but ideologically, technically and culturally oppressive and exploitive.

Thus the post-colonial state in Africa is not in the service of the people, but of the aid donors, the World Bank, the IMF and whoever is prepared to 'help' us by helping him/herself more. As Professor Curle (1971, p. 4) pointed out, the African elite has joined the international exploitative network. Thus the people are only used to acquire the legal authority to qualify those elected to join the service of the network. Accordingly, as Leys pointed out, in Kenya for example, it was no longer the settlers of the New Kenya Group (NKG) who played the political role, but rather Africans with the same interest who had emerged and were now in power (1975, p. 62). While in terms of foreign transnational corporations (TNCs), it was no longer the foreign executives but African executives who held identical views (p. 124).

The imperialist world is against genuine development
Genuine development means the development of man and woman, not of mere things. That is why it is argued in the Cocoyoc Declaration

(1974, p. 359) that: 'the purpose of development ... should not be to develop things but to develop man'. It must be recognized that 'All human beings have basic needs: food, shelter, clothing, health and education.' Accordingly, 'any process of growth that does not lead to their fulfilment – or even worse, disrupts them – is a travesty of the idea of development'. It further declared that 'A growth process that benefits only the wealthiest minority and maintains or even increases the disparities between and within countries is not development. It is exploitation.' The Declaration also 'rejected the idea of "growth first, justice in the distribution of benefits later"'. The experience of Africa has proved as illusory as the idea 'that rapid growth benefiting the few will trickle down to the mass of the people'.

Summing up what development should really imply, the Cocoyoc Declaration declared 'Development should not be limited to the satisfaction of basic needs. There are other needs, other goals, and other values. Development includes freedom of expression and impression, the right to give and to receive ideas and stimulus.' It includes the fulfilment of 'a deep social need to participate in shaping the basis of one's own existence, and to make some contribution to the fashioning of the world's future'. It must also include 'the right to work': meaning that it is just not a matter of 'having a job but finding self-realization in work', and not least, 'the right not to be alienated *through production processes that use human beings simply as tools*' (author's emphasis). The declaration also recommends the development strategy of self-reliance and 'a temporary detachment from the present economic system' because, and as real experience proves, 'it is impossible to develop self-reliance through full participation in a system that perpetuates economic dependence' (pp. 360–1).

According to Professor Paul A. Baran, 'the ... notion of "development" and "growth" suggest a transition to something that is new from something that is old, that has outlived itself'. It follows that development is and has to be a revolutionary process. The entire ideological, technical and cultural aspects of society must undergo revolutionary changes. It therefore means 'a sweeping re-organisation of society, ... an all-out mobilization of all its creative potentialities' all aimed at moving 'the economy off dead center' (1960, p. 13).

But when the colonial powers in particular and the West in general surrendered political power to the African elites, they did not want to see any fundamental changes taking place in the structures they had built in their colonies and in the dominant and dominated relationship between the ex-colony and the so-called mother country. They did not want the black elites who constituted the governing class to tamper with the vertical division of labour bequeathed to them by the colonial officials.

They wanted to see African ex-colonies continue with their role of producing raw materials and providing a market for the manufactured commodities imported from the industrialized capitalist countries. Accordingly, when it came to industrialization, the colonial powers and the West, were not willing to see a genuine industrialization process take place in the ex-colonies. The type of industries permitted were to be of extraction, semi-processing, assembling or repacking. These are what came popularly to be known as import-substitution industries. And they had to be established by metropolitan 'businesses whose main concern is merely to organise initial processing near the point of primary production'(Hanson, 1959, p. 4). Copper processing in Uganda was a good example. The World Bank missions were also 'hostile to projects for the establishment of heavy industry' (p. 101).

The truth is that the industrialized capitalist countries do not want to see the intellectually challenging and stimulating productive activities like research, experimentation, development and design undertaken in the former colonies. They must jealously preserve these activities as their monopoly. The only activities they are prepared to allow in the ex-colonies are those of routine nature like assembling, mixing, repacking and maintenance of imported manufactured commodities, machinery and plant.

In terms of ideological, social and cultural values, the imperialist world was therefore not prepared to see their African ex-colonies develop an independent superstructure, that is, ideological consciousness, social awareness and relations as well as cultural values. Their interest was to see that Africa developed according to what both the United States and Europe wanted Africa to be. And as Leakey pointed out, at the time Africans were attaining formal independence, there were 'people, both European and American, who firmly believe[d] that the only mental and psychological differences between an African Negro and a white man are those which can be attributed solely to education and cultural background'. Accordingly, people who thought like that also believed 'that an African who is given a European or American education will at once become in all mental, intellectual and psychological aspects a white man with a black skin' (1961, p. 16). Thus, immediately after the Second World War, European colonial powers like Britain, France and Belgium which were joined later by Portugal, made 'the effort to draw African territories into a Euro-American economic system' (McKay, 1958, p. 82). The US wanted 'Africa to become ... an extension of the family of Western nations – healthy, vigorous, and democratic'. What they wanted to see was that 'the emergent societies develop national integration without nationalistic jingoism' (Goldschmidt, 1958, p. 187).

What we should note is that both Europe and the US rediscovered Africa during and after the Second World War in terms of raw materials. The European dependence on Africa for few materials was in no doubt. In case of the US, Professor Andrew M. Kamarck writing in 1958, pointed out how 'Africa as a source of supply for raw materials and as a market for United States goods is destined to play a more important part in American economy of the future'(p. 119). And that since the US had 'definitely become a haven't enough nation', in terms of raw materials, Africa was increasingly becoming of interest to her 'as a future supplier of industrial raw materials and unprocessed foodstuff'. Thus:

> Africa has been called 'the continent God kept in reserve'. It is becoming more and more necessary to find out what is in this reserve. Africa, the second largest continent, is large enough to make the chances good, that needed resources can be found which may or may not be immediately exploitable (p. 120).

Both the US and Europe were not prepared to see any real development take place in Africa. The reason was summed up by Professor Baran in the following statement:

> What is decisive is that economic development in under developed countries is profoundly inimical to the dominant interests in the advanced capitalist countries supplying many important raw materials to the industrialized countries, providing their corporations with vast profits and investment outlets, the backward world has always presented the indispensable hinterland of the highly developed capitalist West (1960, pp. 11–12).

For that reason 'the ruling class in the United States' and in Europe, as well as Japan, 'is *bitterly opposed to the industrialization of the so-called "source countries" and to the emergence of integrated processing economies in the colonial and semi-colonial area*'. He then adds that 'this opposition appears regardless of the nature of the regime in the under developed country *that seeks to reduce the foreign grip on its economy and to prove for a measure of independent development*'(author's emphasis). That is, whether the regime is democratically elected and therefore popular, or it is a dictatorship and therefore unpopular, as long as it attempts to seek a path of 'independent development' and therefore undertakes to oppose the foreign domination of its country: 'all leverages of diplomatic intrigues, economic pressures, and political subversion are set into motion to overthrow the recalcitrant national government and to replace it with politicians who are willing to serve the interests of the capitalist countries' (p. 12).

That is, no underdeveloped country can seriously talk of 'building an independent, integrated, self-sustaining national economy' and be left alone to struggle to achieve that objective. And yet without such an economy, 'independence and autonomy are little more than sham as long as the countries in question remain economic appendages of the advanced capitalist countries and as long as their governments depend for survival on the pleasure of their foreign patrons'(p. 14). And as the Hungarian patriotic leader, Imre Nagy pointed out: 'The people cannot be free if the nation is not independent, if it does not possess complete sovereignty, if foreign influences prevail in its internal affairs, as no nation can be independent and sovereign whose people do not possess complete right to freedom' (1957, p. 21).

Under-development and the living conditions of Africans

The living conditions of the people on the continent of Africa can be properly described as appalling, pathetic and inhuman. The people of Africa have been reduced to third-rate human beings. Today, we are the most despised people in the world. But under the World Bank and IMF structural adjustment programmes (SAPs) regime, African leaders dare not point their finger at the real cause of the state and conditions of the people on the continent, because to do so can easily mean losing the necessary handout from 'donors' for survival. The blame for the worsening conditions of the people is therefore heaped on 'bad leadership', on 'lack of multipartyism', 'pluralism' and therefore 'democracy'. That is, on African 'dictators'.

But the truth is that, since independence, no African government has worked completely outside the influence, direct or indirect, of the advanced capitalist countries in its internal affairs; whatever political label it has chosen to wear: capitalist, socialist or African socialist. Through aid, the World Bank 'experts' have always wielded decisive influence on Africa's economic development. The real problem is (although it is now emphasized that the demand for development must be *indigenous* – coming from the community that needs it) that in Africa since independence such ideas have come from outside and are imposed as a condition for aid on post-colonial governments which in turn impose them on the people in the name of development and progress. But when they fail to produce fruits, it is the people who are to blame. The truth was stated by Germa Amare when he observed that 'Communities are required to accept innovations that have no immediate relevance to the solution of their urgent problems. When such measures fail to bring about any significant change, the blame is often directed at the people who are considered stupid and irresponsible' (1970, p. 195).

We therefore believe that the real root cause of the appalling, pathetic and inhuman conditions of the African people today, is to be found in continued foreign domination, oppression and exploitation. For as Nagy said, 'If a nation does not possess its sovereign rights or is unable to attain them, the dependency and subjugation of the country will result in rule of poverty and backwardness for the nation' (1957, p. 21). Accordingly, it is only when their country is genuinely free and independent, that the people can also become rich and prosperous. It is therefore important to stress that 'the fate of the people depends very much on the way in which national independence develops'.

Foreign influence and deepening poverty

Every honest person knows and will admit that the living conditions of the people on the continent of Africa have been steadily deteriorating since independence. It is also true that since independence virtually all African countries have been working under the influence, direction and control of the World Bank, the IMF and Western 'experts'. And as Janheinz Jahn (1958, p. 11) pointed out, Europeans were convinced that the end product of the development process in Africa should be 'a fully Europeanized Africa'. Europe therefore arrogated to itself the right to provide the development model which Africa had to copy. Europe claimed 'to be spiritually the giving, Africa the receiving partner'. Europe posed as the teacher and Africa was deemed to be the pupil; Europe claimed to know better what was 'good for Africa, better than Africa herself'. The responsibility 'to decide when Africa is ripe: ripe for a faith, ripe for action, ripe for freedom' was taken over by Europe! This wish was shared by the dominant nationalist elite.

Those who are old enough to remember the short-lived prosperity that followed the Second World War, continue to wonder why things have become so bad especially since the 1970s. But that period of temporary prosperity was also the beginning of the worst that was yet to come. The worst because a person who has tasted a good life feels much worse than the one who has not. That is why the Abasamia people have a saying that '*Chihutangira chitahutulire nyuma*'('It is better to start with bad times than to suffer them later'). That early post-war period laid the foundation for the appalling state and conditions the African people are suffering today – ideological underdevelopment, technical backwardness and cultural disorientation leading to moral, ethical and aesthetic decay or degeneration.

Economically, the post-war period established conditions for the development of poverty brought about by exploitation. It also established the basis for deepening dependence as a result of producing what we did not need and consuming what we did not produce, and believing in foreign aid as the key to development. The foundation for poverty was laid by the extreme exploitation the people of Africa were subjected to by their colonial masters. According to Professor Fieldhouse, 'A rough calculation suggests that between 1945 and 1951, Britain extracted some 140 million pounds from its colonies, putting only about 40 million pounds under the Colonial Development and Welfare (CD & W) Acts', that is, Britain made a huge super profit of 350 per cent. Fieldhouse therefore notes how the European colonial powers 'squeezed and exploited their colonies in Africa ... in ways never seen before'. These ways included

> a complex network of administrative controls (currency pools to channel all colonial dollar earnings to London, Paris or Brussels, bulk purchase of commodities to keep down prices in the metropolis, limitation of export to colonies of manufactures which might earn hard currency elsewhere, building up credits representing the surpluses of marketing boards, hard currency earnings converted into sterling balances or francs, and so on)' (1986, p. 6).

It is Africa which repaid the European war debts to the US and the post-war European recovery programmes. The degree of exploitation of the African people during the 1950s by the European colonial powers is further indicated by what happened in the then Belgian Congo (now Zaire). There, according to Fieldhouse, in the 1950s, 99 per cent of the population was African, but the 1 per cent of the population which was foreign, owned and controlled '95 per cent of total assets, 82 per cent of the largest units of production and 88 per cent of private savings'. While in 1958, two years before independence, the 1 per cent of 'foreigners received 12.9b[illion] francs in salaries, 7.0b francs from property and business enterprises, 5.9b from amortization and 1.3b from corporate savings'. In terms of consumption, the foreigners accounted for 12.1 billion francs, compared to 19.0 billion by Africans. Thus in that country by 1958, '110,000 whites ... and a few very large overseas firms controlled almost the entire modern economy, possessed very considerable purchasing power and constituted a relatively large market for local manufacturers as well as imports' (1986, p. 44).

It can therefore be seen that such a typical colonial economy was superficial and therefore superimposed. It had no roots among the masses of the African population, and could therefore not benefit them. The masses were mere subjects of exploitation, not of development. For example, in Uganda, the peasant producers of cotton and coffee were deliberately paid very low prices while the Asian comprador capitalists who bought the produce were paid much more. This enabled these Asians to invest in real property and small-scale industries in the 1950s and early 1960s.

As they say, the economy is the base and politics is the concentrated expression of the economy. Undemocratic or superimposed economy also produces a kind of political authority and practice which is superficial and superimposed to serve foreign interests; the colonial and post-colonial state was also superficial and superimposed on African societies in order to force people to serve foreign economic interests.

On achieving formal independence, according to Fieldhouse

> only a partial metamorphosis of the colonial state and society had taken place before decolonization; the new nation state inherited a tradition of autocracy barely tempered by democracy and a society united only by the now irrelevant call to eject imperialists (1986, p. 56).

The call now appeared 'irrelevant' because, the real issue was not imperialism – the system – but the imperialists who now appeared to be going. In terms of economic development, as we have noted, the colonial state got involved in spearheading both economic and social development. This was of course meant to bribe the nationalists who were clamouring for independence and therefore provide 'legitimacy for continuing imperial rule'. As far as the colonial state was concerned, the development ideal justified much greater central government power and intervention. It was expressed in planning, higher taxation, tight economic regulations, state monopoly of commodity pricing and purchase, pressure on peasants to improve production methods and a larger bureaucracy.

But since at the top of the African nationalists' agenda was the ending of poverty, disease and ignorance once the imperialists were removed, it was only natural that these nationalists took over development as a vital political tool, claiming that they could provide it faster than the imperialists. However, as we have noted, the imperialist powers were totally against genuine development. The post-colonial reality had therefore to force even the genuine and sincere African nationalists, to misuse the call for development to justify anti-people policies. But it must also be noted that although the African nationalists wanted the state to play a leading role in economic development, they lacked the ideology to guide the state sector.

It can therefore be seen that the post-colonial state in Africa had to be anti-developmental in terms of the development of the people, by the people for the people. Fieldhouse summed up its true nature thus:

> The political inheritance of the colonialism in Black Africa can, therefore, be summed up in oversimplified form as a tradition of bureaucratic autocracy, scarcely yet affected by democracy and bolstered by the development imperative, and social pluralism only transiently overlaid by the nationalistic myth (1986).

He therefore asserts that such political structures which lacked any base among the popular masses, were actually 'in transition which could either move forward to true democracy or backwards to centralized authoritarianism'. It is the latter that has actually happened. The result of that superficial state has been 'a fundamental political instability usually concealed under monopolistic or oligopolistic authoritarian regimes' (1986, p. 57). That is exactly what Fanon meant when he wrote about 'the national bourgeoisie [turning] its back more and more to the interior and on the real facts of its under-developed country' and instead it begins to look towards the former colonial power and to foreign capitalists and donor agencies and 'donors' of aid as the only people who matter in terms of development. That is when the post-colonial state is said to be set out in Africa. For the national bourgeoisie having turned its back to the people, now rallies behind what it deems to be the 'leader.' Fanon correctly observed that the bourgeois dictatorship of an under-developed country draws its strength from the existence of a leader, a leader whose word is law itself. The point we have therefore to stress is that, today it is not the African governments who decide on what is right or wrong for Africa, but the 'donor community', the 'donor agencies' and the World Bank and IMF resident officials.

The nature of the state and conditions of the people
The national bourgeois governing class, having turned its back on the interior, on the people, and on the real facts of its under-developed country, now has to look to the former colonial power, foreign capitalists and donor agencies, as the source of the survival of its regime. This implies that the governing class has abandoned its responsibility to the people. Experience shows that the real masters of the country become the World Bank and the IMF. As we have already noted, independence was mere sham. Because as Onimode points out, the old masters, the direct colonial officials, who left in the 1960s, merely handed over to the rule of the multinational corporations (MNCs). These have now handed over to IMF and the World Bank which 'represent increasing multilateralism, decreasing direct visibility of imperialism and the current multilateral recolonization of Africa' (Onimode, 1988, p. 280).

We can therefore see that formal independence did not end the foreign domination and exploitation of Africa. Basil Davidson points out, 'The point ... to emphasize [is] that the extraction of wealth from an already impoverished Africa was in no way halted by the "transfer of power".'

Accordingly, 'A transfer of poverty continued as before, even while the means of transfer were modified or camouflaged' (1992, p. 219). That is exactly what happened from the 1970s: adverse terms of trade. For example, while in 1975, one ton of copper from Africa was exchanged for 115 barrels of oil, it could only earn 58 barrels in 1980; African cocoa of the same weight could fetch 148 barrels of oil in 1975, in 1980 its purchasing power had dropped to only 63 barrels; the price of coffee in 1975 was 148 barrels of oil, in 1980 it had gone down to 82 barrels. In 1986 the fall in export prices of African commodities cost the continent 19 billion dollars, but the cost of imported manufactured goods went up by 14 per cent. And not least is the fact that for six successive years up to 1990, the poor countries of the so-called Third World – the ex-colonies – 'increased their net transfer of wealth to the "developed world": that is, to the ex-imperialist and other industrialized countries'. It is also said that in 1991, Africa got a total of 4 billion dollars in so-called aid, but 80,000 foreign experts were paid exactly the same amount, 4 billion dollars. Then think of debt-servicing and other costs. That is why Susan George has asserted that Africa is 'getting precisely little help from outside. Already Africa is transferring more capital abroad in debt-service and other payments than it is receiving in aid and new loans' (1988, p. 86).

The results are clear for all concerned to see. They are reflected in deepening poverty, leading to squalor and misery for the great majority of people. Increasing misery is manifested, in 'the immiseration of the great numbers of ordinary people who had hoped independence would bring relief from the conditions brought about by colonialism' (Turok, 1987, p. 16). This has come about because of increased 'proletarianisation, increased exploitation, and pauperisation'. These miserable conditions that the great majority of African people face are clearly shown by Africa's very low average per capita income: $US 741 in 1980 compared to $US 9,684 for the industrialized countries. And that of Africa south of the Sahara was even more miserable. It was only $US 239. That small average per capita 'income is highly skewed and unequal'. The truth is that no *bona fide* employee in Africa under the SAPs regime is paid a 'living wage'. Even university professors have been reduced to the level of paupers. To make matters worse is the increasing phenomenon of unemployment and under-employment. As Turok points out, in 1980 'unemployment is massive with about half of the 33 million who were available for work during 1970s finding nothing for them'. The situation is even worse today as even graduates and professionals are unable to find employment. Matters are compounded by the retrenchment conditionality of the World Bank and the IMF. This leads to another very glaring problem; that of dependency, which according to Turok was about 'three persons per employed person'. Accordingly, he points out that 'about 70 people out of every 100 were, in 1980, either "destitute" or on the verge of poverty'. The situation is worse now, as the number of job seekers has escalated.

We should also point out that the growth model of development pursued during the two consecutive UN Development Decades, 1960–1980, only worked to make inequalities grow worse. This fact was very clearly stated by the findings of the Commonwealth Conference published in 1971 (see Robinson, 1971). It was noted that economic growth in the Third World instead of creating employment, destroyed it very fast. It deepens social cleavages, while inequality in the distribution of income leads to the widening of 'old and new social' and regional divisions and therefore conflicts (Turak, 1987, p. 16). Under the SAPs regime, these social evils have worsened. All this as noted by Turok is because 'the policies pursued amounted to a massive betrayal of the interests of the people'.

These anti-people policies are responsible for the social turbulence that has dominated Africa since independence, as the popular masses have lost confidence in the governments run by the black bourgeoisie which have proved incapable of serving the people's interests. The phenomenon of coups is one of the important results. These 'coups have overturned both progressive and reactionary regimes, civilian and military governments' (Turok, 1987, p. 17). They are an indication of a society in crisis. In addition to the coups, various strikes, uprisings and popular rebellions and resistance movements are rampant all over Africa. And not least, the demand for popular democracy is voiced all over the continent.

The struggle between the workers and the African neocolonial governments must also be specifically mentioned as an important manifestation of the ongoing social turbulence. There is nowhere in Africa where there has not been a serious confrontation between the trade unions and the government. The following comment by an African scholar Annanaba, explains the nature of the struggle very well. He pointed out the fact that 'since independence the trade union movement in Africa has had a rough existence'. In many African countries, genuine trade union organizations do not exist. Instead they have been replaced by superficial organizations 'created or sponsored by governments, politicians or military leaders' or sponsored by unions from imperialist countries which fear militant trade unionism. Genuine trade unionists have therefore been subjected to persecutions in all forms. Many have been 'arrested and jailed without trial' while others have suffered detentions for very long periods and others 'have been shot in cold blood'. Trade unionists have therefore probably suffered more under post-colonial African regimes than they did under formal colonial rule (see Turok, 1987, p. 18).

The under-development in the rural areas has deepened. Agriculture has remained backward and based on small peasant production using the primitive hoe. The drought experienced by many African countries has of course made matters worse, but the greatest setback causing under-production resulting in famine, is the backward nature of agricultural methods in the rural areas. Deepening under-development and impoverization of the rural areas leads to migration, especially of the youths, into the urban areas thereby compounding the problem of overcrowding and slum development in the towns where conditions of living are most appalling.

Other social evils the people of Africa are faced with because of the adverse effect of SAPs, include an increasing rate of crime – lawlessness, robberies, thuggery, etc. – both in the urban and rural areas; prostitution and other forms of social deviance despite the scourge of AIDS; increasing school drop-outs as many parents fail to raise escalating school fees, and malnutrition both of the children and adults as people cannot afford to feed themselves well. People cannot afford decent clothing – even relatively better-paid civil servants and teachers are forced to resort to buying second-hand clothing from Europe and the US which has an adverse effect on our textile industry. Nor can people afford decent housing. Family instability, drug abuse and alcholism, juvenile delinquency, child abuse, unmarried spinsters as heads of households, uncared-for widows, orphans and the aged are all with us today (Leakey, 1961, p. 20). That is what 'modernization' really means – social rejection! Then there is the increasing mortality rate as many find it too expensive to go to hospitals which have introduced cost-sharing schemes; many women cannot go to hospital for delivery because they cannot afford the fees. It should also be noted that many workers and peasants cannot afford to send their children to school, while higher education is more and more becoming a privilege of only the rich and well-to-do families.

The fact is that African youths are so demoralized, frustrated and helpless due to the working of an unjust inhuman system, that, as someone put it, if they heard that there was a ship at Mombasa taking youths to slavery in the US or Europe, they would rush to it in thousands!

Culturally, the African of today has lost a sense of direction. The African, due to colonial and neocolonial mentality, has lost the core of moral, ethical and aesthetic values that could serve as his or her lodestar to life. As Professor Goldschmidt pointed out, 'the important point about cultural values is that they give direction to life'. Thus, when a person struggles to seek 'after the values of his culture, the individual gives meaning to his life' (1958, p. 167). This has ceased to be the case in Africa. What people seek after is to imitate others as a monkey does a human! This is defended in terms of 'international standards', 'fashion' or 'modernity'. African collective consciousness and social commitment are steadily disappearing, giving way to the worst kind of crude individualism of human-eat-human.

This has led to a loss of intellectual independence and self-respect. Africans have lost confidence in themselves and their people. The African bureaucratic bourgeoisie is therefore incapable of thinking and taking an independent decision (Machyo, 1973). Bureaucrats see their role as that of carrying out instructions from the 'experts' and consultants appointed for them by the World Bank, by the IMF, by the 'donor community'. The African bureaucratic bourgeoisie fits very well in the description by Professor Adam Curle as: 'the local agents of the foreign corporations, officials who smoothe ... the way, ministers and others whose good will it [is] desirable to purchase labour leaders who [can] control workers' (1971, p. 116).

These are the people who, as we have noted, turned their backs on the interior, on the people, on the conditions of their country's under-development. It is they who now look to foreign capitalists, to the 'donors' and foreign corporations. For as Curle points out, it is they who really profit 'from aid and foreign investment. The local contracts, the gifts, the high salaries, the privileges, the opportunities for travel and scholarships abroad.' These constitute a class of people in Third World countries 'who depend on and profit from the link with the rich nations and who are, in turn essential to them'. Curle therefore asserts that it is 'These people with their wealthy masters, [who] constitute *the exploitive network*' (emphasis added) (1971, p. 116). It is that class of Africans on whom the World Bank and the IMF depend for the success of the SAPs' conditionalities like privatization and divesture and therefore the recolonization of Africa.

Poverty has made us undignified beggars. African governments, churches and what have you have elevated begging to a profession. Because all of us are beggars, we have no respect for each other, no mutual trust. We therefore loathe to learn from each other's experience. We all look to the masters, the donors, all the time to tell us what to do.

The fantastic incidence of corruption in Africa is rooted in that class and its foreign masters; so is the syndrome of dependency and begging for aid – even to sink a pit-latrine, protect water springs, construct valley dams (as if we never built them before colonial rule) and to clear garbage from our urban streets! We have a dependency on foreign 'experts' even if they know virtually nothing as compared to our own people. The fact is that a street sweeper from London, Paris, Bonn or New York is an expert on urban management in Africa! But these so-called foreign experts are earning monthly salaries which they would not dream of in their own countries, while their African assistants in the 'authorities' are pocketing salaries way above the average, thus becoming the envy of even professors. Their demonstration effect has to entice corruption for those who struggle to be like the Joneses!

In fact the state and conditions of the people on the African continent with all its fabulous potential wealth, both human and non-human, are not different from those of the people of the island of Haiti which has been referred to as the 'Third World horror'. That is, Africa has also 'become a stage on which it seems every modern plague and curse is now acted out – from rampant AIDS epidemic, drug smuggling' – what is called *magendo* in East Africa, 'child prostitution, and social and class discrimination to unchecked population growth, disastrous environment degradation' – charges for electricity are too high so people have to use charcoal and firewood, 'gregarious human rights abuse and aid dependence' (*The New Vision*, Kampala, 28 November 1993). The difference may be one of degree, but certainly not of kind. The cause is the same: imperialist neocolonial domination, plunder and exploitation of the black people.

As the ranks of the 'haves' become ever more narrow, while those of the 'have nots' increase and widen, social conflicts also multiply and deepen with every step of human degradation. More and more people become frustrated and disgusted and lose hope. In the words of Basil Davidson, what has happened as a result of failure to make independence meaningful to the people, has been 'a steady decline in the moral and political values of those who led or claimed to lead the nation-states'. And although it is true that honesty and hard work could still save the day,

> deepening impoverishment piled tremendous handicaps on every effort at honesty and hard work. Even among those who still hoped for the best, and strove for the general good rather than the individual racket – and there were still many such in this Africa of collapsing expectations – a growing sense of fatal isolation took hope by the throat and gradually choked it in the lassitudes of despair. (1992, p. 221)

That is why many would wish for the return of the former colonial masters (Dumont, 1966, p. 20 and *The New Vision*, Kampala, 1 December 1993). The same sense of despair is reflected in the way we exalt the ability of foreign investors to 'industrialize' our countries as if they had been unable to do so before. That despair is the greatest ideological weakness in the struggle against recolonization.

The struggle for the Second Liberation

The African demand is for genuine liberation and development. But never before in the history of African peoples have they completely surrendered to fate and given up the struggle for liberation. So that, while the bureaucratic bourgeoisie at the helm of the sinking African ship may be too happy and ready to pile up counter-productive 'heavy foreign debts and mortgages on the future of the country and the people' (Robinson, 1971, p. 38) in return for trinkets, in the hope that they can compensate for the undeserved misfortunes arising out of the adverse conditions against us brought about by the exploitive network, there are other Africans who insist that the struggle must continue. A good example is Nzongola Ntalaja, a scholar from Zaire in exile, who urges 'genuine national liberation as the alternative'. According to him, the struggle for the Second Liberation calls for a struggle on two interlinked fronts: that of a liberation from imperialism and a social revolution. That is to say, 'a national revolution or a people's struggle against foreign rule, and a social revolution; one which seeks to destroy the capitalist structure on which the exploitation of workers and peasants is built and to replace it with socialism' (Turok, 1987, pp. 12–13).

The liberation and development Africans are calling for is genuine national liberation and development, not mere sham as the post-colonial experience has proved. For as Professor Robinson observed, despite what appeared to be impressive development of the Third World in the 1960s, 'it often did so in ways that threw existing theories into disarray'. For the more they 'tried to advance, the less they ... succeeded, for the statistics of growth for the 1960s were somehow disappointing' (Robinson, 1971, p. 37). All that this means is that the growth model of development has proved a complete failure. That is why objective and honest economists and other developmentalists have been calling for a development model based on the development of the people, by the people, for the people. The form of development Africans want is that which is capable of creating conditions which are capable of enhancing human dignity. These conditions include safety, sufficiency, satisfaction, cultural and intellectual stimulus. Development must lead to the awakening of awareness of the African peoples. It must assure them the means of life sustenance, esteem, genuine 'freedom from servitudes (to nature, to ignorance, to other men, to institutions) for example, the feudal institutions, churches or mosques and [to beliefs] considered oppressive' (Curle, 1971, pp. 118–19) Development must therefore be a total liberating process.

The question of the social system

The biggest problem in Africa today is lack of a clear understanding of the concept of development and therefore what it really should encompass. As we have noted, for many post-colonial African leaders as well as the pseudo-intellectuals who serve them, development was, and is still, simply seen and understood as 'modernization' which is in turn understood as becoming a blueprint of Europe or the US. Their ambition was coined in the phrase 'to catch up'. The question of what kind of society was to be built did not cross their minds. Thus, when people like Nyerere spoke of *Ujamaa* or socialism in an effort 'to find ways of mobilizing mass support for self-reorganization, [they] were generally mocked by other African governments as "utopian" or "idealist", as though "reality" in this Africa could never do more than serve a narrow and reckless self interest', observed Basil Davidson. But while other African leaders mocked and laughed at Nyerere, 'his "experiments" on behalf of the general good were an object of "outside" scorn while the actual workings of the terms of trade, worldwide, ensured that none of these experiments could do more than limp, or even work at all' (1992, p. 222).

We can therefore assert that the failure of the *Ujamaa* experiment, despite its weaknesses of idealism, was not because it was an essentially wrong approach, but because it had powerful enemies ranged against it both from within and from imperialist circles. Social development is not a matter of just jumping on the bandwagon and aping other peoples. Genuine social development as a process of ideological, technical and cultural revolutions, starts from the minds of the people who want to bring it about. It is an answer to the people's real demands, aspirations and desires, reflecting what people really want to be. What people really want reflects their ideological, socio-economic and cultural longings. The existing social order is not providing or meeting these demands. A social order/system consists of the mode of production – the method people use to produce goods and services; then the production relations and the superstructure or the ideas and institutions established and developed to justify and defend the existing order. A system can operate so that it either meets the demands of the whole community or it can operate to the benefit of only a small minority who control the rest of society through administering the system. That is what capitalism actually does. To those who have, even more is added and from those who have not, even the little they have is taken away. That has been the truth about Europe and Africa since the colonial days.

If the system is anti-people, if it merely works to use people as a means of production for the benefit of others, then it is immaterial as to who administers it. Even if the existing administrators are replaced, as long as the system is left intact, that will only amount to a mere changing of the guards, which is what happened to our so-called independence. The white guards were replaced by black ones

– otherwise everything operated as usual. The only difference was that the black guards were not as experienced and therefore not as confident as the white guards. The mess they have made is due to lack of experience in the management of the system. That is why they have had to depend on white 'experts' to advise them on how to manage the colonially erected system. It is therefore correct to assert that since the colonial system never changed, the real rulers of Africa remain the ruling class of the former colonial powers; the Africans who took over from the white officials have remained mere governors – agents of the foreign ruling class. That is why, apart from Libya (which has since its 1969 revolution maintained a very high standard of living for all its citizens), no government in Africa, whether civilian or military and regardless of the quality of leadership, has brought about any fundamental change. Hence the appalling state and conditions of African people today.

However, without a revolutionary fundamental change in the system, no genuine liberation, development and progress can be expected. Professor Baran clearly states that our situation requires an enabling environment:

> ... where far-reaching structural changes in the economy are required if the economic development of a country is to shift into a high gear and is to outstrip the growth of the population, where technological indivisibilities render growth dependent on large investment and long-run planning, where tradition bound patterns of thought and work obstruct the introduction of new methods and means of production ... (1960, p. 13)

He concludes that it is 'only a sweeping reorganization of society, only an all-out mobilization of all its creative potentialities that can move the economy off dead center' (1960, p. 13). That is what post-colonial African governments failed to do. But again that is what has and will have to be done. The only alternative to that is recolonization.

Intellectual liberation

The biggest obstacle to revolutionary fundamental changes in Africa is what we wish to refer to as a slave mentality: conservative, reactionary and dependent mental outlook of the so-called educated class. Generally speaking, the educated African is not a revolutionary. And the higher up in the educational ladder he or she climbs, the more conservative, reactionary and dependent he or she becomes.

The role of the educated African is always to seek to be on 'the safe side' where the chances of 'falling into things', of 'eating' are brightest. Those who seem to be revolutionary during their youth, slowly but surely shed their revolutionary outlook as they grow up. They change their colours and preach 'moderation' and 'we must be realistic' joining the continuing efforts being made to de-revolutionize the masses – the peasantry and workers – and urging them to 'forgive and forget'. Therefore what Chancellor Williams says of the elected black officials in the US is also equally true of the elected African officials. That is, it 'is well known ... that "black officials" once elected to office, turn out to be as conservative and reactionary as any [white] Congressman from the backwoods of Mississippi' (1987, p. 333). Their African counterparts turn out to be as conservative and reactionary as any conservative and reactionary members of Parliament in the former colonial metroplis. Hence the pride shown in the use of feudal titles like Sir, Honourable, Lordship, Worship, and His Excellency. The African elites in position of power can therefore be comparable to the Church. They become agents trusted by the people 'to run programmes aimed at social change'. But when they are 'threatened by real change', they withdraw 'rather than permit social awareness to spread like wildfire' (Illich, 1974, p. 52). This fear of full-scale revolution, this strong tendency to compromise on principles, is not a natural characteristic of the African people. It is the direct product of colonial and neocolonial education. The aim of that education was and still is, to produce tamed, servile, obedient servants of the colonial system; it aims at producing performers, not critically thinking, growing personalities. Its aim was and is to produce minor servants of the colonial system, not leaders and policy makers; to produce dependent not independent minds. It had therefore and still continues to be, learning by rote-cramming, learning by heart and reproducing facts as one was taught. That is why Rodney described it as 'education for subordination, exploitation, the creation of mental confusion and the development of underdevelopment' (1976, p. 264). According to Professor Curle, '... the children learn to be docile, passive, and conformist because that is the way to get through without trouble. They learn to be thoroughly distrustful of adults because they work to a pattern which is arbitrary, cruel and irrational' (1971, p. 19). Once they are adult they choose to serve the dictators and to distrust others. They are praised as 'good' civil servants, model natives, etc. Explaining the problem, Chancellor Williams points out how 'The present-day confused outlook of the African people is the result of centuries of the white people's acculturation, a quite natural process wherever one people come under the economic, political and social domination of another people' (Williams, 1987, p. 331). This domination results in the dominated imbibing and therefore accepting as his own 'the ideologies and value system of the oppressors ... even when the result is demonstratively against themselves'. In Africa, this unconscious embracing of the oppressors' ideologies and value systems is done in the name of religion, progress and modernization. But, as Williams points out, the Indians, the Chinese and the Japanese, who have also progressed, 'were able to hold on doggedly to their own racial pride and cultural heritage as the last resource for survival as a people' (1987, p. 331).

A country is as good as its people, and the people are as good as their education. A revolutionary people-centred democratic education produces revolutionary democratic people. It follows that if Africa is to struggle and achieve genuine liberation, independence and development, there is a need to revolutionize the educational system and raise the level of awareness of the popular masses, especially through adult or political education. According to Williams, the need for re-education must therefore be seen to be for 'two mandatory changes in attitude: one toward each other in terms of mutual respect and the other attitude about efficiency, expertise in business management and financial responsibility and administration' (1987, p. 339). Therefore, explaining what is meant by education for liberation, Professor Curle wrote that it is that which attempts to liberate us from the habits of thought, action and feeling which make us less human, which enables us in turn to try and liberate others and 'which transforms the system into the counter-system'(1971, p. 127). The objective of education as an instrument of intellectual liberation in Africa must therefore be to 'help nourish the culture'. Which according to Curle should 'mean that it must oppose the alien culture encapsulated in educational practice, or at least present a different model'. It must also contribute towards the development of productive skills. Thus education for liberation 'must provide the appropriate culture and with the culture, the orientation towards skills and material standards' (1971, p. 120).

Pan Africanism and the Second Liberation

Finally, the emphasis has to be made that the greatest obstacle to the defence of African independence against foreign invaders dating to the ancient times, is lack of unity among ourselves. Centuries of struggle against foreign invaders from Asia and Europe, then internecine warfare against each other leading to splits into minor groups, has resulted in what seems to be an irreconcilable disunity. Explaining how so-called tribes came about, Basil Davidson records that it was because of the search for more fertile land, but even more it was the development of 'the iron-pointed spear [which] was undoubtedly a great social and political innovator'. It led to the break-up of the ancient communal democratic stateless communities which existed without government; it led to the rise of strong and ambitious groups which managed to impose their will on the weaker ones. That is how 'centralized political organization, of kingship and a rudimentary bureaucracy, of a systematic social differentiation between masters and servants, rulers and ruled' emerged (1964, p. 13). It is this social fracturing which constituted the process which divided the ancestral stocks into tribes as they are often though misleadingly called – through revolt of chiefs' sons against their fathers, of junior groups against senior groups, of migrant rebels against parent clans and loyalties. That is how present modern African societies originated. But throughout the subsequent history of Africa, peoples have existed on the basis of what Davidson calls *'unity in diversity'*. Thus the root of Pan African unity as a political ambition of modern times is to be traced far back into the past.

Modern Pan Africanism as a political movement was born out of the indomitable spirit of resistance; resistance against European colonial powers grabbing and alienating the Africans from their lands. This resistance took a more organized form globally in the tradition of Pan African Congresses (which began at the first Pan African Conference in 1900), the most famous of which is the 5th Pan African Congress held in Manchester, Britain in 1945. The resolutions of all these congresses had a common feature: anti-imperialism. They therefore centred on the demand for freedom, the dismantling of colonialism, the repudiation of racism, and the call for unity under the banner of a socialist United States of Africa. The 5th Pan African Congress declared the ideological foundation for the post-war anti-colonial struggle. It declared that the African people who were otherwise a peaceful people in the face of centuries of violence and slavery perpetrated upon them by the imperialist powers were prepared to resort to force in the struggle to achieve their freedom. African demands were very clearly stated. They included the determination to be free, the right to education for their children, the right to earn a decent living, the right and freedom of expression of thoughts and emotions and the right to adopt appropriate cultural forms of beauty. They demanded autonomy and independence; they rejected remaining patient any longer, and they voiced their unwillingness to continue to sacrifice and starve while at the same time doing the world's drudgery, in order to support by our poverty and ignorance, a false aristocracy and a discredited imperialism. Monopoly capitalism 'and the rule of private wealth and industry for private profit alone' were equally rejected, and 'economic democracy as the only real democracy' welcomed. They therefore resolved to 'fight in every way' possible 'for freedom, democracy and social betterment' (Thompson, 1969, pp. 58–9). The independence of Ghana in 1957 opened the floodgates to formal African independence. In 1958 Nkrumah called the All African Peoples' Conference (AAPC). It was attended by all African anti-colonial movements. Its guiding motto was 'European Scramble Out of Africa!'

By the mid-1960s, most of Africa had achieved formal independence. But as we have shown, that independence has proved to be mere sham, and today under SAPs with the World Bank and the IMF as the *New Masters*, no African government can sincerely claim to be free and independent. The demands of the 5th Pan African Congress are yet to be realised. But today, unlike in the 1950s and 1960s, Africa is no longer faced with individual colonial powers; we are now faced with a formidable united imperialist front, under the banners of the European Economic Community (EEC) and the North Atlantic Treaty Organization (NATO). Having decisively defeated them on the military front despite their overwhelming military power, they have now regrouped and are using the most effective weapon at their disposal – their superior economic power – to recolonize us. That is the sole purpose of so-called *Aid* and the structural adjustment programmes. With economic power, they are also effectively using the ideological weapon to penetrate and conquer the minds of every African. For as Illich pointed out:

> Next to money and guns, the United States idealist turns up in every theatre of the war; the teacher, the volunteer, the missionary, the community organizer, the economic developer. Such men define their role as service. Actually they frequently wind up numbing the damage done by money and weapons, or seducing the 'under developed' to the benefits of the world of affluence and achievement. (1973, p. 26)

Today the so-called non-governmental organizations (NGOs) have taken over the role that was played by the missionaries during formal colonial rule. Such a formidable and very powerful enemy, cannot be fought by individual African states. For as Cheikh Anta Diop correctly observed, 'The days of the nineteenth-century dwarf states are gone. Our main security and development problems can be solved only on a continental scale and preferably within a federal framework.' Thus, the need for a powerful Pan African movement has never been greater if Africa is to survive recolonization, and achieve real liberation and independence as a condition for genuine development and progress. A Pan African movement is therefore an indispensable prerequisite to the struggle for a Second Liberation. However, as we already noted, the African bourgeois class which inherited the colonial nation-state has proved a complete failure in terms of genuine development. It merely sees its mission as that of maintaining and preserving the inherited system and therefore the status quo. That is what rehabilitating the economy or Economic Recovery Programmes (ERP) really mean. That is also the real objective of SAPs: to rehabilitate the colonial structures. That is why Fanon noted that the phase of this class 'in the history of under-developed countries is a completely useless phase'. After it has destroyed itself 'by its own contradictions, it will be seen that nothing new has happened since independence was proclaimed, and that everything must be started again from scratch' (1963, p. 142). It therefore means that if the Pan African Movement is to spearhead the struggle for the Second Liberation, it has to be rooted in a different social strata, the strata of the popular masses who bear the burdens of SAPs, recolonization and deepening under-development. Therefore in the words of Walter Rodney in his contribution at the 6th Pan African Congress: 'The Unity of Africa requires the unity of progressive groups, organizations and institutions rather than merely being the preserve of the states' (1976, p. 34). Let the people take over if African unity is to be genuine and permanent. For as Diop pointed out, attempts to form regional organizations by African states or governments have proved not only a useless and expensive exercise, but also a total failure. They depend on the whims and personal ambitions of the individual presidents and their governments. The moment there is any change of government in any country, the organization they formed also collapses, causing great suffering to the people. However, African presidents and their governments will come and go, but the people of Africa will always be there. They have to be the real basis of unity.

Conclusion

It must be emphasized that the state and conditions of the African people on the continent is the direct product of continued foreign domination, oppression and exploitation under neocolonial rule. Independence has proved a mere sham and meaningless for the popular masses. Development has never taken place; rather Africa is now threatened with recolonization. The stage is therefore set for the struggle for the Second Liberation. This can only be achieved by a Pan African movement based on the popular masses as the prime mover and the spearhead of the struggle. If we can build that powerful movement, the victory will definitely be ours. Without it, poverty, immiseration and pauperism for the great majority will continue, as will chaos and instability which, for example, have dominated the people of Latin America for over two centuries since they achieved formal independence and were reformed into neocolonies. The vast army of the Afro-pessimism industry and their imperialist masters and lackeys who believe that we Africans are too weak to challenge the present super-imperialist recolonization should note the words of the Hungarian patriotic leader, Imre Nagy, who asserted that 'historical experience decisively proves that economic, political, military, and other power groups are built on quicksand and cannot entice the masses of the people into the service of their cause or with their allegiance'(1957, p. 23). It follows that with a Pan African movement based on the popular masses cutting across the artificial borders of the nation-states, there is hope for Africa. And not least, let us reiterate Rodney's call upon the Pan African Movement to be internationalist and anti-imperialist and ideologically socialist-oriented. The movement must therefore forge links with all world forces struggling for genuine independence, sovereignty, peace and the betterment of all human beings.

Lastly, let us suggest that the challenge to the 7th Pan African Congress should be seen as the declaration to the whole world that Africa is ready and willing to fight and struggle for genuine liberation and development, and therefore for genuine freedom, independence and sovereignty. On these demands there will be no compromise. That struggle for the Second Liberation must start today, not tomorrow. All Africans who wish to frustrate the imperialist efforts to recolonize Africa must therefore rise up, unite and go into battle against imperialism and its internal African allies.

References

Amare, Germa (1970). 'Considerations of some of the important social functions of African Education' in Robert K. Gardiner *et al.*, *Africa and the World*, Addis Ababa: Oxford University Press.

Battuta Ibn (1929/57). *Travels in Asia and Africa 1325–54*, trans. by H.A.R. Gibb, London: Routledge and Kegan Paul Ltd.

Baran, Paul A. (1960). *The Political Economy of Growth*, New York: Afzan.

Curle, Adam (1971). *Education for Liberation*, London: Tavistock Publications.

Davidson, Basil (1992). *The Black Man's Burden: Africa and the Curse of Nation-States*, London: James Currey.

DeGraft-Johnson, J.C. (1954/55). *African Glory: The Story of Vanished Negro Civilization*, Watts and Co.

Dumont, Rene (1966). *False Start in Africa*, Transl. by Phillis Nauts Ott, London: Andre Deutsch Ltd.

Fieldhouse, D.K. (1986). *Black Africa 1945–1985: Economic Decolonization and Arrested Development*, London: Unwin Hyman.

Fanon, Frantz (1963). *The Damned*, trans. by Constance Farrington, Paris: Presence Africaine.

Goldschmidt, Walter (ed.) (1958). 'Culture and Changing Values in Africa', *The United States and Africa*, Columbia University, New York: The American Assembly.

George, Susan (1988/89). *A Fate Worse than Debt: A Radical New Analysis of the Third World Debt Crisis*, Harmondsworth: Penguin Books.

Hanson, A.H. (1959). *Public Enterprise and Economic Development*, London: Routledge and Kegan Paul Ltd.

Illich, Ivan D. (1973). *Celebration of Awareness: A Call for Institutional Revolution*, Harmondsworth: Penguin Books Ltd.

'International Class Struggle in Africa, the Caribbean and America', *Resolutions and Selected Speeches from the Sixth Pan African Congress* (1976) Dar-es-Salaam: Tanzania Publishing House.

Jahn, Janheinz (1958). *Muntu*, trans. by Marjorie Grene, London: Faber and Faber Ltd.

Kamarck, Andrew M. (1958). 'The African Economy and International Trade', in Walter Goldschmidt (ed.), *The United States and Africa*, Columbia University, New York: The American Assembly.

Leakey. L.S.B. (1961). *The Progress and Evolution of Man in Africa*, London: Oxford University Press, 1961.

Leys, Colin (1975). *Underdevelopment in Kenya: The Political Economy of Neo-Colonialism 1964–1971*, London, Heinemann.

Machyo, Chango B. (1973). *Africa and Foreign Intervention*, Makerere University: Publication of the Centre for Continuing Education.

McKay, Vernon (1958). 'The African Operations of United States Government Agencies', in Walter Goldschmidt (ed.), *The United*

States and Africa, Columbia University, New York: The American Assembly.

Nagy, Imre (1957). *On Communism*, New York: Frederick A. Prager, Inc.

Onimode, Bade (1988). *A Political Economy of the African Crisis*, London: Zed Books Ltd.

Robinson, Ronald (ed.) (1971). *Developing the Third World: The Experience of the Nineteen Sixties*, Cambridge: Cambridge University Press.

Rodney, Walter (1976). *How Europe Underdeveloped Africa*, Dar-es-Salaam and London: TPH and BL.

Rwachewiltz, Boris de (1966.). *Introduction to African Art*, trans. by Peter Whingham, London: John Murray.

The Charter (1962). Cairo: Information Department.

'The Cocoyoc Declaration' (1975). *The African Review: A Journal of African Politics, Development and International Affairs*, vol. 5, no. 3 (Dar-es-Salaam University).

Thompson, Vincent Bakpetu (1969). *Africa and Unity: The Evolution of Pan-Africanism*, London: Longman.

Turok, Ben (1987). *Africa: What can be Done?*, Institute of African Alternatives, London: Zed Books Ltd.

West, H.W. (n.d.). *The Mailo system in Buganda: Preliminary Case Study in African Land Tenure*, Uganda Government: Government Printer, Entebbe.

Williams, Chancellor (1987). *The Destruction of Black Civilization: Great issues of a race from 4500 BC to 2000 AD*, Chicago: Third World Press.

2

The African Woman on the Continent: Her Present State, Prospects and Strategy

Victoria Sekitoleko

Introduction

The fact that man and woman are partners in society has for long been recognized. Each needs the other directly and in complementarity. What is, however, not so clearly recognized is that man and woman should and can coexist as equal partners. This arises out of society's failure to view the men's and women's diversity in characteristics as attributes which, when properly tapped, benefit both men and women.

That perceptual failure on the part of society has led it to believe that women are second-class citizens. Hence women have not only been relegated to second-rate positions in society, but have also been assigned inferior stereotyped roles. These man-made stereotypes can be changed by society and women themselves need to be at the forefront of their struggle. Certainly, women need not accept that all their current lower roles and positions in society are a fate predestined by God. Even if they were, why shouldn't women themselves lead the prayers to God to remove the anomalies? African women, though living on a continent well-endowed with natural resources, live in deprived cultural and socioeconomic environments.

The African woman lives in a state of abject poverty, poor health and ignorance, deprived of her human rights, social status and means of livelihood. The conditions which determine the African woman's state are imposed on her by a society which maintains rigid social-cultural values and practices against her.

Women over the ages have been acculturated to believe that their secondary position and the subordinate roles assigned to them are honourable and need not be changed. Challenging age-old roles and practices, is not 'lady-like'. So the African woman remains subdued by her own attitudes, even perpetuating the practices she is best-placed to stop. Creating a gender-balanced society in which women are not discriminated against in any life endeavour merely because of their sex will require massive women's awareness, education and mobilization for collective action. There is no easy way.

Concepts of woman and state

The concept of woman as a female human being or a mature one of the class, is generally well-understood. What is not so well-understood of women, especially when we are discussing their state, is that females start being women right from birth and continue as women till death. Women shoulder burdens and responsibilities, and suffer discriminations which are generally disguised as privileges or appreciations, right from birth. However, the modern woman has discovered that her so-called rights, privileges and appreciations provide the mechanisms by which society suppresses her. Hence the struggle by women for emancipation from the age-old bondage toward equality with the men.

The African woman is the female human being who by descent, birth and upbringing, belongs to the continent of Africa, who experiences the African socio-cultural and economic environment right from her mother's womb to death in old age. The African woman is what one cartoonist depicted as substitute for ploughing ox and water tap, as well as carrier of heavy loads, cook and, of course, bearer of children. She is what Okot B'Itek depicted in the *Song of Ocol* as

> Woman of Africa
> Sweeper
> Smearing floors and walls
> With cow dung and black soil
> Cook, ayah, the baby on your back,
> Washer of dishes,
> Planting, weeding, harvesting
> store-keeper, builder
> Runner of errands
> Cart, lorry, donkey ...
> Woman of Africa
> What are you not?

The African woman is the deprived member of society. To understand her better, ask three questions: What is happening to poverty, especially her poverty? What has been happening to employment (rather unemployment)? What has been happening to equality?

Webster's dictionary defines state as: position or standing; a set of circumstances or attributes characterizing a person or thing at a given time, way or form of being, a condition, a particular mental or emotional condition as in a state of melancholy, a condition as regards physical structure, constitution, internal form, stage or phase of existence, conditions or position in life, social status, rank or degree; style or living characteristics of people having high rank and wealth, rich, imposing, ceremonious display; dignity or pomp.

This long definition brings out a few essential elements of the concept of state we are after, namely, under what conditions does a woman live? What effect have those conditions had on her? What is the magnitude and complexity of what can be done to raise her social standing; unposition or projection as a strategy for women's emancipation and enhancement.

Settlement of man

From time immemorial, men lived by hunting both wild fruit and animals, while women kept home: it is known that she played a key role in the domestication of plants and animals. Society being unfair as it has remained to the present day, permanently bonded women to low-subsistence agriculture instead of rewarding her for the great invention of the science and art of domestication of crops and livestock. It then appears that in women's very great contribution lay their greatest curse, to remain a second-rate partner to men.

Fora like the 7th Pan African Congress strive to change this second-rate position to which women are relegated in society. Change for the betterment of women must surely come and that time is *now*. The international community is already playing its part as can be seen below.

Milestones in advocacy for women's equality

Efforts towards achieving women's equality with men started in the 1940s. Continuation of those efforts and their outcomes will, to a large measure, depend on an enhanced awareness of women's situation, of their rights and of the machinations used by men to keep women down. The milestones include:

- 1946 – The United Nations Commission on the Status of Women was formed to monitor the situation of women and promote women's rights around the world.
- 1952 – The Commission initiated the Convention on the Political Rights of Women, the first global mandate to grant women equal political rights under the law: the rights to vote, hold office and exercise public functions.
- 1957 and 1962 – Conventions were initiated on the equality of married women, guaranteeing them equal rights in marriage and on the dissolution of marriage.
- 1967 – Declaration on the Elimination of Discrimination against Women.
- 1975 – International Women's Year. The World Conference on Women in Mexico City proclaims 1976–1985 as the UN Decade for Women's Equality, Development and Peace.
- 1978 – The Alma Alta declaration: Health for All by year 2000, although general in scope, brought some hope for women's health through Community Based Primary Care, for example, the training of traditional birth attendants.
- 1980 – The World Conference on Women in Copenhagen adopts the Programme of Action for the Second Half of the Decade for Women: Equality, Development, Peace. Agencies are asked to prepare the most recent data and time-trend analyses on the situation of women.
- 1985 – The Nairobi Conference reviews progress during the Decade for Women and adopts Forward-Looking Strategies for the Advancement of Women.
- 1992 – World Health Assembly in Geneva requests the Director General, World Health Organization (WHO) to utilize all existing mechanisms within the WHO system to ensure incorporation of a gender perspective in all its programmes and the allocation of 30–50 per cent of each programme's resources to women's health issues.

I have listed the above women's equality landmarks to show that the formal recognition for women's struggle for equality is a relatively young phenomenon starting only in the middle of the twentieth century. The struggle is about deep-rooted values and the task is not an easy one. Women, therefore, must prepare for the gigantic task ahead of them if equality is to be achieved. The above fora were to draw world attention to the woman's plight in the hope of improving her participation in all human endeavours as an equal partner with men. The last two landmarks are specially noteworthy; for they created the strategies for the operationalization of women's equality. The strategies demanded that governments:

- Play key roles in ensuring that both men and women enjoy equal rights in such areas as education, training and employment.
- Act to remove negative stereotypes and perceptions of women.
- Disseminate information to women about their rights and entitlements.
- Collect timely and accurate statistics on women and monitor their situation.
- Encourage the sharing and support of domestic responsibilities.
- Call for 30–50 per cent allocation of all resources of World Health Organization Programmes for women's health issues.
- Call for data and information gathering, analysis and utilization for national and international planning.
- Call on women to form grass-roots pressure groups to alleviate the torments and contradictory situations of women, that is, call on women to protest against discriminatory practices of all kinds.

Other important strategic areas included access to fertility management, education, credit and financial facilities to enable women to engage in economically viable projects which would, in turn, contribute to improvements in their health.

Indicators of women's well-being

The World Conference of the International Women's Year held in Mexico City in 1975 listed the following indicators and called on the United Nations Statistical Services to compile and monitor their situation:

- Family life – How are women's responsibilities in the family changing relative to men's? How are changes in households providing greater opportunities and affecting what women do?
- Leadership and decision-making – How many women are represented in government, business and the community? Is their influence on the rise?
- Health and child-bearing – Are women living longer, healthier lives? How does the health of women and girls compare with the health of men and boys? What choices do women have in child-bearing? And what are the risks connected with child-bearing world-wide?

- Education – Are women better educated today than twenty years ago? How does their education compare with men's?
- Economic life – What do women contribute to production – and to development? How is that contribution valued and measured?

The African woman's situation

Generally the situation women face in many countries in Africa, is the result of cultural, socioeconomic and political trends. Women are prone to pressures and practices which suppress their potentials for personal fulfilment from birth through childhood, adolescence to ultimate senescence. The relegation to a second-rate position in society permeates through all women's endeavours and becomes so embedded that not only do they accept fewer rights and less education for their daughters; some would even regret giving birth to more girls than boys. The women's roles, likewise, closely follow the situation the women face.

Socioeconomically, women form more than 50 per cent of the world's population; more than 75 per cent of the world's women live in the Third World. Women agricultural labourers in Sub-Saharan Africa make up about 30 per cent of the world's agricultural labour force. Women make up 87 per cent of the Ugandan agricultural labour force and contribute 60–80 per cent of the total agricultural production, of which they almost wholly process and market 60 per cent. In Uganda, 90 per cent of the locally consumed food is produced by women.

Despite their socioeconomic importance, women's share is only 10–17 per cent of the wealth, 20 per cent of employment and only 1 per cent of property at world level. The African situation is even worse. For example, in Uganda, in the civil service, there are relatively fewer women than men and women generally occupy the bottom or lower-middle posts. This obviously limits their prospects for promotion to positions of higher responsibility. Women are also torn between being career officers and family mothers.

On top of that is men's chauvinism which suppresses the women. The women, because of tradition and culture, are discriminated against in other ways. Social institutions such as the family, land laws, education, extension services in agriculture, training, credit and marketing are male-dominated. The laws of inheritance are either skewed towards or favour only sons rather than daughters. Women and their daughters are discriminated against purely due to male chauvinism and gender ideologies which deny women equality. The women have been yoked to drudgery and servitude and spend more than 16 hours a day on home chores. Yet even this drudgery need not be and could easily be reduced or eliminated should society decide to introduce simple technologies which are appropriate for women. But women continue working the gardens, preparing meals, fetching water and a host of other chores without efficient tools and technology.

African women and education

Gender discrimination is reflected in the fact that generally the literacy rates of women are lower than those of the men within the same society. In Uganda, female literacy is only 35 per cent while that of men is 50 per cent. In Sub-Saharan Africa, as a whole more than 70 per cent of women aged 25 and over are illiterate which compares very poorly even with other under-developed regions such as the Caribbean and Latin America where it is 20 per cent. To make matters worse, as populations in some African regions outpace educational efforts and facilities, the actual numbers of illiterate girls and women are bound to increase. The illiteracy rate is, of course, worse in rural areas, yet it is in the rural areas where food and wealth are produced by women. In rural Africa female illiteracy is estimated at more than 75 per cent as compared to less than half in urban areas. Also the widest gaps between literacy of men and that of women are in Africa. Both primary and secondary school enrolment for girls lags behind that of the boys, and this is worse at the university level.

The situation in Uganda elucidates this inequality. The number of primary schools has doubled since 1978 from 3969 to 7955 in 1987 and secondary schools from 120 to 515, all mainly due to self-help initiatives (see Table 2.1). The jump in the number of schools is indicative of the importance parents place on education, but those numbers are still inadequate to cater for all children. In addition, education is not free. Given the limitations on space and other resources, the boys get into school in preference to the girls.

Table 2.1 Schools by level, selected years (up to 1987)

Institution	1981	1983	1985	1987
Primary	4 585	5 695	7 025	7 955
Secondary	178	285	500	515
Teacher Training Colleges	33	59	83	102

Source: UNICEF, Children and Women in Uganda: A Situation Analysis

Table 2.2 Total education enrolment by level, 1987

Level	Students	Percentage of total
University	6 318	0.25
Other Post Sec.	29 153	2.14
Secondary	226 875	8.90
Primary	2 286 580	89.70

Source: UNICEF, Children and Women in Uganda: A Situation Analysis

Table 2.3 Gross primary school enrolment by region, 1980

Region	Population in 6–12 Age group	Primary school enrolment	Gross enrolment ratio (%)
Eastern	584 525	349 521	60
Central	631 818	366 244	58
Northern	506 672	275 233	54
Western	692 350	365 799	53
Total	2 415 365	1 356 797	56

Source: UNICEF, Children and Women in Uganda: A Situation Analysis

In a situation where children first herd and graze cattle and goats before starting school, as in Western Uganda, and where priority is given to the boys, obviously it is the girls whose enrolment will suffer.

Female enrolment in educational institutions as illustrated in Table 2.4 has stagnated around 30 per cent and 22 per cent on average for senior one year and senior six year respectively. The situation is similar in the whole of Africa, with girls registering 70 per cent in North Africa and 60 per cent in Sub-Saharan Africa respectively on average.

In a situation governments' programmes and budgets for literacy campaigns, and extension agencies, target male clientele (perceived as the official farmers), women's opportunities for literacy and education for productive living become minimal. It is, therefore, not surprising that Sub-Saharan African women have one of the highest illiteracy rates: now at 50 per cent for women between 20–24 years against just over 40 per cent for North Africa, and 9–12 per cent for Eastern Asia, Latin America and the Caribbean.

Table 2.4 Progress of female enrolment in secondary schools, Uganda, 1976–1983

Year	Sex	SS1	SS6
1976	Male	10 922.0	1 970.0
	Female	4 427.0	486.0
	Female % of total	28.0	19.7
1977	Male	10 011.0	2,046.0
	Female	4 564.0	510.0
	Female % of total	31.3	19.9
1978	Male	10 639.0	2 138.0
	Female	4 440.0	520.0
	Female % of total	29.4	19.3
1980	Male	12 289.0	2 600.0
	Female	5 594.0	720.0
	Female % of total	31.3	27.6
1983	Male	23 882.0	4 073.0
	Female	12 651.0	1 027.0
	Female % of total	34.6	20.1

Obviously, the high illiteracy rate is bad news for not only the individual woman, but her family and her nation, for the producer of wealth is not equipped with the requisite technology for better living and development. A writer in *The African Crisis* put it in plainer language:

> Women are never told about training schemes, and if they were, they would not have time to attend to them. As women are more and more the farmers of Africa, then research and extension which does not reach them will have little chance of improving African farming.

It is also important to note that although proportionately the increases in enrolment for girls are more than for boys, women's educational situation is bad because of starting at a far lower base than that of boys. Even in Makerere, the 1.5 point shift has not changed that trend much. The 1.5 point 'boost' was introduced as an affirmative action to increase the number of women who will qualify for places in the university. This action, established by Uganda's Ministry of Education, is especially helpful for students whose grades are at the borderline for admission.

Education is the master key to women's equality for the following reasons:

- At survival and health level, there is a positive correlation between the education of the mother and the survival of her children through improved hygiene and nutrition.
- Education improves women's employment opportunities in a male-dominated and discriminatory world.
- Education improves the women's awareness of the situation they face and its effects on them and their communities. It is no accident that only those of us who have been educated, by accessing either affirmative admission policies or private family income, are assembled in this Congress.
- At the family level, education empowers women to participate in making decisions about the work they do and the number of children they have.

Policy gaps

Agriculture

Despite the fact that in Africa, women constitute more than 50 per cent of the population (currently about 53 per cent of Uganda), women's concerns and interests have not been incorporated into the mainstream development policies in most countries. Gender-blind policies and programmes continue to be formulated and implemented without regard to equal opportunities for the women. Women's roles and contributions in society are taken as a matter of course. A recent Gender Policy Document in the Ministry of Agriculture, Animal Industry and Fisheries, Uganda, recognized the leading role women play in the agricultural sector in addition to their other enormous responsibilities in the family and recorded:

> Unfortunately the women's role has not been adequately reflected in the formulation of the agricultural policies and strategies leave alone production statistics. Gender-blind terminologies like farmers, farm operators, rural people have been used in projects and policy documents. In practice however, such terms as farmers turned out to refer to men only. Hence it is men who have access to the production resources like land, credit and purchased inputs.

I have started with agriculture, which I know best, but the situation on policies affecting women are similar in any sector in most African countries. Perhaps the most serious policy gaps are to be found in laws which deny women equal rights with men to own land, borrow money and enter contracts. It is, for example, known that there are countries in Africa where a woman cannot open a bank account unless she is guaranteed/witnessed by a man. Even in countries where equality laws or regulations are in existence, like Uganda, their implementation leaves a lot to be desired and in the final analysis, women are denied their rights all the same, as one Ugandan observed in *The World's Women: Trends and Statistics, 1970–1990*: 'We continue to be second-rate, no, third, since our sons come before us. Even donkeys and tractors get better treatment.' The laws of inheritance are against the women; these laws are worsened by tradition, for example, where widows are inherited as property or dismissed from their deceased husbands' land.

Women's work

The socioeconomic importance of women cannot be over-emphasized. But their contribution as bearer of children, and as the main provider of all the household work, family care and food production is not counted in national statistics. Yet it is known that women's household work constitutes 25–30 per cent of the total work output. How long can biased policies allow policy makers to ignore known and quantifiable facts?

Investment gaps

Investment in women's education, health and other social services seldom receives the attention it deserves from governments and families. Yet according to a study in Malaysia, the net return to education at all levels of wages and productivity is consistently 20 per cent higher for girls and young women than for boys and young men. Biased or non-existent supportive policies steer women into less productive endeavours, limiting overall development.

Pay gaps

Pay gaps exist between what women produce and what they are paid. Occupational segregation and discrimination relegate women to low-paying, low-status jobs. Even where women do the same work as men, they receive less than the men; at a global level 30–40 per cent less. An obvious gap is that not only is much of the women's work not recognized in statistics, but it is not paid for. Household work, family care, etc. is considered of no economic importance. Recent UNICEF surveys clearly show this relegation thus:

Table 2.5 Household population by industry and sex (urban)

Industry	Women	Men	National
Trade, Hotels	35.74%	24.06%	29.18%
Community, Social Services	26.74%	19.91%	22.91%
Agriculture	87.64%	74.43%	78.76%
Manufacturing	4.25%	9.00%	6.92%
Transport, Communications	0.54%	12.86%	7.46%
Financing, Business Services	6.74%	8.74%	7.86%

Table 2.6 Household population by occupation and sex (urban)

Occupation	Women	Men	National
Professional/Technical	7.64	12.82	10.55
Administration/Managerial	0.80	3.02	2.04
Clerical	5.97	4.52	5.16
Agricultural/Allied Workers	25.42	11.67	17.70
Sales Workers	38.98	27.67	32.76

The rural situation where women do most of the work is even worse. Agriculture is predominantly female, with 94.24 per cent women in the sector versus 81.57 per cent men, against the national position of 87.41. Even in rural areas, trends in employment point to women in low-status jobs.

In Africa most public and waged employees are men, leaving women to work in subsistence agriculture or to create whatever opportunities they can in the informal sector, for example handicrafts. Women are becoming more and more overburdened as the number of female-headed households increases due to a rise in the number of unmarried, unsupported mothers and as the young generation desert their mothers. In Uganda, female-headed households constitute about 20 per cent of the total number of households.

Health

Although women outlive men almost everywhere in the world, in Africa where life expectancy is as low as the age of 45 for men, the burden on those women left to fend for the family is obvious. But even when men are still living, since policies do not focus on special health needs of the women, and their education is poor or nonexistent, women are in poor health due to under-nutrition and high birth rates, which stand at about 5.5 per woman in Africa versus their counterparts in developed countries like say Sweden, 2.1 and Germany, 1.4.

Most African countries do not have clear-cut policies on services such as appropriate health care, family planning and education which would help in reducing the women's reproductive burdens. Some countries have vague health policies to support family planning for health reasons, but not as a means of population control.

It has been estimated that women in developing countries face the risk of death, due to pregnancy at rates some 80 to 600 times higher than their counterparts in the developed world due to lack of trained personnel, malnutrition and non-existent back-up services for high-risk pregnancies. When health services deteriorate, it is the woman who suffers most: she has to attend to the pregnancy, the children, the husband and even other relatives when they are sick in hospital or at home. When policies such as cost-sharing for medical services are formulated, it is the woman who earns less or nothing who suffers most. Once it is time to be born, the baby will come out regardless of whether the cost-share has been paid or not. The woman suffers all the attendant consequences. As shown by Uganda's situation (Table 2.7), the health situation of most African countries is becoming worse and worse due to wars, civil strife, outright mismanagement and the effects of drought on agricultural production.

Table 2.7 Some indicators of health situation, Uganda

Life Expectancy	1960s	1990s
Male (years)	60	45
Female (years)	65	47
Infant Mortality (per 1000)	80–90	120
No. of Doctors (per 1,000,000)	1171	337

Source: UNICEF: School Health Project

There are other variables which women do not control, but which are critical to their health, for example, determining when she gets her first child. In countries where parents give their daughters away for marriage at an early age, women have little control over when to have their first child. Such young girls do not know any fertility management technique – they get pregnant, but with the increased likelihood of failure to deliver.

Sexual assault and rape are also, in these days of the AIDS pandemic, obvious health risks; sexual abuse is on the increase in Uganda. Unfortunately, much of the abuse is not reported and when it is, the punishments are light, probably because those in authority are men.

Justice

The African woman suffers injustices not only by written laws, but by tradition and outright cultural biases. From birth, she is told 'do' or 'do not' do this or that because you are a girl: kneel, wash the dishes, do not eat chicken, etc. The machinery for administration of justice – the police, the judiciary, the prison service and the army – are all male-dominated. If arrested, a woman experiences injustice and injury right from the time of her arrest. She is roughed up because those who are arresting her are men; as she makes her statement she is mocked or tormented by men, only to go to prison where the prison warders are men. It is a sad story to tell what happens there.

There is an urgent need to evolve policies which will promote the recruitment and development of women in these institutions, though the process will be very difficult.

Public life and leadership

As already indicated, woman make up more than half of the populations and electorates in most countries. More and more women are working in public offices, but very few of them achieve elective offices or have equal access to political parties, trade unions, government, business and even special interest associations. Society does not even acknowledge their vital role in environmental protection and the struggle for peace.

By December 1990, of the 159 United Nations member states, only seven heads of state and nine prime ministers had ever been women.[Editor's note: It is most welcome that in 1994 the first ever female Vice President in Africa, Dr Specioza Wandire Kzibwe was appointed in Uganda.] Only 3.5 per cent of the world's cabinet ministers are women. Even then, women head ministries such as women's affairs, culture and social welfare. Generally women are least represented in executive, economic, political and legal ministries in Africa.

Women are allowed to vote, but their representation in parliaments in Sub-Saharan Africa is about 8 per cent and about 3 per cent for North Africa. The reasons for that trend are of course not democratic, but range from lack of awareness of women's rights and education to religious restraints and outright suppression.

Women are blocked in the two main paths leading to decision making: political candidacy and the Civil Service. Changing women's situation in these areas will of necessity call for deliberate policies and efforts in order to uplift the women. Uganda's position has ably been articulated by President Yoweri Museveni himself when he stated at the establishment of the Women in Development (WID) Ministry 'Our policy aims at strengthening the position of women in the economy by raising the value and productivity of their productive resources. By productive resources, I mean land, capital, credit, seeds, fertilizers, tools, water, energy, education and information ...'

Uganda's efforts to pursue that policy in addition to creating the WID ministry have included appointing special women representatives to the National Resistance Council. There are now 42 women council members in the parliament, three of whom are cabinet ministers and two are deputy ministers. Women are slowly entering what traditionally have been men's jobs and positions: for example, the Head of Administration in the Ugandan police is a woman. We also, at least, have a woman lieutenant colonel in the National Resistance Army. In the Ministry of Agriculture women's situation is fast improving. Of the five directors of major research institutions, one is a woman, 42 out of 90 researchers at Kawanda are women, 23 out of 66 in Namulonge and the prospects for higher positions for women in the ministry are bright. The number of women in agricultural colleges has increased from 62 to 140 and in the near future, female students will form 50 per cent of the enrolment in the agricultural colleges. All this may not have happened without an enabling political environment which included putting women and men who are gender-sensitive in charge.

One important contribution from women is their participation at the grass roots in community-based programmes and non-governmental organizations though it is often ignored. Grass-roots organizing is good strategy because that is where the majority of folk live and work and where the greatest of women's hardships and drudgery occur. Many women have mobilized their colleagues in environmental efforts like tree planting.

Peace

Women's contribution to national and international peace is fairly well-understood and acknowledged. Indeed exceptiional women have won the Nobel Peace Prize, but when there is a war, it is the women and children who suffer most. They suffer due to wartime violence directed against them and, if they survive that violence, they suffer as refugees. Wars increase defence budgets and reduce those for social services, creating greater suffering, particularly on the part of women. At household level, there is now increasing violence against women. Rape, defilement and outright murder are on the increase against women. Court cases involving the defilement of even two-year-old girls are now common. Women need to rise up to fight against all these forms of violence. It is our responsibility to see that we promote peace, not only nationally and internationally, but also in our homes. The solution for more peace lies in achieving high levels of education. Education not only enables you to know your rights, but will make you articulate them better. Women need to make noise, but not empty noise. We should learn to bargain and not allow ourselves to be used as tools.

Other issues
There are other areas of a general nature which affect women more than they affect men:

- Food crisis – When there is shortage of food, for whatever reason, the man can afford to stay away from home leaving the woman with the children. The food crisis which Africa has gone through in the recent times, has of course, affected women more.
- Heavy dependence on external funding – The African economies are donor-driven, with debt-servicing ratios of over 50 per cent. In such situations subsistence agriculture suffers.
- Inflation – This requires that more money is raised to pay for goods and services. Most of the social services are needed by the women and children who are the least able to pay. Even structural adjustment programmes hit the women worst.
- Urbanization – The elderly women are left in the countryside with the burden to produce more food for everyone. The development of mega cities is not good news for the African woman either. Lack of support networks – especially the loss of the extended family system as people drift to the cities – means that many women live and single-handedly raise families in bad housing and sanitary conditions. Resultant ill-health is treated by an inadequate health care system. Without traditional rural support networks, some women turn to or are coerced into prostitution and criminal activities in order to survive, exposing themselves to potential violence or sexually transmitted disease, especially HIV/AIDS.

Some challenges

Now that women understand their situation and the odds against them, what challenges do they face?

Women constitute more than 50 per cent of the populations of most countries of Africa. Why is it that their representation, even where elected government exists, is so low? Why not vote for women?

Women are the custodians of culture. Women teach the culture to the children, why can't women free culture from the fetters of the past? How do women expect change when they themselves perpetuate bad cultures?

The majority of our sisters live in the rural areas. Are the educated women, the members of the elite (including ourselves) not alienated from the rural women by our lifestyles, values, by what we say and do or fail to do? Actions speak louder than words: what have we done to show that we are determined to improve the situation of rural women? What demonstrable sacrifices have we made for this cause?

As we demand equality with men, are we not ambivalent in our class relationship to our rural sisters and even urban poor women? Are women prepared to accept all rights together with the responsibilities that go with them? Or do we want equal rights only up to a point? Wanting to have the best of two worlds will no doubt arouse opposition and we might lose the struggle. There is the need for some trade-off. Equality need not be mathematical. Already in Sweden, renowned for its equal rights legislation, there are problems: women will not take all the 360 days' maternity leave entitled to them, and some men are opposing the 40 days given to them because of a 10 per cent loss on salaries.

Women work more than 16 hours a day. Why then are they portrayed as the weaker sex?

Women are stigmatized as having low learning capacity. Why, then, are they burdened with so many responsibilities and functions? Are men wise to entrust so much to the unintelligent? We have seen that education is the key to emancipation and development. Why do women stay home when there is a course of instruction or meeting?

What can be done to promote the African woman on the continent?

- *Education and training*: Influence women's participation in development activities, nutrition, health status and decision-making opportunities. Deliberate efforts, therefore, must be made to accord equal education opportunities to both girls

and boys. Women, too, need to be active in training and other fields.
- *Productivity*: Women should be given opportunity to improve their productivity by reducing drudgery. Provide appropriate technology, clean water in the home and electricity, especially rural electrification, credit and other inputs because lack of capital is closely linked to the vicious circle of poverty.
- *Participation*: Governments should ensure equal opportunities for men and women in political decision-making, the Civil Service, industry and development activities. Deliberate shifts need to be put in place such as Makerere University's example of awarding few extra points to girls on admission, reservations for parliamentary representation and other enabling positive discrimination packages.
- *Clientele*: Women should be targeted as a category since they have special problems and are at the lowest of bases in all fields, rather than use general terms like 'farmers'.
- *Laws*: Laws and customs which relegate the woman to second or third-class citizenship and deny her rights to property, borrowing, etc., must be changed.
- *Family*: Family-level responsibilities, rights and privileges should be distributed equally among men and women, boys and girls. While the girls should get equal opportunities for education, there is no reason why the boys should be denied the privilege of preparing meals and doing the dishes.
- *Fora*: Women should have the opportunities to interact with their colleagues in the developed world and within Africa.
- *The individual*: Women everywhere should resolve and commit themselves to stop the perpetuation of bad customs. Promote the good ones and get involved in efforts for their betterment. Make noise, stop stigmatization as unintelligent and all forms of discrimination and, above all, *act productively*.

Conclusion

Women have occupied and continue to occupy second-class positions in all fields of human endeavour. I have shown here something is being done to address the situation, but starting from very low bases. Given men's chauvinism, any achievements made in education, health, employment, politics and other forms of participation, are but a drop in the ocean. A lot still needs to be done and our best bet is massive awareness and education of women. Women themselves need to be at the forefront.

In doing so, women need to watch out for too much rhetoric and too little action. Real issues may be lost in excessive rhetoric. There is a need to prioritize problems and to adopt clear strategies for each problem. The tendency had been to try to handle all women's issues at the same time. In the process the real issues and messages may suffer from what communicators call 'verbal overkill'.

Lastly, advancing the women's cause has assumed war-like tactics. There has been a lot of militancy spearheaded by women activists. It may, therefore, be worthwhile to consider the principles developed many years ago by a Polish commander, Clausewitz, which still guide modern warfare today. These principles apply to other areas of social change and women can use them gainfully too: 'maintain the aim, concentrate force, ensure cooperation of forces and remain flexible'.

Further reading

Isabirye, J.L.K., 'Women and Development Seminar paper', 1991.
L.W.F., *Uganda Annual Report* (Department of World Service, 1992).
MAAIF, *Proposed Gender-oriented Policy Document*, MAAIF, 1993.
MOFEP, *Key Economic Indicators*, 15th Issue, October 1993.
Mubiru, J.B., 'Institutional Factors Affecting the Role of Women in Uganda', 1992.
Ojacor, F.A. & Isabirye, J.K.L., 'Current Status and the problem of rural youth in Uganda', 1991.
Sekitoleko, V., 'Country Statement', 27th Session of FAO, United Nations Conference, November 1993.
Sekitoleko, V., Budget Statement, 1993/94.
Tipoteh, T., 'Dimensions of Rural Crisis in Africa' Workshop paper, Ibadan, Nigeria, 1985.
United Nations, *The World's Women: Trends and Statistics*, New York: 1970–1990.
World Bank, *Uganda Growing Out of Poverty*, Country Study, Washington DC: 1993.

Part II

Africa and the World

3

The New World Disorder – Which Way Africa?

A.M. Babu

The 7th Pan African Congress took place at a critical time internationally when the old post-Cold War world system was dead and a new one was/is yet to be born. Old political assumptions and economic certainties are crumbling one by one. Old alliances are rapidly being replaced by new ones. Old contradictions: ideological, north/south, economic, environmental, have not gone away; but new ones: ethnic, religious, territorial, have emerged with a vengeance, threatening global stability. It is an unsettled multi-polar world in which old centres of power and influence are gradually shifting to new, but as yet to be identified, spheres.

African people's situation in the new multi-polar world

In this volatile international scene, we see Africa inevitably embroiled in dramatic changes of her own, reflecting the new situation. New political leaders, of different political persuasions, are emerging everywhere. Mass political consciousness is spreading across the continent with one clear message: 'We want change in this changing world!'

Africans in the diaspora are equally in a state of flux. They are confronted with new challenges which demand new solutions. The rise of racism and Neofascism in the US and Europe (both eastern and western) is targeting Africans and people of African origin as scapegoats for economic failures of the racists' own governments.

It is against this background of uncertainty and racism that the historic 7th Pan African Congress was convened. Its primary task was to address these challenges in a realistic way, helped by inputs by African activists from all over the world where Africans and people of African origin live in large and small communities.

To achieve any meaningful understanding of this new situation and to arrive at a realistic 'African position', it is important that we study the phenomenon dispassionately without any preconceived notions. Realism should be our guiding principle, because the issues at stake are not only urgent but too serious to be left to the mercy of demagoguery and confused thinking. Our actions must take into account the concrete reality of Africa as it exists here and now, not an idealized one, and must pay attention to the people's aspirations. We must assess, without any exaggeration, our true capability to influence events at home and abroad. Above all, we must evaluate the material foundation on which our position in the world context must be established. This is also true for the people of African descent in the diaspora. Needless to say, the continent is in a serious crisis. What needs to be identified are some of the key elements that led to this crisis in order to subject them to serious analysis. There are several political as well as cultural and social issues to be taken into consideration. While such issues should not be ignored, it is ultimately the economic base which must be our starting point. This will then naturally enable us to define appropriately these elements of the superstructure.

The economic foundation

Briefly, the economic weaknesses of Africa can be traced to the following roots:

- We have inherited our economic backwardness from the primitive structure of colonial economy and aggravated by our post-colonial involvement in the world economy from a position of extreme weakness.
- We have failed to formulate policies for restructuring these economies soon after independence which would have enabled each of our countries to start on a path to an independent national economy. This failure has condemned our countries to be wholly dependent on, and heavily indebted to, the old imperialist world system.
- A proliferation of weak and self-seeking leadership and coup makers has helped to disrupt the development process which has resulted in putting the continent firmly at the mercy of foreign interests. These come in the form of aid donors, creditors, financial speculators, multilateral agencies and also in the form of foreign 'experts'. Their primary task is not to help us, but to create the material conditions for multinational corporations (MNCs) to exploit our labour and natural resources, and to

- perpetuate the colonial structures which facilitate this brutal exploitation.
- As a result of the above inherent weaknesses, the mangled African economies have emerged structurally unfit to take part in profitably, and benefit from, the world market; the continent has thus remained perpetually the loser in this venture.
- Failure to correct the above shortcomings and the ensuing lack of economic complementarity among and between African countries has created conditions for continental disunity. Africa has thus been rendered not only disunited but the majority of our nation-states have remained too small to be economically viable. They are too poor to take advantage of modern technology and unable to benefit from the vast human and natural resources of the continent.

While this condition is now universally known, no appropriate strategy to correct this situation has yet been proposed. Many 'alternative' policies have been recommended by some of the highest 'authorities' on Africa, but results have been disappointingly negative. The reason for the failure of these 'alternatives' seems to lie in the fact that they all start from assumptions and premises set earlier by the very traditional exploiters of the continent. All are based on the simplistic proposition of 'export in order to import' (a shopkeeper's notion of wealth creation!). They make no attempt to look into the structure on which our economies are based, a precondition to working towards a viable solution. This lack of proper diagnosis of our backwardness has had the effect of challenging only the form but not the essence of what has to be changed. This is yet another variation of the strange notion of seeking a solution to the status quo from within the status quo!

Is there a way out of this mess?
Our discussion must, first of all, take into account our food situation which is threatening to be the most serious crisis on the continent for the next decade. We are in a situation where our populations are rising but our food supply is diminishing, owing to a topsy-turvy order of priorities to which Africa has been subjected since independence.

The rapid expansion of deserts which eat up most of our fertile land, from the Sahara southwards, is a serious cause for concern; and this phenomenon too is directly linked to our wrong order of priorities in agriculture and land use. We must devise a sound policy on **agriculture** which will correct this imbalance and which will determine the whole direction of African economies, and create the essential conditions for continental unity.

The following discussion is a tentative attempt to set the ball rolling. It makes no claim to being the only way out. Rather, its purpose is to provoke critical thinking on the topic. Many of the points raised and solutions recommended are the result of several years of practical experience in the field of development strategy, later refined by contemplation, debates, exchange of views and rethinking which was made possible by a few years in the academic world.

A tentative Pan African alternative

The real meaning of the African crisis is that our countries, collectively and individually, are at a dead end, thanks entirely to the economic and 'development' policies pursued since independence.

The situation is so untenable that no 'reforms', whether inspired by the World Bank or IMF, or whether initiated locally, can get us out of the mess. What is needed is not reforms but a different outlook which calls for a decisive change of direction, a change from the primitive colonial structure of the economy to a national economy; above all, a change in the structure of production. This entails a change from an outward-motivated to an inward-motivated development strategy, whose guiding principle must be one based on the recognition that external causes are only a condition of change and internal causes the basis of change.

This African crisis is reflected in, among other phenomena, the total destruction of our national currencies, thanks to the IMF and the World Bank and their structural adjustment programmes (SAPs). In practically all African countries, there are no national currencies, only fluctuating tokens of the US dollar or of the French franc. All real business is conducted in terms of these two foreign currencies. The reason for this is that, except for the franc zone whose currencies (until 1994) were tied to and backed by the French treasury, the destruction of the national currencies is at once the cause and effect of the 'disunity' between the economy and the financial sector which it is supposed to service.

The disunity of these two most important sectors in the national economy has led to a killing-fields situation for speculative capital and foreign-exchange dealers. And as long as this disunity remains, there can be no reform because the two sectors remain in a perpetual state of disharmony, of one negating the other.

It is the US dollar which takes advantage of the resultant chronic disparity between the official and the so-called parallel exchange rates. All that the IMF and the World Bank can instruct to correct this disparity is to call for a better management of monetary and financial sectors. It is the monetarists' prescription for all kinds of economic ailments. But the result has always been disastrous to the well-being of the 'second liberation of Africa'. As a result, a new theme of Pan Africanism therefore requires us first of all, to ask ourselves: Do we want to continue in that prescribed role? It is clear that Africa's leadership is reconciled to this status, while at the same time calling for a 'new international economic order'. This position is also echoed by United Nations Economic Commission for Africa and the African Development Bank (which has now turned itself into a mini-IMF and a spokesman for international financiers) and even by the Organization for African Unity (OAU) itself. But the elusive new world order does not seem to be anywhere near the horizon and the reason for this delay is simple: the existing world economic order is the only possible one under the conditions of the 'free' world market economy. To wish for something else is to indulge in metaphysics.

But if we want a 'second liberation' in the real world, we must change our outlook, the direction of our economies and the order of our priorities. The starting point must be the satisfaction of the people's basic needs: food, housing and clothing. We must abandon, as a precondition, the old notion of looking outwards for our survival and instead, orientate the economies to look inward for solutions. External factors – trade, aid, foreign investments and loans – must only complement internal activity, but not the other way round, as is the case in Africa now.

In order to embark on this new path we need to have general, broadly applicable, principles to guide us but which at the same time could be modified to suit local conditions. In an unevenly developed continent like Africa, each region, if not each country, has its own specific characteristics which have to be taken into account before any strategy is formulated. That is why the following will remain essentially general principles to guide us in our analysis and in organizing for radical political and economic action in each specific case and region.

As Africa is undergoing rapid democratic transformation away from the political culture of the one-party states and military dictatorships to multi-partyism, it may be useful for us to have a clear view of what all this means and what our role and responsibility is in providing political leadership.

Although 'free marketeers' want to link free-market objectives as part and parcel of the democratic transformation, we must keep in mind that the two are not necessarily linked. You can have one without the other. The fact still remains that there are two contending social systems, one of which is represented by social democracy, in which the interests of the society as a whole or the community are paramount. The radical tradition stems from this. The reason why the radicals pursue this social system with a bias to society is simply due to the realization that it is the natural condition of the human being. As the clumsiest among all like species, we owe our survival as a distinct species to our social instinct. We always grouped together and invented mechanisms to defend ourselves as a group. Therefore social responsibility is the essential attribute of human nature. For radicals, therefore, democracy must mean social democracy, which promotes and encourages positive aspects of individual initiatives.

We may thus categorizse this new era of democratic revival as the era of the New Democracy for Africa, by which we mean, if the current democratic upsurge means anything, it must mean a movement for seeking, in Nkrumah's memorable phrase, the 'Kingdom of Self-government' – a movement towards upholding the principle of 'Government by the People'. At any rate, this seems to be the interpretation and expectation of the ordinary people in Africa since the days of the struggle for independence, although the 'born-again democrats' may have a different motive in misinterpreting democracy and confusing it with 'free market'. For a government by the people to be realized and ensured that it is by the people and for the people, Africa must have a policy and a radical programme necessary to bring about a change, to *empower* the people in directing and giving meaning to their political, economic and social aspirations, and to chart a new path that will take us out of the post-colonial rut and dilapidation and the current threat of recolonization.

In order to do so we should begin by at least recognizing what it is that we are rejecting and what we want to replace it with. Going by our hellish experience of the post-colonial past, we can say that we are rejecting excessive reliance on a political and economic strategy of *outward* orientation, and in its place we need to firmly establish and adhere to a strategy of *inward* orientation in the political, economic and social direction, as outlined below.

The political direction

The political principles of 'New Democracy'
We must pursue the policy of 'New Democracy' which in essence means putting power in the hands of the people. That is to say, establishing the principle and practice of government by the people.

We must accept the thesis that, while it is absolutely essential for the radical Left to recognize the importance and role of classes in society in its theoretical perspective, we must not, at this economically backward level of our development, follow the line of 'class reductionism'. In this respect, we must accept the dialectical reality that there is 'struggle' as well as 'unity' of opposites. That is to say, struggle is only one side of a contradiction and unity is its other side. Each plays its appropriate role in the course of development. Thus, in conditions of economic under-development, the stress must be on unity rather than on class struggle, without of course neglecting the primacy of class relations, especially for the study of the evolution of modes of production.

New Democracy, as government by the people, must be based on broad-based 'people', and on institutions that will ensure their democratic representation and control, as well as accountability.

While multi-partyism is essential for parliamentary democracy and for ensuring democratic representation, its establishment as a system does not in itself ensure New Democracy. Nor does it ensure the creation and equitable distribution of the national wealth. A society of mass poverty, on the one hand, and massive wealth in the hands of a few, on the other, cannot develop the necessary conditions for the creation of the national wealth to its fullest potentiality, nor can it be democratic.

To bring about New Democracy, the parliamentary system must be supplemented with and strengthened by other popular institutions and associations like the local governments, cooperative movements, independent workers, women, student and youth organizations, assemblies or organizations for environmental concerns and for minority rights, and so on. These will help unify the people at all social and territorial levels. They will also help devise a sound economic strategy reflecting the people's interests.

To ensure the above is firmly established and sustained as the dominant political culture, with enough flexibility to allow for changes when changes are needed to strengthen and further consolidate that culture, is ultimately the responsibility of Pan African radicals. It is only they, with their commitment to social justice, who must bear the responsibility to remain the 'conscience of their society'.

Radicals must, therefore, play full part in the multi-party system of their country and must ensure the supremacy of their ideas and their aspirations. They should be proud to be 'patriotic' in defence of real 'national' (people's) interests. To ensure leadership, they must have sound policies on all major national issues, and those policies must make sense to the people. They must, above all, project a credible vision of a future which the people can recognize and with which they can identify.

They must take into account what others in the political field are doing, but they must not be influenced by them. They must be influenced by their own perspective, their own world-outlook and remain faithful to their own vision of the future, single-mindedly.

These are the qualities that are needed for leadership in societies mired in poverty, but which have the will and determination to get out of it by sheer effort and reliance on the diligent labour of its people. Their immediate political goal must be the establishment of the 'hegemony of the people'. This objective can be realized only if the following is adhered to strictly: commitment to unify all the popular forces that are for radical change and struggle against all forces that seek to divide them or those who seek to sell the country to external bidders. They must commit themselves to struggle against those who seek to obstruct the democratic process or seek to hamper people's economic aspirations or undermine their well-being through exploitation for individual interests of the more powerful and more privileged.

Radicals must lead the movement to conserve what is positive in the national heritage, and change what is negative; they must commit themselves to direct national assets and natural resources to serve the people and the development of the national economy. The political aim of the radicals must of course be to achieve state power, singly or in alliance with other popular forces, in order to consolidate the New Democracy and prepare the ground for economic revival and reconstruction and the promotion of social well-being of the people.

Political organization for New Democracy

In order to reach state power, the radicals must organize themselves in a 'political party' that will lead the people to victory. The party must be guided by its constitution, its rules and codes of discipline. It must have a programme covering the political, economic and social policies it proposes to pursue when in power.

The party must train its cadres for day-to-day political work among the people, take up issues that affect them directly and look for ways to resolve them; learn from the people, and promote direct people's own leadership at all levels of the party organization.

The party of radicals must not be simply a vehicle to state power, but it must also be a means for establishing the political culture of political affiliations of people in a community.

In taking over state power the radicals must establish their administration as distinct from the political organization of the party. The administration must serve the entire people within the state without regard to their political affinity or class position. The aim of the administration must be to mobilize all the people in the national effort for reconstruction. The people must always remain the object and subject of national development.

The economic and social direction of New Democracy
Before we can chart a future economic direction, the radicals must first make clear what has so far blocked the way to Africa's prosperity since independence. These obstacles can be summed up as follows:

- dependence on the developed world to help our development;
- excessive use of our socially necessary labour time in the production of useless goods for export, instead of producing useful goods for our own human and development needs;
- continuous deterioration of commodity prices which weakens our capacity for capital formation;
- unproductive use of borrowed money (and the corruption that this entails) and the consequential debt-servicing at very high and unjustified rates;
- poor energy policies that make our countries heavily dependent on oil imports for our needs thus depleting our meagre foreign exchange earnings, and
- an irrational world economic order which we cannot change from a position of weakness.

A radical economic strategy therefore must take into account all the above factors in the course of outlining its corrective policies for laying the foundation for rapid economic and social development.

A realistic alternative strategy for development
Africa won its independence on the strength of its 'political' nationalism. Unlike European nationalism, which has mostly expressed itself in jingoistic terms, African nationalism is anti-imperialist, anti-predatory and anti-jingoism – it is a nationalism of resistance and therefore, progressive in essence. But we must not limit it only to political aspiration, it must extend to the economic struggle. While we remain internationalist in outlook, we must base our internationalism firmly on our nationalism – this time it is the nationalism of survival!

What then is the scientifically-based common-sense approach?
Our primary purpose is to change the economic structure from its present colonial orientation. The new structure must seek to increase the production of goods needed by the people. To achieve this objective the national economy must establish sound relations between its different branches, within each branch, and between all the links in production. The human resources, and material and financial resources of society must be utilized rationally.

Lastly, the improvement of the people's livelihood must be directly linked with the development of production and construction in such a way that they promote each other. This structure will ensure a continuous growth of the national income.

The strategy for this objective in principle, with each country devising its own detailed strategy taking into account specific national conditions, can then be summarized as follows:

1 Discard any illusion about export-led development for economies with extremely backward agriculture and no industry to speak of. We must, as a cardinal principle, look internally for our progress.
2 Recognize that neither the Western model of relying on the 'invisible hand' of the market, nor the Soviet model of lopsided development of heavy industry and indiscriminate nationalization, is any good to us. What we need is to make use of both the 'invisible hand' of the market and the visible hand of central planning and long-term programmes.
3 Move as quickly as possible, as a matter of top priority, from the primitive mode of production inherited from colonialism and enter the realm of expanded reproduction. It is the most decisive threshold on the way to an independent national economy.
4 Develop the production base in agriculture and industry, initially for the purpose of fulfilling the basic human needs – food, clothing and shelter; in the course of producing these basics the rest will follow: employment, expansion of the domestic market, increased output and surplus funds for investment, social welfare, etc. This will arouse mass enthusiasm for production and social harmony.
5 Raise standards of living of the people by improving the quality of life.
6 Understand fully the laws of economic development and seriously study our own national conditions. On the basis of this knowledge, devise a sound policy (in addition to agriculture and industry) on energy, environment, communications and transport; promote small and medium enterprises to serve the growing home market with emphasis on labour-intensive industries to provide

employment opportunities, promotion of skilled labour and the expansion of the cash economy; raise educational and modern technological standards and culture; constantly improve medical care, and develop a sound policy on foreign investment in order to make effective use of foreign capital without losing national economic independence. We must also develop a sound foreign trade policy in order to put foreign earnings to full and productive usage. All these objectives must be guided by a policy of prudence and frugality in both the public and private sectors.
7. On the debt question: short of declaring 'odious debt' we must negotiate urgently for a twenty-year moratorium on debt-servicing and interest-freeze to allow the national economy to pick up reconstruction momentum. To be effective, this can best be done maximally, on a continental or at the minimum, regional basis in collaboration with other African countries.
8. All this requires a dedicated leadership, honest and incorruptible.

It can and must be done if Africa is not to be recolonized!

Creating conditions for an economic strategy necessary for the 'second liberation of Africa'

Unify financial and economic work and stabilize prices

The key problem in most of the mangled African economies is the division between the financial and the economic sectors. Upon gaining state power, the New Democratic government must strive as a precondition to bring about the unity of these two vital sectors. This is primarily a struggle against speculative capital whose strategy and tactics can be worked out in accordance with a given concrete situation. In principle, though, we can generalize by observing that the breakup of the economies in Africa has led to the emergence of a large number of profiteers and speculators as a result of prolonged inflation and currency irregularities. Most of the private funds are therefore used for direct or indirect speculation. A large percentage of private capital is illegally used for what amounts to usury and illegal marketeering, which leads to sky-rocketing prices, a tight money market and soaring interest rates. As a result the entire market is dominated by speculators, with a flourishing illegal trade in foreign currencies and precious stones.

As a rule, soaring prices stem from the imbalance between the amount of currency and commodities in circulation. Under these circumstances, speculative activities cannot be effectively checked by mere administrative means. To restore the balance between currency and commodities in circulation depends on a country's approach to economic development. For the neo-liberals and the 'monetarists' who seek all economic solutions from the point of view of money in circulation, their way of restoring balance is via monetary and fiscal policies, no matter what damage this does to the well-being of the population – unemployment, lower incomes for the masses, deteriorating standards of living for the majorities, bankruptcies for small businesses, etc. It is the way of the IMF and World Bank.

But for an economy which is concerned more about the welfare of the people, the way to restore the balance is by increasing commodities in circulation. African countries that have followed the IMF route, like Ghana, Uganda, and others which claim to be 'success stories' may show impressive economic growth figures at the cost of a fall in the living standards for the people. The current plight of the Russians and other Eastern European people shows that the IMF cure is worse than the disease. China, on the other hand, in the wake of its economic reforms, chose the way out by raising production and flooding the markets with commodities and the results are quite impressive. This is the *direct* method of restoring the balance.

For this kind of solution, that is, the non-administrative or 'direct' methods or 'frontal onslaught', useful lessons can be learnt from the experiences of the post-war West Germany when Dr Erhard, then Finance Minister, had to deal with the runaway inflation and the speculative capital. Lessons can also be learnt from the Chinese experience of the same kind after the revolution in 1949. Both these countries, with diametrically opposite social and economic systems, utilized the same direct method to achieve price stabilization.

Expand the economy

This implies moving as rapidly as possible from the primitive mode of production, in other words, the 'simple reproduction' inherited from colonialism and enter the realm of 'expanded reproduction'. 'Simple reproduction' refers to a situation when a society produces its social wealth and then consumes all of it, including the surplus value, so that it is left with only its means of production with which to start the next production cycle. In other words, it is a *static* society.

'Expanded reproduction', on the other hand, refers to a situation when society conserves or saves some of its surplus in order to invest it so as to start the following production cycle from a higher level and *expand* its social wealth thus creating a *dynamic* society. A more dynamic society saves and invests more of its surplus to start the production cycle at a much higher level. In the contemporary experience since the advent of Thatcherism/Reaganism in Britain and the US respectively, and their introduction of dogmatic 'monetarism', the distinction between a more dynamic and less dynamic society is signified by the difference between, on the one hand, the successful German and Japanese economies which conserved and invested a larger proportion of their surplus value; and on the other hand, the Anglo-Saxon economies, starting from the US downwards, which consumed most of their surplus value through money exchange in currency speculation and stock exchange gambling, instead of investing in the production of goods and the creation of new wealth. Making profit out of currency speculation or stock exchange may enrich a few individuals but it does not *create* new social wealth; only manufacturing and agriculture create new wealth.

This movement from simple to expanded reproduction crosses the most critical and decisive threshold essential for moving from a dependent to an independent national economy. Economic expansion needs rapid development of the productive forces directed at producing basic needs, an industrialization fully integrated with agriculture, and a balanced or proportionate relation between heavy industry (i.e., capital goods-producing industries, or 'machines that build machines') and light industry for consumer durables as well as wage goods. In other words, agriculture must serve industry, and industry must serve agriculture.

Learn from historical experiences in economic development

What lessons can we learn from the developed industrial world which now dominates the world economically, diplomatically and militarily? Let us look at each region's experiences

The European and North American experience

Europe and North America have developed on the basis of industrialization. They achieved this mainly due to specific historical circumstances that obtained at the time. These include excessively cheap (almost free) labour: slavery and colonialism. This led to rapid capital accumulation and a ready 'captured' market abroad and an unprecedented population expansion at home.

In spite of its brutal history of slave labour which accelerated capital accumulation, the US experience has some useful lessons in the logic of its economic foundation which has eventually turned it into the strongest capitalist economy in the world. The US economy was founded on the production of food grains and cotton. In promoting food grains production it made the country self-sufficient in food, which is the most important basic need.

Cotton production on a massive scale, first for export to Britain, later for internal consumption, helped the United States not only to develop and expand the textiles industry, but it also helped to revolutionize that industry by the invention of the cotton gin which transformed the manual separation of seeds from cotton into mechanical operation and raised productivity several folds.

What is more it made cotton products affordable to poor people world-wide. (In East Africa the Kiswahili word for the printed grey cloth is 'Mrekani', that is, 'American'!) The most important point in the US national economy, however, was that textile industry provided a key link between heavy industry and agriculture. Agriculture formed the base; textile and other light industries (for example, housing construction, household appliances, consumer durables and many others) evolved around agriculture by supplying its needs and consuming its products. Eventually, heavy industry developed to supply the machines needed to build light industries and the latter in turn became the market for the heavy industry, as well as its supplier of consumer goods for the workers in heavy industry/light industry/agriculture, which made the US economy so well integrated internally with an ever-expanding home-market which provided the stimulus and motive force of the national economy. However, in spite of these advantages, the US economy is still undermined by the weaknesses inherent in the capitalist mode of production with its periodic and very damaging crises.

If the US economy developed on the basis of internal (settler) colonialism and slavery, European economies developed largely on the basis of external colonization and from the income that came from the surplus labour of the slaves in both North and South America. Their economies, however, cannot provide a model for developing Third World countries because, being so dependent on foreign trade, they are extremely vulnerable to external shocks. It is only the weaknesses of the Third World countries as suppliers of cheap raw materials and consumers of imported industrial goods from Europe that keep Europe's economies more or less flourishing.

The Japanese experience
The Japanese bourgeoisie also developed their national economy at about the same time as their Euro-American counterparts. They too helped themselves to some colonial exploitation after the Meiji restoration in 1868. In 1889 Japan emerged as a modern state with ambitions to be an industrial power. After the war with China in 1895,

Japan colonized parts of China. In 1905 it won the war against Russia, and in 1910, annexed Korea, and in 1915, presented China with the notorious 'Twenty-one Demands' which sought, among other things, to control China's mineral resources, especially coal deposits in North China. Japan's 'primitive accumulation of capital' was enormously helped by conquest and exploitation of foreign labour and resources. ('Primitive accumulation of capital' refers to the earliest stages of capital accumulation out of the surplus (the value of wealth created by the whole of society and then *appropriated* by one part of that society for its own use).) The country's development strategy followed the same path as that of Europe, and although now a manufacturing superpower, thanks to the post-war special relationship with the United States, which injected massive capital and technology into the economy, and opened the US market to Japanese goods, Japan is nevertheless extremely vulnerable to external shocks and cannot be a model for Third World development. Although the newly industrializing countries (the NICs) of Southeast Asia are flourishing on the Japanese model, thanks to massive Japanese capital and technology, they too cannot be a model for us because the circumstances and the conditions that gave them a boost – the Cold War, the Korean War, the Vietnam War, the US/Japanese market and technology – no longer exist for the majority of countries, especially in Africa.

The Soviet experience
Before the 1917 socialist revolution, Russia was a colonial power with vast resources, and was beginning to emerge as a capitalist industrial economy, enjoying large investments and loans from the West. After the revolution, foreign loans and investments dried up and the new leaders of the Soviet Union were faced with the problem of finding sources for the 'primitive accumulation of capital'. After some serious disagreements among the policymakers, Stalin (then Secretary-General of the Communist Party) and his faction got the upper hand and adopted a policy of transferring massive surplus from the agricultural sector, that is, from the peasantry, in order to invest in the industrialization programme, mostly heavy industry. They called this policy 'the law of primitive socialist accumulation'. (In the socialist theory of accumulation there is only socialist accumulation, and only under capitalism do you have 'capital accumulation', primitive or otherwise.)

Serious socialist economists, led by Bukharin, opposed this proposition, arguing that impoverishing the peasantry would hamper the development of the home market, distort the balance between agriculture and the industry and stifle the growth of light industry, which by its nature yields more profits owing to its quick turnover and a very short 'gestation period'. And this trend would inevitably lead heavy industry as a primary objective to enable the Soviet Union to develop a strong armament industry to defend herself, surrounded as it was by hostile capitalist countries of Western Europe and the United States. Bukharin and his friends ended in front of the firing squad as 'enemies of the people'!

As predicted, the Soviet policy turned into an economic disaster. Just as Bukharin foresaw, it led to a permanent imbalance between agriculture and industry, mass poverty in rural areas, and seventy years later, the mighty Soviet Union was reduced from a superpower to a humble follower of the United States. Stalin was right in one important respect. As he had predicted, his political decision to favour heavy industry as a top priority helped the Soviet Union survive the Second World War. Moreover, the Soviet Union was instrumental in the defeat of the most powerful and highly technical army of Fascist Germany. Twenty million Soviet people died and saved humanity from the brutalities of Fascism. However the imbalance in the Soviet economy led to a situation in which she was a superpower in military and space technology, but with a Third World economy characterized by mass poverty of the peasantry.

The Soviet experience was unique in that it was the first socialist country in history to challenge the imperialist powers when the Soviet Union was itself still economically and technologically extremely backward. The dilemma of choosing either economic or political priorities that faced the Soviet leadership at the time was exceptionally critical and it may not be fair to judge them purely on economic grounds. However, as those circumstances are not likely to face any African country, it is important for us to learn from the Soviet Union's economic misjudgments so that we do not repeat them in a planned economy.

The Chinese experience
After the revolution of 1949 up to 1956, China followed the Soviet model. But very soon they saw in the model the inherent tendency towards imbalance between the major sectors of the economy and therefore decided to abandon it. In rejecting the Soviet model Mao put forward his famous Ten Major Relationships thesis which were essential for developing a balanced economy. The most important of these relationships was that between heavy industry, on the one hand and light industry and agriculture, on the other. Mao stressed that the Soviet's lop-sided stress on heavy industry to the neglect of

agriculture and light industry results in a shortage of goods on the market and an unstable currency. This conclusion was not due to an inspired prophetic vision, but rather due to a full grasp of the laws of economic development. In any case, 35 years after that observation, events have proved the Maoist thesis to be realistic and correct, confirmed by the tragic collapse of the Soviet model in Europe. China, in the meantime, is making great strides and by mid-1992, it had become the fastest growing country in the world with an annual growth rate of 12 per cent, and a trade surplus with the US alone of some 20 billion dollars, which is second only to Japan's!

What can we learn from the Chinese miracle? The one thing that is most outstanding is that while the US has achieved its balanced development, as noted above, by unique historical circumstances (slave labour, settler manpower from Europe, etc.) in a haphazard and unplanned manner, China is reaching her balanced development through:

- efficient deployment of the nation's socially necessary labour time and
- through a sensible and realistic planning mechanism of observing the cardinal principle of proportionate and balanced development of the national economy.

At her rate of current growth, China will be a medium industrial power at par with, say, Italy, by about the year 2020. As the only fastest developing (ex-semi-colonial) country without external conquest or colonization, China is probably the perfect model for all African countries to emulate.

Ideal conditions for industrialization and development

A combination of several factors as noted above, including Anglo-Saxon settler economies in America, Australia, Canada and New Zealand, created ideal conditions for advanced agriculture, industrialization and development, which followed more or less the same pattern:

- Agriculture expanded in order to feed the growing domestic populations. But that agriculture was not based on the production of coffee or tea or cocoa, the standard Third World crops, but largely on food grains, cotton, oil seeds and other industrial crops as raw materials for domestic industry.
- Influx of labour from the rural to the urban industrial areas resulted in labour scarcity in agriculture and created conditions

for innovations and capital-intensive farming, labour-saving techniques and raised productivity.
- The growing demand for labour-saving techniques in agriculture induced industries to go for the production of producer goods and created conditions for capital-goods production.
- Population growth created demand not only for more food, but also for more clothing and housing, which promoted textile industrialization and the housing and construction industry, which constituted the foundation of national economies by creating massive employment opportunities and raising living standards. Expanding industrial capacity needed wider markets beyond the home market for the finished products. Expanded industrial activity in turn demanded more raw materials from abroad.
- The ensuing competition among the industrializing countries for external markets and for sources of raw materials stepped up colonization, 'settler-ization' abroad, further technological expansion and naval superiority which facilitated further colonization. All this gave Europe, the United States and Japan the power to dominate the world economy which they exploit to this day.

What can Africa learn from these various experiences?

The above experiences of the developed countries in Europe, the United States and Japan and with the exception of China's, were exceptional historical circumstances which no longer exist for the developing Third World.

There is no going back to the 'birth throes' of capitalism (slavery and colonialism) which helped Europe and the US to develop, although not for want of trying in Africa by the International Monetary Fund and the international bankers it serves. People are everywhere resisting any attempt to reintroduce the humiliating conditions of subjugation familiar under slavery and colonialism.

In other words 'primitive accumulation of capital' in our case cannot take place in the same fashion as was the case in Europe, the US and Japan, through slavery or through the savagery inflicted on the native Americans and through colonialism.

But the fact still remains that we must have the wherewithal for our own 'primitive accumulation of capital' if we are to develop the productive forces and move on to expanded reproduction without which there can be no development.

Again, if in Europe and the US the massive expansion of urban centres was indicative of economic growth and has created the necessary conditions for industrialization, in Africa the expansion of urban population, on the contrary, is only indicative of the condition of rural stagnation and under-development, which in itself obstructs national development.

Nor can the mass poverty in towns and cities that we are now experiencing in Africa provide a stimulus to modern agricultural farming, as it did in Europe and in other developed countries. Nor can it be a source for accumulation as in the above cases; on the contrary, it has the effect of obstructing development and of worsening rural impoverishment, for the simple reason that our economies hardly respond to internal conditions. We only respond to 'external shocks'!

This situation in which the majority of African countries find themselves today is what is refered to as 'contracted reproduction'. In this case, a society goes through several production cycles without allowing social wealth to maintain itself and instead allows it to shrink and become less and less. Then, as in the days of 'easy money' in the mid-1970s and 1980s, society goes out to borrow money from the international money markets, not to enhance its production cycle, but on the contrary, in order just to keep it in the vicious cycle. Apparently, these economies are not even *static*; they are declining!

Can Africa emulate the past?

What can an African country do in order to develop a self-sustaining, independent national economy? We cannot of course re-create the above 'favourable' historical circumstances that have helped advanced countries to develop; nor will the latter help us develop and become their competitors. On the contrary, ever since the beginning of the 1980s, Europe and the United States have been doing everything to destabilize our economies through the IMF and the World Bank. The Bretton Woods system itself, since its inception in 1945, has been the main source of Western prosperity by ensuring a steady flow of wealth from poor countries to the rich (the net outflow, which includes the effects of debt-servicing, brain-drain and resource transfer, is currently estimated to be around 200 billion dollars a year, or about 23 million dollars per hour!). We have, therefore, no alternative except to find our own way of starting the capital-accumulation process, which includes putting a stop to this massive outflow of wealth. For Africa alone the net outflow of value from the continent to the Western world is estimated at 200 million dollars per day! This amount, if retained in the continent, can be an important starting point for our 'primitive accumulation of capital'.

This means that we must be realistic and discard any illusion that anybody else can help us develop except ourselves. If we cannot recreate historical circumstances, it is within our means to at least create 'artificial' conditions which can and will induce development.

If the West achieved its primitive accumulation of capital at the expense of Africa and other colonies, and the Soviet Union achieved hers at the expense of her peasantry and her Asiatic colonies, who will Africa exploit for our primitive accumulation of capital?

Our experience since independence has shown that we cannot hope to start our accumulation via the export of primary commodities to the world market. The world market, on the contrary, has been and is the main contributing factor to our poverty and under-development for two reasons. First, we waste almost all our socially necessary labour time in the production of useless agricultural commodities primarily for export, yet we earn hardly anything to set our accumulation in motion. Thus we put more into the world market than we get out of it, which means a net loss. Any waste of socially necessary labour time has its penalty, and in our case we pay the penalty by being condemned to absolute poverty and mass starvation.

A strategy for initial capital accumulation

If we seriously want to set in motion the process of accumulation for productive investment, it is essential to first of all adopt a different world outlook in our approach to development. In other words, we must start with a different frame of mind. This outlook must be based on accepting the fact that *external* causes are only a condition of change, while *internal* causes are the basis of change.

We must learn to utilize our socially necessary labour time more efficiently, concentrating more on the production of what we actually need for our own development rather than on what we hope to gain from exports. If a society wastes a large proportion of its social labour time mostly in the production of agricultural commodities for export, and gets less and less in return, as is the case in many African countries, then that society is bound to head for serious economic and social problems.

This is the state in which many African countries find themselves. We are paying the penalty for wasting our socially necessary labour time in the production of commodities which we can only sell, but which we cannot ourselves use. If there is no demand for them, or if we are offered an unacceptable price which will not enable us to buy goods needed by the society in compensation for the social labour time so wasted we face financial crisis. We cannot eat coffee or tea if no one wants to buy them! In other words, we produce what we do not consume, and consume what we do not produce. The penalty for this kind of dysfunctional national economy is, in some extreme case, to expose the people to famine and starvation on a mass scale. Gains from exports can begin to be economically useful only when the economy is soundly based internally and the needs of the people are regularly met.

To start the accumulation process we must rely entirely on the diligent labour and skills of our own people (now wholly exploited by external forces), and on our own resources and on an expanding internal market. To achieve this we must have a people's own leadership at the helm instead of the wasteful and corrupt petty-bourgeois ones we have so far experienced. We cannot, realistically, immediately abandon production of 'cash crops' as a source of foreign exchange earning. We must have a long-term plan to minimize our dependence on such crops the production of which takes so much of our labour time without commensurate income; and at the same time neglecting to produce what we need for our own development. We should utilize our weakness in the world market to strengthen our economic base by importing new technology and capital goods as needed for that objective. After setting in motion the process of real national development, we will then be able to fully enter the world market on our own terms, and from a position of relative strength, like any other developed country.

We must learn to be frugal; to be, collectively, a nation of savers and not of the waste-makers and vulgar consumerism that we are at the moment. This requires exceptional discipline because we cannot afford to be anything less at the start of our long journey to national prosperity.

As we are so heavily indebted, thanks to the sins of the previous governments, there are two ways of resolving or minimizing the pain of the problem. We may either renounce the debts on the 'odious debt' principle, which is a perfectly legitimate ground in international law because the people were not consulted when the debts were contracted, and the governments that contracted the debts were mostly illegal either because they were military regimes who came to power through coups, or one-party dictatorships which did not enjoy the mandate of the people. Finally, we do not have anything to show for it on the ground. Indeed most of the debts are held in Western bank accounts of our corrupt leaders.

It is obvious that most of these loans were corruptly contracted and therefore, the people are not obliged to honour them. The bankers must suffer the consequences of their wrong decisions, as in any business that runs at a loss. Or they and the corrupt leaders must settle accounts between themselves, either via the Swiss banks or through courts.

The second way out is, if we accept to bear the debt burden, then Africa can collectively start to negotiate with our creditors for a twenty-year moratorium on debt-servicing and immediate freeze on interest, both of which are a major source of capital outflow. Smart bankers would naturally accept this second option.

The meagre foreign exchange that we are currently earning from our exports must be spent most frugally by carefully choosing between importing either absolutely essential consumer goods, that is, on social consumption like health service, education and transport, on the one hand, or on goods to advance our technology and on producer goods, especially machine-tool industries, that is, machines that build machines, on the other.

We must gradually change the composition of our exports and imports to conform with our reorientation strategy. Stepped-up export of manufactured or processed goods will increase our foreign exchange earnings and enable us to import advanced technology and equipment. That is to say, by gradually minimizing the production of cash crops for export and instead diverting our efforts to the development of food, housing and textile and garment industries, to begin with, in order to expand the home market and raise people's incomes. By doing so, we will be creating favourable conditions for utilizing our socially necessary labour time more efficiently and productively for people's needs. The foundation of our economy, as that of any developed economies, must be home-based.

As 90 per cent of our populations are engaged in agriculture, then initially the modernization of agriculture must be our top priority, and the raising of rural incomes the motive force of our economies. By improving rural skills through production and construction – irrigation work, water conservation, fish farming, flooding control, soil improvement through intensive use of natural manure, afforestation, proper training in the introduction of technical know-how and modernization of agriculture – we will help promote rural industrialization and promote economic complementarity between the urban and rural sectors of the economy, thus solving one of the most disabling contradictions in under-developed economies, namely the urban/rural dichotomy. It will also help stem the rush to the cities by rural youths. As the Chinese slogan aptly puts it in its campaign to keep the youth in the rural areas: 'Leaving the farmland, but not the village: entering the factory, but not the city'.

Our industrial development, therefore, must initially be geared towards serving agriculture, which in turn must serve industry. This strategy will help set in motion the process to self-sustaining, independent national economy, gradually put a stop to capital outflow, and will accelerate the process of accumulation, of the development of the productive forces and thus enter the realm of expanded reproduction.

Identify areas where savings can be affected
To start with we must drastically reduce spending on the military and cut down official foreign travel, now widely abused and a big drain on our foreign exchange. Overseas embassies must be cut to an absolute minimum; limit these to five or six essential areas of significance for promoting real 'national interest', for example, the UN, Washington (IMF and the World Bank), London (British Commonwealth), or Paris (for the Francophones), Brussels (EEC), and at the OAU. Embassies are notorious for squandering foreign exchange resources, legally and illegally.

We have to learn to utilize every potential internal resource first before resorting to imports. This is most essential in the early stages of capital formation, for example, the use of natural manure instead of (imported) chemical fertilizers. For instance, one cow produces one tonne of manure annually. Tame and train some of the wildlife for production work. Wildlife is potentially a great source of energy which in many cases can be used to replace (imported) oil-driven machines. In Burma, the entire timber industry is based on elephants; in Zanzibar, the entire clove and coconut transport was based on animal-driven carts which brought much prosperity to the nation; oil milling was based on camel energy, and so on. We can resort to modern machinery only when we have a sound and prosperous basis at home. Japan utilizes the most ancient and most modern technologies side-by-side, and as a result they have achieved what we now call the 'Japanese miracle'.

We must strive to establish a most efficient public transport system which will make large-scale importation of private cars unnecessary and the foreign exchange thus saved could be diverted to importing productive inputs in the form of new technology and machines essential for increased production of consumer goods needed by the people, creating more employment and raising people's standards of living. There are several other areas for saving our limited foreign exchange resource, which can be investigated. For instance, Cuba, after being abandoned by the Soviet Union and embargoed by the US, has embarked on ingenious methods of saving their meagre foreign exchange earnings in order to continue to maintain their socialist system. There is a lot that can be learnt from the Cuban experience, both as a warning and as an economic necessity.

Above all, special attention must be paid to develop a scientific economic management capability which is essential for rapid economic transformation. So far our experience with the leadership in Africa is that it tends to be excessively 'political'. The civilian leadership pool (that is to say, where the Idi Amins of this world have not taken over state power) ranges from university graduates of one kind or another to semi-literate rabble-rousers, depending on the needs of the top man in authority at any given time, that is, to increase his popularity, to step up his security or secret police; to isolate a certain section he thinks dangerous; to step up political thuggery and intimidate the population and so on.

National economy is normally given lowest priority. An economist would be appointed as a minister of finance or economic affairs or agriculture or industry, without the faintest idea of economic management or the intended direction of the economy. Managing the national economy and knowledge of economics are two separate fields and they must be distinguished as such, otherwise the economist will make a mess at managing the economy and the trained manager will make a mess at forecasting economic trends. Economic management entails formulating policies like, for example, who is responsibile for decision making? How many kinds of ownership – state ownership, private ownership, cooperative ownership, planned or market economy or a combination of both, in which case which is to be primary? What are the intrinsic relations within the economy? How to coordinate production with marketing? How and where to invest the accrual surplus funds, for what national, regional or district objective? What are the principles guiding the national economy and how best to attain them within a specific time frame? How to balance the two major departments of social production, that is, means of production and means of consumption? What and how to set priorities and for what specific or general purposes? Are all these to be left to the 'market forces' to determine or to a national plan or a judicious combination of the two? And so on and so forth. All these need special orientation which a university graduate or a mob-rouser may not share or be aware of. Scientific management of the economy needs training and orientation in all these aspects before launching the economic transformation exercise.

Three basic approaches to development

Within the two main social systems mentioned above, that is, the *neo-classical* and the *social democratic*, there are three methods usually adopted as a strategy for development:

- the ideological, that is, either capitalist or socialist or 'mixed';
- the economy, that is, responding only to the 'economic imperative', for better or worse, and
- serving the people, that is, the economics of the New Democracy, which is a scientifically-based common-sense approach to development, giving priority to the long and short-term needs of the people and then organizing the economy accordingly for the attainment of that objective.

Experience has shown that the first approach has many dangers because going exclusively by the dictates of one's ideology, unchecked by the scientific method of verification, one very often tends to lose sight of the concrete realities of a given situation. Ideology must remain only as a guide to action, but never turned into a dogma. Serious mistakes have been made by both capitalist and socialist 'fundamentalists' who have refused to alter their course even when danger signals indicated disaster ahead. This shortcoming has become obvious by the catastrophic results of the ideology of 'monetarism' in the Anglo-Saxon countries in the 1980s and by the rigid Soviet model which distorted the very essence of socialism and socialist planning.

The second approach too has many shortcomings. For one thing, economics on its own has no foresight; it can forecast figures, but it cannot predict their social outcome. It can probably work for 'good economic results' but these are not always in conformity with the social or people's needs and their welfare. It is rather like the proverbial doctor who performs a technically 'successful surgical operation' although the patient dies. That is why it is said that 'national economy is too important to be left to the economists'.

The last approach is more pertinent because it is guided constantly by what society or the people need. That is why we should call it a common-sense approach. Of course, if you are dealing with developing a national economy you must have economists, but only as technicians and not as initiators of policy. The common-sense approach uses economics to justify or to subject to critical analysis what has been ordained by the 'authority of the people', to give 'indicative figures' of what might happen to the growth of the economy in the abstract if action A or B were to be taken, but not to decide whether to take A or B. That is a political decision.

The key factor contributing to the current African crisis is that ever since independence, African countries have been run on the principles of the economics-driven approach. Where you had 'five-year plans', it was the economists, mostly foreign and not the political representatives of the people who laid down 'national objectives'. This has been the root cause which has led Africa down blind alleys to virtual economic ruin. The crisis is made worse by once again following the dictates of the same foreign economists in the hope of bailing us out! In every case these economists tend to be steeped in capitalist ideologies, which have no relevance to our conditions. And they always 'get it wrong'. On the other hand, their radical opponents, mostly with socialist orientation, often tend to challenge them on the same grounds, but from a different direction. The result is a 'dialogue of the deaf' which does not reach the people because they cannot follow what the fuss is all about.

Where national economies were not planned, no specific economic objectives were set; it was only hoped economic prosperity would be achieved by encouraging full play of individual greed operating in the 'market place'. Countries like Kenya or the Ivory Coast operated on this basis and they were hailed as *success* stories, but actually only a handful, again mostly foreigners, benefited at the expense of the majority of the impoverished masses. There has indeed been a lot of 'economic activity', impressive office tower-blocks and so on, which gave the impression of 'growth', but in real terms the people at large have become worse off. In both these 'success' models, there are currently intense political and economic upheavals.

That is why we should stick to the common-sense approach as the guiding line of the economics of New Democracy. Whereas the traditional development theories have treated the question of poverty and deprivation as an outcome of some amoral international arrangement, and that to alleviate the situation is by means of changing the world economic system and stepped-up exports, the common-sense approach treats the situation more seriously. The causes of our poverty are not external but internal, although the external causes help to aggravate the already rotten situation. And to correct it we must seek internal solutions and then and only then, external factors may be resorted to in order to stimulate the corrective or transformatory process. But at the same time the common-sense approach must thoroughly understand the situation in the external world, that is, the world economy, because only in understanding who controls it, its history, its mechanism, its motive force and our position and role in it, can we best use it to our advantage and not allow ourselves to be used by it.

The international perspective: the slide to the status quo

As part of the world economy Africa cannot help but play her part in it and seek answers and solutions to her problems by taking into account what is affecting the continent in the context of the political economy of the world.

But there is an important distinction between trying to understand the world political economy and seeking our role in it, on the one hand and, on the other, to simply be subservient to it and only react to it as if we are helplessly reacting to the forces of nature. In the latter category we should put the new African elites, the decision makers, who are inordinately influenced by the multilateral agencies, like the old elites before them who were brainwashed by the colonialists. They do not seem to be able to take the initiative on any major issue affecting their countries. They simply sing the tune of the prevailing refrain orchestrated by the imperialist powers. They are propagating the notion of the 'global management of an interdependent world', which really means managing the status quo for the benefit of the imperial powers and at the expense of the poor countries. This is not the way of looking for solutions to our problems within the context of the world economy. This is a futile pretext of seeking solutions to the status quo from within the status quo!

It is an attempt at seeking adjustments within the same old economic world order without attempting to change our own role in it, beginning with changing our own economies as a precondition to a new order. It is a negative way of seeking to establish the 'new international economic order' while we remain in the same economic status of commodity producers. That kind of 'globalism' is meaningless; it is only a way of intoxicating the poor with hope.

The real world economy, in fact, is not interdependent; it is an exploitative arrangement whereby one section of the world benefits from the weakness and backwardness of the other. And it is in the interest of the former to maintain the situation as it is. Africa has no power to change it, shout as we may. We can only change what is in our power to change and that is our own economies first – their structure and direction.

We made a fatal mistake right at independence. We had a choice then between siding with the emerging world socialist movement and (mercifully) being cut off from the capitalist 'world economy', or remain junior partners in an economy dominated by the US and the ex-colonial powers from whom we had just emerged from colonialism. In Asia, only China, North Korea, Laos and Vietnam chose to join the world socialist movement which sought to bring about a completely new world order, a socialist world. In Africa none went that way, although we invented various forms of 'socialisms'(African socialism in Tanzania, 'Workers' or Peoples' republics in Guinea, Ethiopia, Angola, Mozambique, Somalia, etc.) to fool the masses while we were putting them more firmly under the grip of Western domination.

In a comparatively short time, China and North Korea became medium-sized industrial powers, largely self-sustaining, while the rest of us became more and more mal-developed, with millions of new social problems emerging by the day. But in the case of China, with extraordinary foresight she had abandoned the Soviet planning model by mid-1956 which had the fatal weakness of emphasizing the development of heavy industry at the expense of light industry and agriculture. Instead, China decided to put in practice the Maoist strategy which came to be known as the Ten Major Relationships. Among these relationships, the key one was that between heavy industry, on the one hand, and light industry and agriculture, on the other. In rejecting the Soviet and East European model, the Maoist thesis pointed our that: 'Their lop-sided stress on heavy industry to the neglect of agriculture and light industry results in a shortage of goods on the market and an unstable currency.' Thirty-five years later, this observation has proved to be remarkably correct with the tragic collapse of the Soviet system in Europe, while China continues to make great strides in her economic performance and modernization.

In spite of the inherent weakness in the Soviet model, however, the West could see in it the potential for becoming a serious challenge to the West's strategy of world domination, or hegemony. The West, therefore, decided to fight it to the finish, with all its enormous advantage over the young emerging socialist system. When Africa began to gain its independence, this war against socialism was at its peak. Africa, consciously or unconsciously, decided to side with the West against socialism, and at the same time declaring ourselves to be non-aligned between East and West! It was never explained how anyone can honestly be non-aligned between a just and an unjust system. In any case, we decided of our own free will to place our countries under the sphere of influence of the West as junior partners and in effect, signed our own death warrant: we were to be condemned never to see any serious development of the continent, collectively or individually. As long as we remained in this demonstrably unjust world economic system from a position of weakness, with circumstances so heavily weighted against us, there was no way we could attain any form of development beneficial to ourselves.

What, therefore, are the causes, both external and internal, of the African crisis?

External causes of the African crisis
The 'modern' world economic order was created soon after the anti-Fascist war in 1945. It was designed to continue with the war by other means; this time against the socialist order which was then emerging as a system that could provide an alternative to the status quo, especially to the poor countries. Thus, the first Conference to re-establish the old system in a new guise was held at Bretton Woods in the United States, and the system became known as the Bretton Woods System. Its declared objective was to stabilize international monetary and financial regimes which were disrupted in the pre-war period of the 1930s, to help the Western world's economic recovery and to combat socialism in the post-war era. The main institutions created for the job were the World Bank, the IMF and GATT (the General Agreement on Tariffs and Trade), all of which were at the same time designed, in addition to recovery, to strengthen the Western grip on the world economy. We became members of all of these institutions soon after independence. Thirty years on, we have already been demoted from the status of independent and honourable members of these institutions to that of their 'obedient servants'.

It will be useful for those who urge us to deepen our involvement in this economic arrangement in the spirit of 'interdependence' to remember that at no time has the system ever worked in our interest and there is no evidence to show that it might do so in the future. The alleged 'interdependence' can only be of the kind in which we are permanently dependent on the West's massive exploitation of our human and material resources. The system itself, has a long history starting from the dark epoch of the slave trade, to colonialism and imperialism, and in all of these phases Africa has remained its constant victim. An interdependent world indeed! But we need not go too far into the past. Our immediate purpose is to have a full grasp of the current international economic order in order to find the way out of our problem.

The nature of the contemporary global economy
To come to the nitty-gritty of this modern world economy, it is of primary importance to first of all understand the role of international finance as a major force that lubricates it. Very briefly, there have been three significant areas of international finance. The first was

between 1870 to 1914 which was dominated by Britain. The second was between 1920 to 1929 when the centre of international finance shifted from London to New York, but it collapsed in 1930 with the Great Depression followed by the Second World War. The third era – the era of US hegemony, the Bretton Woods era – started in 1947 until 1985 when the US itself was reduced from a creditor to debtor country as Japan replaced it as the world's foremost creditor nation.

The decline of US hegemony, which inevitably cost Africa a lot owing to her dependence on the dollar (for example, for every 1 per cent rise in interest rate, the debtor countries have to pay four to five billion dollars in interest!), was brought about by excessive irresponsibility of US policies: the over-printing of the paper dollar (more than 600 billion dollars!), mismanagement of the international monetary and financial systems, adventurist wars of aggression (Korea, Vietnam and others), the advent of Reaganomics and its monetarist orthodoxies and so on. In other words, the US used the system to its own advantage and became the root cause of the global economic problems of the 1980s, the debt problem being the most significant one for Africa.

The debt burden made debtor countries even weaker while correspondingly the creditor countries, under the IMF leadership, gained strength through its insistence on conditionality and reliance on the old imperial policy of divide and rule over debtor countries, so that they would not form a united front of debtor countries and negotiate from the strength that position will have conferred. Although the debt crisis, like the crisis in the monetary and financial systems, was brought about by the actions of creditor countries themselves, the responsibility is placed on the debtor countries: the developed countries dumped loans and capital into the Third World, seeking a large return in interest. Unequal trade terms cut into Third World export income, weakening their ability to service their debts on time. And of course, the rise in interest rates has compounded the African crisis.

Furthermore, the failure of the misdirected struggle launched by the Third World for the so-called New International Economic Order which had sought to bring the multilateral financial agencies, the IMF and World Bank, under the jurisdiction of the UN General Assembly, has helped to absolve creditor countries from any responsibility for the debt crisis. That failure has actually strengthened the position of the IMF *vis-à-vis* Third World countries. From then on, it has continued to impose its own 'conditionality' on African countries with impunity, resulting in massive unemployment, a steady decline in the living standards of the people and spreading domestic political instability, with all its devastating consequences. Ironically, one of the original purposes for which the IMF was created, in addition to facilitating world trade, was to promote employment and general well-being!

Under the existing conditions of this 'interdependent' world, there is no way that Africa can repay its external debt, estimated conservatively at 300 billion dollars, while the net outflow of wealth from Africa to the West continues to mount, leaving nothing for domestic capital formation and investments. Conservative estimate puts that outflow at nearly 200 million dollars *per day*, and mounting!

The declared principles of the multilateral agencies and their relationship with the new countries, as they were emerging from colonialism and joining the institutions, were defined as providing aid to assist developing countries to reach a point where they could 'participate fully in an open, market-oriented international economy' and that aid policies were to be subordinate to the norms of the market system. But even in those early days it was clear that, as far as the emerging countries were concerned, this objective contradicted the principle of national sovereignty because it frustrated the right to development of these young countries by forcing them into a world market system which was itself not open, not free and extremely imperfect, favouring only the strong against the weak.

Comparative advantage and free trade

For their part, the dominant nations always insist that 'all's fair in trade and war'. But this is acceptable only as long as you are in a dominant position! Their interpretation of 'fairness' was elevated, long ago, to a principle known as the 'comparative advantage' principle. Its history, as we know, goes far back to the philosophy of the British philosopher, David Hume, and later expounded in the economic theories of Adam Smith and David Ricardo in the post-Industrial Revolution Britain when it dominated the world trade. To this day, this 'law' has remained the basis of liberal 'free trade' theory. Our elites who are now blindly advocating the notion of an interdependent world base their rationale on the theories based on this 'law', ignoring the fact that it was conceived and applied by Britain at a time when it had all the advantages over all other nations.

But even then weaker nations had a different approach and were very critical of the comparative advantage thesis. They saw in it a serious threat to their own national security, domestic welfare and industrial development. This must be even more so today for countries whose economies and foreign trade are largely based on primary commodities. Can there really be any comparative advantage between the peasant producer of, say, coffee or tea and the industrial producer of the tractor from whom the former has to buy his inputs? The only advantage is the *absolute* advantage to the industrial producer? As a matter of fact, our present experience proves to us, again and again, that the industrial producer countries find this system of 'free trade' so advantageous to them that they are prepared to use force, via the IMF and the World Bank, (or even in a bilateral form as in the case of Cuba versus the US), against any poor country that tries to embark on an independent route to development or which dares to resist their dictation or challenge their hegemony.

Historically, even the mighty Germany of the last century found it necessary to protect its economy, dignity and sovereignty against what they dubbed the 'imperialism of free trade'. This was at a time when Germany was already becoming an industrial power in its own right, but it still realized that it would not be to Germany's disadvantage to abide by the thesis of comparative advantage and free trade when they were still weak compared to Britain, which then had only a decade or so head-start over Germany.

Similarly, for the poor and weak countries of Africa today, like the then poor and weak countries of the last century, the primary preoccupation must not be a blind adherence to the international trade norms or belief in the 'law' of comparative advantage which is really the law of the strong over the weak, but to produce for their own needs, that is, the need to strengthen their state systems so that they do not become vulnerable to the dictates of other interests. Secondly, they must struggle for the attainment of unity of state and nation in a continent so mangled and fragmented by slavery and colonialism. Thirdly, it is vital to reorient the economy so as to achieve a unity between industry and agriculture, a precondition for integrating the economy internally and evolving an independent national economy in place of the present colonial economy. You may call this 'economic nationalism', but all countries that started late on the road to development (Germany, the US, Japan, the Soviet Union, China, etc.) had to resort to this development strategy and history has proved them right. Why should Africa be an exception?

Internal causes

In the wake of the economic crisis and the debt problem which have put Africa in its most serious socio-political plight, various 'alternative' strategies are being offered from different perspectives. As noted above, there are three main approaches to development, the ideological, the economistic and the common-sense approach. So far the alternatives that have been outlined for Africa are either of the first or second type, but none from the point of view of the 'common-sense' approach.

The Lagos Plan of Action was designed to be operative from 1980 to the end of the century. Its objectives are the achievement of:

- regional food self-sufficiency,
- the provision of shelter, health care, housing,
- sustained growth and development and
- national and collective self-reliance.

There is also the African Priority Programme for Economic Recovery during 1986–90, adopted by the United Nations. This was followed by the African Alternative Framework to Structural Adjustment Programme, by the UN Economic Commission for Africa (UNECA). All these ambitious programmes were motivated by honourable intentions, no doubt, but so far none of them has produced any hopeful signals. On the contrary, we are more than halfway through the Lagos Plan of Action, and indications are that Africa is worse off now than it was in 1980 when the programme was launched.

We have already gone beyond the target of the UN Priority Programme for Economic Recovery and we have seen no recovery at all, anywhere. The African Alternative Framework sounds more like a theoretical debate between UNECA and the World Bank rather than a serious strategy for Africa's alternative policy. That is why it has failed to be anywhere near achieving its stated objectives. The reason why all of these so-called alternative programmes have failed is because they all start from the same premise, namely that Africa has no alternative except to go for an export-led development strategy. That is to say, Africa must rely on the export of its primary commodities to earn foreign exchange to enable it to import its domestic needs. That is why, on the basis of this rationale, we see Africa's cities and towns jammed with all types of foreign cars when we cannot even produce spare parts locally to service them! The concrete reality is that this strategy is inapplicable to Africa's current level of development based on its present production structure. Its acceptance as the linchpin of policy goes counter to the basic law of development which, as we saw, asserts that *internal* causes are the basis of change, while external causes remain only as conditions of change and not the other way round. Any country that tries to alter this reality is doomed to failure.

Conclusion

The internal causes of the crisis aggravated by the debt burden may be summarized as follows. In addition to the topsy-turvy structure of our economies which gravitated outwards rather than inwards, a new phenomenon entered the world economy. The oil crisis of 1973, the transfer of massive surplus 'unwanted' dollars to the oil-producing countries and their recycling them back to the Western banks created a crisis of surplus of unusable funds (unusable because no developed country wanted to take responsibility for the over-printed 600 billion US dollars). As foreign banks were thus eager to dump their 'petro-dollars' and other surplus funds in the mid-1970s, African countries recklessly borrowed and fell into the debt trap. They failed to draw up comprehensive repayment timetables, taking into account the total amount of the debt incurred, the investments absorbed, interest due for payment, their foreign exchange reserves, development of the productive forces, exports, the foreign exchange to be earned, the growth rate and target of their national economies. The resultant imbalance between the debt incurred and income forced them to incur new debts to pay for the old ones.

Secondly, inappropriate use of foreign loans resulted in poor economic performance and low foreign exchange earnings. Loans largely went into financing consumption (for example, building brand new capital cities, ultra-modern airports, and so on) and hardly any went into the development of the productive forces, which in turn weakened economic efficiency and earned no surplus.

4

Global Africa: From Abolitionists to Reparationists

Ali A. Mazrui

Introduction

Africa has experienced a triple heritage of slavery – indigenous, Islamic and Western. The reparations movement seems to have concluded that although the indigenous and Islamic forms of slavery were much older than the transatlantic version, they were much smaller in scale and allowed for greater upward social mobility – from slave to sultan, from peasant to paramount chief. Indigenous systems of slavery were unracial – black masters, black slaves. Islamic forms of slave systems were multiracial, both masters and slaves could be of any race or colour. Indeed, Egypt and Muslim India evolved slave dynasties. Western slave systems were the most racially polarized in the modern period – white masters, black slaves (i.e., biracial).

Because the transatlantic slave trade was tied to expansionist global capitalism, the Western slave trade itself accelerated dramatically. Millions upon millions of African captives were exported in a very short period. Today in the Western Hemisphere there are some 150 million people with African blood.[1]

The agenda for the reparations crusade must therefore begin with the horrendous consequences of the transatlantic slave trade. That crusade alone may take a generation. Perhaps in the future there has to be a different kind of crusade for reparations from the Arab world – where the calculations have to be of a different kind.

Once upon a time, there were abolitionists, who were committed to the proposition that slavery and the slave trade were evil, and engaged in a struggle to end them. Now a new moral and political breed is forming or expanding – the reparationists, committed to the proposition that the injustices of enslavement and bondage could not have ended with formal emancipation. They can only truly end with the atonement of reparations.

While the abolitionists' movement in the eighteenth and nineteenth centuries was mainly inspired by benevolent changes in the Western world, the reparationist movement in the twentieth century has been partly inspired by malevolent continuities in the black world.

The benevolent changes in the West which had once favoured the abolitionist movement were partly technological and partly socio-normative. Innovations like the cotton gin made slave labour less necessary and less efficient for Western capitalism. The abolitionist movement found a more responsive political establishment as slave labour became technologically more anachronistic.

In addition, the values of the Western world were getting more liberalized in other fields such as the extension of the franchise to the working classes in the nineteenth century and the beginnings of movements for women's rights. The convergence of more efficient technologies and a more liberal ideology helped to boost the abolitionist movement in Europe and the Americas. These were the benevolent changes in the West whose cumulative impact favoured the abolition of the slave trade and subsequently of slavery itself. Even the political emancipation of Roman Catholics in Britain was a cause which William Wilberforce championed just a decade before he was converted to the more radical cause of abolishing the slave trade and slavery.

The consequences of colonization are not merely research topics for scholars, but are also horrendous civil wars and a normative collapse in places like Rwanda, Liberia, Angola and Somalia. Hence the more malevolent continuities of colonialism. The consequences of both enslavement and colonization are not merely themes for plenary lectures at African Studies conventions, but also the malfunctioning colonial economies in Africa and the distorted socio-economic relations in the African diaspora. Hence the malevolent continuities of both colonialism and racism.

On the other hand, the inspiration behind the reparations movement was not change but continuity: the persistence of deprivation and anguish in the black world arising directly out of the legacies of slavery and colonialism. The consequences of enslavement and colonization are not chapters in history books but pangs of pain in the ghettoes of Washington DC, and the anti-black police brutalities in the streets of Los Angeles, Rio de Janeiro, London and Paris. These are some of the malevolent continuities of racism.

From Fredrick Douglass to Moshood Abiola

While the most historically visible heroes of the abolitionist movement were disproportionately white, the emerging visible heroes of the reparationist movement are disproportionately black.

The historically visible white abolitionists in Great Britain included William Wilberforce (1759–1833) while those in the United States included the martyred John Brown (1800–59) and in a special sense of abolitionism, the martyred Abraham Lincoln (1809–65). William Lloyd Garrison (1805–79), founder of the American Anti-slavery Society, was for a while, the best-known white American abolitionist. This is quite apart from Harriet Beecher Stowe (1811–96), the author of *Uncle Tom's Cabin* (1851), arguably the most important white female abolitionist influence in the history of the movement in the United States, alongside Lydia Maria Child.

There were of course also black abolitionists, including such towering and brilliant activists as Fredrick Douglass (1817–1895).[2] But by the very nature of the power structure of the period, black abolitionists had less influence on their own than did either slave rebellions, on one side, or white abolitionists, on the other. Black slave rebellions sought to challenge the power of the slave system; white abolitionists sought to challenge the legitimacy of the slave system. Black abolitionists attempted to be allies of both, but were weaker than either. Yet even in their lonely isolation, black abolitionists like Douglass and William Wells Brown displayed remarkable courage and heroism.[3]

While the abolitionist movement in the eighteenth and nineteenth centuries was thus disproportionately led by liberal members of the Western establishment, the reparationist movement in the twentieth century has been disproportionately advanced by the nationalist wing of black global opinion.

The reparationist movement is a child of black frustration and black nationalism rather than white liberalism. It originally arose in the African diaspora, especially in the United States: 'Where are my few acres of land and a mule?' There was a sense of betrayal among blacks following Lincoln's Emancipation Proclamation of 1863. The minimum social contract of emancipation had been violated. It was only a matter of time before blacks of the United States raised the flag of compensation.

And yet diaspora reparationists were usually concerned with reparations strictly for the diaspora. In the United States the effort reached the Congress, at least to the extent of mobilizing the Congressional Black Caucus (CBC) to be more attentive to those of their constituents who were demanding restitution.

When the reparations movement finally captured the imagination of Africans in Africa, a wider normative shift had to occur. It was the African side of the reparations movement which shifted it from a demand of diaspora blacks for restitution in their countries to a new, wider crusade for reparations for both the African and the wider black world as a whole.

The most resilient African culture in the diaspora is arguably the Yoruba culture. Defiant remnants persist from Cuba to South Carolina, from rural Jamaica to the ghettoes of Brazil. Old Yoruba culture dies hard even in conditions of enslavement. And yet by a strange twist of destiny, the demands for reparations on the eve of the twenty-first century in West Africa are also led disproportionately by the Yoruba. Chief Moshood Kashimawo Olawale Abiola stands out as a central figure in the latest reparationist phase. Without Chief Abiola, the reparations issue might not have become a concern for the OAU. Again paradoxically, it was Chief Abiola's friendship with President Ibrahim Babangida of Nigeria which helped to put the reparations issue on the agenda of the organization. President Babangida was the Chairman of the OAU at a crucial time in the reparations saga. Of course, Babangida himself was not Yoruba, nor was the ethnic issue likely to have been on his mind on the reparations debate. Nevertheless, this was a case where the Yoruba, who had proven to be a cultural vanguard under enslavement, were now part of the vanguard in the demand for reparations. But of course the movement is not ethnic, but Pan African. The vanguard is expanding.

Empowering people and centring the state

Damaged governance is part of Africa's case for reparations. After all, the older indigenous institutions of political accountability were effectively destroyed by Western colonization. In their place the West attempted to transplant new Western-style institutions of accountability. Unfortunately the new-fangled mechanisms turned out to be culturally unsustainable. Parliamentary systems were reduced to a mockery within a decade of independence. Political parties rapidly atrophied. Electoral pluralism shrunk in one African country after another. And soldiers quite often threw the politicians out of State House with a painful regularity.

Is Africa owed reparations for this brutal political limbo? The West had enclosed ancient societies in new states. It had enclosed the age-old Yoruba in the new Nigeria, the age-old Wolof in the new Senegal, the age-old Baganda in the new Uganda. The underlying tension in Africa is how to reconcile ancient societies with the new states. The tension was created by the West because the new states were manufactured by the West. Is Africa owed reparations for the anguish of this dichotomy? If so, what form should reparations take?

Two forms of reparations are, at least in principle, non-monetary: first, how to empower the African people in relation to the new states, and second, how to empower the new states in relation to the world system.

Empowering the African people in relation to the new states is the challenge of democratization. Empowering the new African states in relation to the world system is the challenge of international centring.

How can the West help in empowering the African people in relation to the new states manufactured by the West? First, by reducing Western support for African tyrants. One of the happier consequences of the end of the Cold War is that the West can judge African rulers without the distorting prism of whether they were pro- or anti-communist. Many countries now, especially the smaller ones, are using stricter criteria of performance in human rights as a basis for determining their relations with African governments. Withholding support and legitimacy to more overt African tyrants is therefore definitely a contribution to the empowerment of the African people.

More positively, the West can increase material and moral support to democratic trends in Africa. Since 1990, some twenty African countries have taken steps towards democratization, if only to give greater freedom to the political opposition. Greater material and moral support to these trends by the West over the next half-century may itself constitute the beginnings of democratic reparations.

Third, the West may help democratization by helping to eliminate or reduce economic impediments to democratization. In some African countries the debt burden is not only a handicap to economic recovery, but also a serious obstacle to the consolidation of the new fledgeling democracies. In such situations, Western debt-forgiveness could be a democratization measure.

Fourth, the West could help Africans deal with some of their own socio-cultural impediments to democratization, but without excessive Western intrusion. For example, the West may help African programmes designed to empower women or increase female participation in development and governance.

If the democratic empowerment of the African people can be an aspect of Western reparations to Africa, Chief Abiola may be forgiven for having come to the United States in search of support against the Nigerian military government's veto on his election as President. Was this crusader for Western reparations to the black world demeaning his cause by asking the West to help him become President of Nigeria? Not if an aspect of reparations is Western help to empower the African people to control the new states (like Nigeria) which the Western world itself had helped to manufacture. Ancient societies like Yorubaland and Hausaland needed to find a *modus vivendi* with new states like Nigeria.

The West created 'the political mess' called 'Kenya' or 'Nigeria'. Should the West be called upon to tidy up that political mess? Western contributions to African democratization is one approach towards bridging that historic dichotomy. In that sense, to help democratic forces in Nigeria was an aspect of his crusade for Western reparations. But Chief Abiola did not get what he asked for. On the contrary, he damaged himself at home without gaining abroad.

But it is not merely the empowerment of the African people over the African state which is at stake in the politics of reparations. It is also the empowerment of the new African state in the wider global system. How is this kind of global empowerment to proceed?

In fact one of the paradoxes of the 1990s is that the African people in countries like Zaire, Zambia and indeed Nigeria have been trying to assert greater control over their governments at precisely the time when African governments have been losing influence on world events. Since 1990 some twenty countries on the continent have taken steps towards democracy, sometimes voting out incumbents. The African public is beginning to get empowered but at precisely the time when the African state is more deeply enfeebled.

The momentous changes which have occurred in the wake of the end of the Cold War have, on the whole, marginalized Africa further. Former communist enemies in Europe have become more important to the United States than former friends in Africa. With the disappearance of socialist allies, Africa's influence in the United Nations has declined sharply and Africa's share of world trade, global investment and foreign aid continues to shrink.

How is the enfeeblement of the African state to be reversed? What role can reparations play in the future towards reducing Africa's marginalization while enhancing its global leverage?

One form of reparations would involve 'capital transfer' in the tradition of the Marshall Plan after the Second World War. From 1948 to 1952 the Marshall Plan transferred 12 billion dollars from the US to help reconstruct Europe after the devastation of war. In real terms the value of that amount was probably 14 times the 1993 value of the dollar. The newly proposed Middle Passage Plan would in part also involve capital transfer from the Western world as a whole towards the reconstruction of both Africa and its diaspora, after the devastation of enslavement and colonialism.

But the Middle Passage Plan need not limit itself to capital transfer. A parallel form of reparations could be 'skill transfer' to help transform the marginal and skill infrastructure of Global Africa as a whole. International scholarships for Africans would only be a minor part of this effort. More fundamental would be institutional changes in Africa itself in the direction of more genuine capacity building on a large scale, at different levels of society. Current capacity-building projects encouraged by the World Bank are at best touching only the surface. The Middle Passage Plan would be designed to lead to a true managerial and skill revolution in Africa.

The third form of reparations after capital transfer and skill transfer is direct 'power transfer' or 'power sharing'. Giving Africa greater voting power in the World Bank and the International Monetary Fund (IMF) would constitute one kind of direct power transfer. The basis of the proposed Africa's leverage in the Bretton Woods' institutions would not, of course, be because Africa was now wealthy, but to compensate Africa for being denied for so long a capacity to become independently wealthy in spite of all its resources.

Another form of direct transfer would be to give Africa a veto on the Security Council of the UN; not as a recognition of Africa's power outside the UN (as the other vetoes are) but as a recognition of the need to bring Africa into the mainstream of global decision making after centuries of deprivation. How the permanent African seat would be occupied on the Security Council is something which may have to be worked out between the United Nations and the OAU. The seat could rotate between East, West, Southern, North and Central Africa over a period to be agreed upon.

All these options concerning the future empowerment of the African state are against the background of both its historic colonial artificiality and its contemporary diplomatic marginality.

Of course the distinction between empowering the African people (through democratization) and empowering the African state (through international leverage) may be analytically neater on paper than in real life. The crusade for reparations has inevitably to be multifaceted. Western direct support for African democracy and Western direct support for institutionalized African leverage in the world system have to be included in the agenda for reparations. If love is a many-splendoured thing, so is reparations.

Ledger of reparations and calculus of causality

One dilemma of the reparations debate is whether the compensation should be based on the damage done to the victim or the benefits obtained by the violator. Should the restitution be calculated on the basis of the pain of the slave or the profit of the slaver? We are dealing not merely with the history of bondage, but also with the bondage of history. The history of bondage includes of course the history of enslavement and the slave trade. The bondage of history, on the other hand, is the extent to which, to a considerable degree, we are all prisoners of our history.

But how much of the here-and-now is a consequence of history? What are the limits of the bondage of history? If one were to construct a *calculus of causality*, the proportions' determination may be roughly in the following broad percentages in Global Africa: the direct bondage of history, the consequences of what happened in the past, is about 40 per cent of the causation of the present condition. In the African continent this includes the repercussions of the colonial boundaries and the entire imperial experience. We are all 40 per cent history. In black America the bondage history includes the consequences of enslavement and centuries of racial humiliation and cultural deprivation.

In the calculus of causality, 25 per cent in Global Africa is determined by the contemporary global system and political economy. The contemporary global system continues to reaffirm the marginalization of the black world in the global scheme of things, from the prices of African commodities to black stereotypes in the Western media. This includes the roles of the IMF, the World Bank and the whole agenda of North–South relations.

In this calculus of causality, 15 per cent of the determinism comes from ecological factors. This includes problems of drought, soil erosion, floods, tropical diseases affecting animals and humans and the like. Another 15 per cent in the calculus of causality is for African leadership and choices of policies. Africans are in control of only 15 per cent of their destiny. This is the arena of black choice and black political will. This is where philosopher-kings, ideology, diplomacy, and negotiations make a difference.

The final 5 per cent of causation concerns pure luck, chance and coincidence. This could range from an unexpected bumper harvest to an unforeseen global event.

The domain of reparations concerns especially the first two categories: the 40 per cent bondage of history and the 25 per cent contemporary marginalization of Global Africa. Where do we turn for additional resources for Africa?

The consequences of slavery in the United States did not end with the Emancipation Proclamation of 1863, but continues today in the disproportionate black presence in US jails, the disproportionate black infant mortality rates, the disproportionate self-destructive juvenile black violence. The damage of the past is in the present. The black community is chained to the bondage of its own tragic history.

With regard to the benefits which the West derived from Global Africa, there were at least three phases:

- 'The era of the labour imperative' was when the West was interested primarily in African labour and was prepared to promote slave raids, the Middle Passage and slave plantations to ensure that kind of exploitation of African labour.
- 'The era of the territorial imperative' was the era of colonization when Africans lost their lands as well as their labour. Almost the entire continent fell under European imperial rule.
- 'The era of the extractive imperative' concerned the political economy of Africa's minerals, many of which were quite fundamental to certain sectors of Western industry. There were periods when Africa sometimes had 90 per cent of the world's cobalt, over 80 per cent of the world's reserves of chrome, half the world's reserves of gold and so on.

Should reparations to Global Africa be based, at least in part, on the benefits the West has derived from the imperatives of labour, territory and extraction across generations? This would be in addition to assessment on the basis of benefit obtained by the violator.

The most difficult category to access is one in which armed struggle against the villain turns out to be more advantageous to the villain than to the freedom-fighter. It may be worth juxtaposing three very different visions in this regard: the vision of the black revolutionary writer from Martinique, Frantz Fanon (1925–61); the vision of the rather shy English poet, Oliver Goldsmith (1730–74), and the Christian concept of the crucifixion as a form of redemption.

Frantz (alias Omar) Fanon was convinced that anti-colonial violence was a healing experience for the colonial freedom-fighter: 'At the level of individuals, violence is a cleansing force. It frees the native from his inferiority complex, from his despair and inaction ...' (Fanon, 1968, p. 94).

If the crucifixion of Jesus was an act of violence and it was at the same time an act of atonement and redemption, there are moments when Fanon's thought has points in common with Christian doctrine. In the words of Frantz Fanon: 'Violence is thus seen as comparable to a royal pardon ... The colonized man finds his freedom in and through violence' (Fanon, 1968, p. 86). The crucifixion was violence as the ultimate royal pardon – redemption by the King of Kings. The son of God was killed; so that human beings might live.

With regard to Oliver Goldsmith, he enunciated a vision of a good man who was bitten by a mad dog. Under normal circumstances the man would have developed rabies or hydrophobia and experienced one of the most painful forms of dying in human experience. But the man's inoculation against rabies was his moral worth. His morality was his vaccination:

> That still a godly race he ran,
> whene'er he went to pray ...
> the naked every day he clad,
> when he put on his clothes ...

On the other hand, the mad dog had evil appetites when it bit the good man. The moral fibre of the man was not only a protection for the man; it turned out to be fatal to the dog:

> The dog, to gain some private ends,
> went mad and bit the man ...
> The man recovered of the bite
> the dog it was that died.[4]

What really happened in the anti-colonial wars in places like Algeria, Mozambique and Angola, was a remarkable reversal of who gained from the violence. Frantz Fanon was wrong about who gained by violence. In the short run, the greater beneficiary of armed struggle in Algeria was not Algeria but France. France was purified by the violence, not Algeria. The war in Algeria destroyed the Fourth French Republic and inaugurated the more stable Fifth Republic. The Algerian war brought Charles de Gaulle back to power in France and he helped to launch France into new European and global roles. France emerged stronger after losing Algeria than before. And yet Algeria itself continues to bleed in new forms of post-colonial trauma.

Anti-colonial wars in Angola, Mozambique and Guinea-Bissau helped to destroy Fascism and political lethargy in Portugal. Portugal had resisted every progressive formative European force in modern history: the Renaissance, the Enlightment, the Reformation, the legacies of the American and French Revolutions and the Industrial Revolution. It took anti-colonial wars waged by Africans to dislodge Portugal from its age-old lethargy. In April 1974 a coup took place at last in Lisbon, Portugal, as a direct result of the colonial wars. The coup turned out to be the beginning of the modernization, democratization, and re-Europeanization of Portugal. And all this because African liberation fighters had challenged the Portuguese Fascist state in its imperial role.

It is here that the paradox arises which contradicts Fanon and revises Oliver Goldsmith. It turns out that anti-colonial violence is a cleansing force not for the original victim but for the imperial villain. Angola and Mozambique are still in a desperate condition while Portugal is experimenting with modernization and democracy. Algeria is struggling with problems of instability and cultural conflict while the Fifth Republic in France remains relatively firm. Anti-colonial violence has helped the imperial villain but has it helped the colonial victim? Fanon was right that anti-colonial violence led to moral rejuvenation. But who was rejuvenated – the colonized or the colonizer?

With regard to Oliver Goldsmith, let us assume that the mad dog was the imperial and the morally upright man was Global Africa. When the mad dog bit Global Africa what really followed? We have to amend Goldsmith as follows:

The dog, to gain some private ends,
went mad and bit the man ...
The man *suffered* from the bite
– the dog it was that *healed*!

This is very different from 'the dog it was that died'! In the imperial order the villain has been healed; while the victim still suffers.

It is in this context that the case for reparations becomes stronger than ever. Even when Africans fought for their independence, the short-term consequences were of greater benefit to the imperial order than to the former colonial subject.

African–Western encounter: A cost-benefit analysis

Reparations should be calculated partly on the basis of the suffering of the colonized person (the criterion of damage to the victim). But reparations should also be calculated on the basis of the healing of the hegemonic powers (the criterion of benefit to the villain).

One of the most obscene and perverse ironies of the slave era is that emancipation did result in compensation, but to the wrong party. In the British West Indies those who had slaves were regarded as property-owners. The forceful loss of their property was regarded as worthy of compensation. Most slave-owners therefore received reparations.

Ex-slaves, on the other hand, were regarded as moving from a worse condition to a better condition; from bondage to emancipation. There were no major voices in Britain in favour of compensating blacks for prior racial degradation, humiliation and exploitation of labour. Property was sacred, but labour apparently was not. Loss of property demanded compensation, but forced labour apparently did not. In the final analysis, there is therefore an unfulfilled moral debt yet to be paid to those whose labour had been plundered during slave days.

Emancipation in the United States had once included a form of reparation for each black slave – a few acres and a mule. This was fulfilled only for a few ex-slaves. The founding of Booker T. Washington's Tuskegee College was also a kind of partial reparation but on the whole, in the US, reparation was honoured more in the breach than the observance. The unpaid void remained horrendous.

In the 1990s, African-Americans have been trying to reactivate the reparations crusade right up to Capitol Hill, in Washington DC. Those meagre acres and a mule have accumulated considerable interest over the generations. Led by black Congressman, John Conyers, Jr from Michigan and sometimes supported by such dissidents as Louis Farrakhan, the reparations crusade in the US is seeking out appropriate strategies for action. In this case the demand for compensating African-Americans is the most immediate responsibility of the US.

But US responsibility does not end with survivors of the Middle Passage. What about those who did not survive the Middle Passage? What about the casualties in slave forts like Goree and Elmina on the West African coast before the captives were exported? Many of them died on land. What about the casualties in the slave raids before the capturing was accomplished? Slave markets in North America were responsible not merely for the captives who finally arrived intact for use on the plantations; the markets were responsible also for those who perished on the way from the slave raids to the American plantations. The demand for the end of the slave trade was especially culpable for the whole system. The history of bondage includes those who were captured in Africa but did not survive to be enslaved in America. The bondage of history includes the consequences and aftermath of all these momentous events for subsequent generations in both Global Africa and the Western world.

And yet it cannot be denied that the civil rights movement of the 1950s and 1960s in the US, the anti-colonial movements in Africa from the 1940s and even aspects of the global Cold War, all helped to reinforce each other and produced important gains for Global Africa as a whole, as well as for African-Americans.

While 'hot' wars like those of Korea, Vietnam and the Gulf endangered a disproportionate number of US blacks, the Cold War in its literal sense (military preparedness without actual war) gave disadvantaged groups an additional career of potential advancement. In the US military-industrial complex, blacks are over-represented on the 'military' side and under-represented on the 'industrial' side. The doors of military opportunities are more open for African-Americans than the doors of industry. The military-industrial complex is lopsided for blacks. General Colin Powell became the first black Chairman of the Joint Chiefs of Staff in the military. There has never been such a high-ranking equivalent in industry.

There is a school of thought which regards the black condition in the United States as a kind of internal colonialism – that African-Americans are still a kind of subject people (Asante, 1993, p. 167). But if the colonial paradigm is applied today, we must recognize a shift from the early twentieth century whereby the US as a system treated its African-Americans very much as British colonialists treated the natives in their African dependencies. The British colonial order at that time combined paternalism with highly institutionalized segregation. The natives were kept at arm's length. Schools, social clubs, public places, lavatories, and so on, were all racially differentiated. The US doctrine of 'separate but equal' was just a rhetorical American version of British racist paternalism.

Then came the second half of the twentieth century, with such US constitutional and legislative milestones as Brown *vs.* the Board of Education of 1954 and the empowerment legislation of the Great Society under President Lyndon B. Johnson. What was overlooked was the unconscious shift from a British model of colonialism to a French model. French colonial policy allowed their subject peoples to rise very high as individuals in the central institutions of the metropole. Individual natives from the colonies rose in France itself, while the group to which they belonged still remained subordinate in the total French hierarchy.

For example, individuals like the late Felix Houphouet-Boigny, a native of Cote d'Ivoire (Ivory Coast), was able to serve as a member of several French Cabinets in Paris under the Fourth Republic in the 1950s. But Cote d'Ivoire itself remained a colony. Leopold Sedar Senghor, a native of Senegal, also served as a member of French Cabinets in Paris in the Fourth Republic while his people as a whole were still being subjugated. The French colonial system permitted considerable *individual* social mobility while retaining *collective* ethno-cultural subordination.

The question which arises therefore concerns the condition of neo-colonial status. Individual African-Americans may rise to become a Secretary of Commerce or Chairman of Joint Chiefs of Staff. Clarence Thomas can be confirmed to succeed Thurgood Marshall on the Supreme Court of the United States; just as Leopold Senghor of Senegal helped to draft the Constitution of the Fifth Republic of France. The Reverend Jesse Jackson has tested the system to its limits – exploring whether it is ready to live with a black head of state. Alas, no!

At the collective level, there has continued to be a *master* nation and a *subordinate* nation both in the French world and in the US. But the struggle continues; African-Americans are part of the vanguard for change, a force for progress.

What Harold Cruse did not realize when he published his important book *The Crisis of the Negro Intellectual* in 1967 was that the crisis of the black intellectual in America was potentially a permanent crisis – world without end. The manifestation will vary, but the basic crisis is a bondage of history and ultimately irredeemable, until reparations are paid.

Conclusion

Perhaps one of the more basic cultural returns to the past concerns the issue of collective compensation. In ancient times, if one member of a tribe was killed by a member of another tribe, a debt was immediately created, owed by the tribe of the killer to the tribe of the victim. This debt was not subject to any statute of limitation. The debt stood until it was paid. It could be paid with heads of cattle – or with blood.

If the debt was not paid there was a serious risk of a long-festering feud between the two tribes. Because responsibility was collective, individuals in each community could be unnecessarily at risk for a killing for which they were themselves not directly responsible. They were, however, indirectly culturally responsible. The civilized way out was to pay the debt in cows and goats. In other words, the civilized response was to pay 'reparations'.

This whole issue of reparations has, as we indicated, re-emerged in black politics in both Africa and the US; reparations for hundred of years of black enslavement, colonization and racial victimization.

A debt is outstanding between the West and the black world; a debt which is not subject to the statute of limitations.

At a summit meeting of the OAU, the heads of state of Africa appointed me and eleven others to constitute a Group of Eminent Persons to explore the modalities and logistics of a campaign for black reparations world-wide. Our group of twelve members did indeed elect as our Chairman, Chief M.K.O. Abiola, who was subsequently elected President of Nigeria in June 1993 but was prevented from taking office by the military.

Our Group of Eminent Persons on reparations elected as our Co-Chair, Professor Mohtar m'Bow, former Director-General of the United Nations Educational, Scientific and Cultural Organization (UNESCO). We elected as our Rapporteur-General, Ambassador Dudley Thompson QC, a distinguished Jamaican jurist and diplomat. The Nigerian government under President Babangida promised us a preliminary budget of $500,000 to enable us to make a start.

We do believe that the damage done to black people is not a thing past but is here and now. It lies in the disproportionate number of black faces in US jails; the disproportionate black infant mortality rate in the US; the ease with which a black man in police custody in London (like a certain Mr Lumumba) or in Paris (like a 17-year-old Zairean boy) can get killed by the police; the cheapness of black lives from the sadistic streets of Rio de Janeiro to the masochistic streets of Soweto in South Africa. The damage is *here*. And the debt has not yet been paid.

How are the reparations to be paid? I have explained that there are at least three alternative modes – modern versions of the ancient payment of heads of cattle from one tribe to another:

- 'Capital transfer' from the West to the black world, comparable to the grand precedent of the Marshall Plan to Europe.
- 'Skill transfer' in the form of a major international effort to build the capacities and skills of Africa and the rest of the black world. Redress is needed for the damage which is here.
- 'Power-sharing' by enabling Africa to have a greater say in global institutions; such as more effective representation in decision making in the World Bank and the IMF, not because Africa is rich but because it has been systematically enfeebled.

And why should all the permanent seats of the UN Security Council be given to countries which are already powerful outside the UN? Is there not a case for giving Africa a permanent seat with veto; not because Africa is powerful but because it has been rendered powerless across generations. We need to redeem the damage which is here.

In the 1960s, the United States invented the concept of *affirmative action* – an effort to make allowances for historic disabilities whenever minorities applied for jobs or sought other opportunities. It was a progressive step (though currently under serious attacks) towards racial equity and socioeconomic justice.

We now need to make a transition from affirmative action to a more comprehensive *affirmative reactivation* in the form of reparations. It is in fact a logical next step after affirmative action. Conservatives believe that the next step after affirmative action should be the free play of market forces. But the bondage of history denies the market autonomy. Residual racism is an impediment to the market. We have to move beyond affirmative action to the affirmative reactivation of black peoples the world over.

There is a primordial debt to be paid to black peoples for hundreds of years of enslavement and degradation. Some of the causes of global apartheid lie deep in that history. It may take a generation to win the crusade for reparations but a start has to be made. This will be one more aspect of reverse evolution back to ancient ways of settling moral debts between tribes. The damage is here. It is time to mend.

Notes

1. We define 'Global Africa' as the Continent of Africa plus, firstly, the diaspora of enslavement (descendants of survivors of the Middle passage) and secondly, the diaspora of colonialism (the dispersal of Africans which continues to occur as a result of disruptions of colonization and its aftermath). Ali Mazrui and his children are part of the diaspora of colonialism. Jesse Jackson and Edmond Keller are part of the diaspora of enslavement. Jamaicans in Britain are a dual diaspora of both enslavement and colonization.
2. See Douglass (1960, 1962), and Quarles (1981, pp. 319–25). Also consult Douglass and Ingersoll (1883).
3. See Brown's *Clotel* (1969); a novel that denounced slavery and was intended to strengthen the abolitionist cause. Also see Brown (1850, 1852, 1867, 1968).
4. See Oliver Goldsmith's 'An Elegy on the Death of a Mad Dog' (1910, pp. 72–3). The relevant stanzas of the poem went as follows:

This dog and the man at first were friends;
But when a pique began,
The dog, to gain some private ends,
Went mad and bit the man.

Around all the neighbouring streets
The wond'ring neighbours ran,
And swore the dog had lost his wits
To bite so good a man.

The wound seem'd both sore and sad
To every Christian eye;
And while they swore the dog was mad,
They swore the man would die.

But soon a wonder came to light,
That show'd the rogues they lied:
The man recover'd of the bite,
The dog it was that died.

Bibliography

Asante Molefi Kete (1993). *Malcolm X as Cultural Hero and Other Afrocentric Essays*, Trenton, New Jersey: Africa World Press.
Brown, William Wells (1968). *The Negro in the American Rebellion: His Heroism and His Fidelity*, Massachusetts: Lee and Sheperd, 1867 and New York: Johnson Reprint Corp.
Cruse, Harold (1967). *The Crisis of the Negro Intellectual*, New York: William Morrow.
Douglass, Fredrick (1960). *Narrative of the Life of Fredrick Douglass: An American Slave Written by Himself*, Cambridge, MA: Belknap Press.
Douglass, Fredrick (1962). *Life and Times of Fredrick Douglass*, New York: Collier Books.
Douglass, Fredrick and R.C. Ingersoll (eds) (1883). *Proceedings of Civil Rights Mass Meeting Held at Lincoln Hall 22 October 1883, Speeches of Hon. Frederick Douglass and Robert G. Ingersoll*, Washington D.C.: C.P. Farrell.
Fanon, Frantz (1968). *The Wretched of the Earth*, New York: Grove Press.
Goldsmith, Oliver (1910). *Poems and Plays*, London: J.M. Dent & Sons Ltd.

Quarles, Benjamin (1981). 'Fredrick Douglass: Challenge and Response' in W. Augustus Low and Virgil A. Clift (eds), *Encyclopedia of Black America*, New York: McGraw-Hill, pp. 319–25.

Further reading

Boahen, Adu A. (1985). *Africa Under Colonial Domination*, abridged version, Berkeley, CA: University of California Press.
Brown, Williams Wells (1950). *Narrative of William Wells Brown: an American Slave*, London: Charles Gilpin.
Brown, Williams Wells (1952). *Three Years in Europe: Places I have seen and People I have met*, London: Charles Gilpin.
Brown, Hedley and Adam Watson (eds) (1984). *The Expansion of International Society*, New York: Oxford University Press.
Clarke, J.H. (1993). *African People in World History*, Baltimore: Black Classic Press.
Cruse, Harold (1987). *Plural and Equal*, New York: William Morrow.
Davidson, Basil (1984). *The Story of Africa*, London: M. Beazley.
Farley, R. and Walter Allen (1987). *The Color Line and the Quality of Life in America*, New York: Russell Sage Foundation.
Graham, Richard (ed.) (1990). *The Idea of Race in Latin America*, Austin, TX: University of Texas Press.
Harris, J.E. (ed.) (1982). *Global Dimensions of the African Diaspora*, Washington: Howard University Press.
Holloway, Karla (1992). *Moorings and Metaphors: Figures of Culture and Gender in Black Women's Literature*, New Brunswick, NJ: Rutgers University Press.
Klein, Herbert (1986). *African Slavery in Latin America and the Caribbean*, New York: Oxford University Press.
Lewis, Bernard (1990). *Race and Slavery in the Middle East: An Historical Enquiry*, New York: Oxford University Press.
Low, W. Augustus and Virgil A. Clift (eds.) (1981). *Encyclopedia of Black America*, New York: McGraw-Hill.
Mazrui, Ali A. (1986). *The Africans: A Triple Heritage*, Boston: Little Brown.
Mazrui, Ali A. (ed.) (1993). *Africa since 1935*, UNESCO.
Mazrui, Ali A. (1994). *General History of Africa*, vol. VIII, Oxford: Heinemann; Berkeley: University of California Press.
Mazrui, Ali A. and Michael Tidy (1984). *Nationalism and New States in Africa*, Nairobi: Heinemann.
Reis, Joao Jose (1993). *Slave Rebellion in Brazil: The Muslim Uprising of 1835 in Bahia*, Baltimore: Johns Hopkins University Press.

Robertson, Claire C. and Martin Klein (1983). *Women and Slavery in Africa*, Madison, WI: University of Wisconsin Press.

Skinner, E.P. (1992). *African Americans and US Policy Toward Africa 1850–1924*, Washington, DC: Howard University Press.

Thompson, V.B. (1987). *The Making of African Diaspora in the Americas 1441–1900*, White Plains, New York: Longman.

Washington, Booker T. (1986). *Up from Slavery*, New York: Penguin Books.

Williams, Juan (1987). *Eyes on the Prize: America's Civil Rights Years*, New York: Viking.

Willis, J.R. (1985). *Slaves and Slavery in Muslim Africa*, 2 vols, Totowa, New Jersey: Frank Cass.

Winks, Robin W. (1972). *Slavery: A Comparative Perspective*, New York: New York University Press.

Wright, Marcia (1993). *Strategies of Slaves and Women: Life Stories from East and Central Africa*, London: J. Currey.

Part III

Continental and Regional Unity

5

Creating an African Common Market

Sam Tulya-Muhika

Introduction

Historical overview

The redrawing of global economic boundaries that visibly started with the commitment of the EEC to completion of the European Internal Market at Hannover in 1988, leading to deeper integration under the Maastricht Treaty (1993), continental developments in North America (leading to the North American Free Trade Agreement (NAFTA)) as well as current movements of Asian economies on the Pacific Rim, make it imperative for Africa to unite, and to do it fast. *Economic integration is a virtual precondition for development in Africa.* In the short to medium term, it is a necessary direction to avoid recolonization through total external economic control. As the saying goes these days, 'the State is now too small for big things and too big for small things'. The world is, indeed, rapidly becoming a Global Village.

Not only has economic cooperation become a world-wide phenomenon, but it has also deepened from 'creation of desirable structure of international economy' of the 1960s (see, for example, Tinbergen, 1964, p. 12) to redefinition of viable boundaries of political economies. Individual African economies as they exist now, are unviable as political economies. Unless they integrate, they will disintegrate. They will then be recolonized.

The desire to integrate exists and is not new to Africa. It can be argued that, historically, integration pre-dates written history in Africa. Efforts of African chieftains and warrior kings to create large empires, some of them somewhat successfully (for example, Ghana, Nuba, Zimbabwe, Mali, Ethiopia, Songhai, Zulu), bear testimony to this innate wish of Africa to extend control over large areas for efficiency of management of resources (including war-makers). That this was often done on the battlefield is a debate on means rather than end. Some scholars (for example, Yoweri Kaguta Museveni,

1991, pp. 7–8) argue that without 'colonial interruption', this process would have matured into large, integrated and viable African states.

In more recent history, it could be said that the earliest step towards regional efforts in solving African problems was the 1st Pan African Congress held in Paris in 1919, later followed by the epoch-making 5th Congress in Manchester (UK) in 1945 (attended by latter-day great African leaders like Kwame Nkrumah and Jomo Kenyatta). Later, in 1955, a gathering of African Pan Africanists issued the Bandung Declaration. However, continent-wide movement caught momentum after the independence of the first black African state (Ghana, 1957), leading to the formation of the Organization of African Unity (OAU) in Addis Ababa in 1963 by the then 32 African states (having gained their independence in a space of only six years!).

Typology of cooperation

Since then, African economic cooperation has taken a diversity of attempts through various institutions and sub-regional organizations (see Appendix 2) as well as a number of plans and declarations, for example, the African Declaration of Cooperation, Development and Economic Independence (1973), the Kinshasa Declaration (1976) on Principles of the African Economic Community, the Monrovia Strategy for Economic Development (1979), the Lagos Plan of Action and Final Act of Lagos (1980), and the Abuja Treaty for Establishment of a Pan African Economic Community (PAEC) on 3 June 1991.

In a relatively more modern setting African states have tended to pick on various possible forms of cooperation as below (see also Appendix 2):

- common defence pacts (for example, East African High Commission 1948–1961, Sene-Gambia, 1982),
- single commodity trade treaties (for instance, various bilateral arrangements such as that of the East African Community (EAC) on tyres),
- multiple commodity trade treaties (for example, Preferential Trade Area (PTA)),
- common facility utilization treaties (for example, Northern Corridor in East Africa, Central African Airways in Northern and Southern Rhodesia and Nyasaland, East African Development Bank, ADB and so on),
- Preferential Trade (for example, PTA),
- common market (for example, East Africa, 1948–67),

- free trade area (for example, between Uganda and Kenya 1900–22).
- customs union (for example, East Africa 1922–67 and *Union Dovaniere et Economique de l'Afrique Central* (UDEAC) since 1959),
- monetary union (East Africa up to 1965/66 and Southern African Customs Union (SACU) which is still going strong),
- economic community (for example, East African Community, 1967–77),
- confederation (Early States of Union of South Africa in the nineteenth century), and
- federation (for example, Central African Federation of Southern Rhodesia, North Rhodesia and Nyasaland).

Most of these attempts have not been very successful. Appendix 2 samples 24 of these and comments on them. Altogether, it is estimated that there are over 200 organizations for regional cooperation in Africa. Over 150 are inter-governmental. The rest are NGOs (non-governmental organizations), but most receive governmental support (directly or indirectly). There is clearly a need for some 'ruthless' scissor-work for purposes of rationalization.

The (defunct) East African Community (EAC) was once a shining example of regional cooperation not only in Africa, but also the entire world. In fact, the EEC took a few leads from the EAC in its early years. The collapse of the EAC, which had up to then been seen as a model for cooperation in Africa (with Zambia, Ethiopia, Somalia, Burundi lodging applications to join), was a blow and a reversal in the process of integration in Africa. Most of the problems of the EAC stemmed from 'nationalized cooperation', which seems to be a recurrent theme in the Treaty of East African Co-operation (1967) (see, for example, Mtei *et al.*, p. 6).

Problems of regional cooperation

There are two well-known routes to economic integration. The first type is the 'planning approach' which was adopted in the economic association of the former Eastern Communist Bloc (COMECON). In this approach, production (especially industrialization) is planned at a regional level between various countries. This would tend to be the choice of countries that integrate in order to develop, rather than trade only and tends to be a sensible approach for less industrialized countries. In capital-driven and developed economies, for example the European Union, integration tends to focus more on market creation and liberalization of factor movements, especially goods and services, that is, the 'trade approach'. The EAC was a mix of both approaches, although it could be said that the balance fell more on the trade approach than the planning approach. For Africa, both approaches will need to be adequately and mutually balanced.

The fastest route to integration, historically, has always been military conquest. Modern times mitigate against this. Consensus-building and formal treaties have taken over from instruments of violence. However, this makes integration a complex, arduous, slow and tortuous process typified by fits and starts, displayed in periods of leaps forward, often followed by periods of stagnation, consolidation, and (at worst) reversal (as was the case in East Africa in 1977).

Lessons from recent successful integrative efforts, for example the EEC, indicate that it would be advisable to start the integration process with small, well-measured, but tangible, low-cost or cost-free projects. Other important aspects of integration to be built into the management of integration should include: treaty, common market operations, institutions, funding arrangements, and decision-making processes that ensure checks and balances which would mitigate against reversal of any level of integration reached. Emphasis should be on *consolidation* (or at worst stagnation), but 'backward never'.

But even with the best cooperation treaty and the best of intentions, typical problems do tend to arise in the process of integration. The following are readily identifiable:

- political will and decision-making mechanisms;
- common market issues including:

    – Unbalanced industrialization and development
    – 'Stag Bull Syndrome' symptomized by domination of the 'Union' by one (or two) countries.
    – trade balance/market share;

- funding the process of integration, including the secretariat, which touches on division of costs and benefits;
- political, social and economic convergence (or, rather, divergence);
- private-sector involvement in the processes of integration, including making the integration processes a 'union of peoples' rather than a 'union of governments', and
- creation of an integrated – human, institutional and infra-structural – identity of the union.

Definition of a common market

Though the Abuja Treaty aims at creating a continent-wide community, I will talk about 'a lesser form of integration', though hard enough to achieve: the creation of an African common market.

A common market often involves 'free movement of goods and services ...'. Creation of a common market for Africa would involve common policies, strategies and plans to attain the following objectives, though each has its own problems. All involve the free movement of:

- Persons and labour across national frontiers. Most of this movement is likely to be economic or political refugees or informal traders unless cross-border investments and trade is enhanced.
- Goods grown or produced or manufactured in African countries using *local raw materials*. The main constraints to this are likely to be political infrastructure, similar typology of production and soft infrastructure, for example, information and physical infrastructure.
- Goods that use *a mixture of imported and local raw materials* provided that the mixture ratio did not violate agreed Rules of Origin. This shares the constraints of the usage of local goods plus possible non-convergence of interpretation of the Rules of Origin.
- Capital goods (including machinery, transport equipment, agricultural implements and building materials) produced in African states within agreed Rules of Origin. But typology of production and production structures are unlikely to promote trade in capital goods initially. Other trade barriers may crop up. There is a need for 'regional' planning to 'create' capital formation centres.
- Raw materials, between African states, mainly minerals and agricultural commodities, grown or produced within African countries. This will create a need for resource inventories and comparative cost-advantage assessment in order to facilitate attempts at regional planning.
- Livestock and livestock products (including skins, hides, hoofs, animal and game trophies). The problems here are the same as for other 'raw' materials and continent-wise trade in general.
- Invisible transactions, inclusive of all services, provided such transactions originate from one African country destined for

another African country. This would call for early harmonization of economic, monetary and fiscal policies together with financial institutions as well as 'regionalization' rather than 'nationalization' of development aid as is currently the case.

A common market is to do with the free movement of various economic factors. For this to be done sustainably, there is a need for a steady convergence of political, economic, social policies and systems, and the development of relevant soft and physical regional infrastructure. ('Soft infrastructure' includes good governance, permanent security of the right of ownership, and supremacy of knowledge.) These two necessitate regional planning.

Since the independence of the first black African state (Ghana, 1957), there has always been some apparent realization of the need for regional cooperation and some of its benefits. The problem has so far been the internal cohesion of African states as well as adequacy of national economic structures to bear the 'costs' of economic cooperation against both internal and international pressures.

The state of African economies and the need for a common market

The call 'Africa Must Unite!' is not new. The 1st Pan African Congress (1919) took place more than seventy years ago. The late Dr Kwame Nkrumah, one of the greatest Pan Africanists of all time, wrote a book (by the same title) in 1963, the year of the establishment of the Organization of African Unity (OAU). At that time, large parts of Africa were still under colonial rule. So, as Nkrumah argued, it was 'Freedom First'. The accent of the OAU has been on *political* liberation rather than *economic* liberation. But, as the last 40 years have proved in Africa, political independence without economic independence is a sham. Only the oligarchy in power and its allies benefit. The masses remain pauperized.

As already mentioned, various attempts have been made through regional cooperation to facilitate faster economic development in Africa. Unfortunately, while regional cooperation in Africa is a *necessary* condition, it is not a *sufficient* condition for development. Other problems can neutralize its potential impact. Some of the problems that have mitigated against past attempts at economic cooperation and integration in Africa include:

- lack of *political accountability* of leaders (the biggest problem), and hence,
- lack of *democracy* in (many) African countries has also been identified as a major obstacle to economic cooperation;
- lack of *political will* (this was also responsible for the break up of the EAC);
- general *ignorance* (lack of education) on the part of the electorate as to the opportunities for economic cooperation and advantages and benefits of such co-operation;
- lack of *free movement* of people and weak national economies;
- lack of clarity on the *distribution of benefits* of cooperation is always a problem area and needs to be adequately researched;
- weak or inadequate *institutional* (and other) *arrangements* as well as infrastructure for cooperation;
- weak and/or non-participation by the *private sector*, and
- some adverse *international forces* and factors, for example 'colonial' borders, metropolitan economies, some IMF/IBRD policies and adverse terms of trade.

These problems are still with us, and will need to be researched and addressed honestly in detail before we can move towards an African Common Market.

An African Common Market (or large 'building blocks' like preferred trade areas (PTAs)/COMESA, the Economic Community of West African States (ECOWAS) towards the same end) would create:

- larger markets out of the 'balkanized' states inherited by African leaders at independence;
- a sustainable environment for a major transformation of African economies, without which economic integration is unlikely;
- a larger economic basin for capital flows and investment as well as facilitation of other factors of production; and
- a stable framework for social development of the African peoples.

Social welfare has retrogressed steadily in virtually all African states since independence. This is due to both internal and external factors. One major internal factor has been lack of democracy. Although Nkrumah (1963, p. 11) states that the colonial 'Governor was not responsible to a *local* electorate; and here the truly authoritarian nature of the regime becomes apparent', many African leaders have been no more responsible to the electorate. Consequently, politics has consistently assumed total priority over economics as indicated by the preponderance of politics of *power* in place of politics of *development.* Economic management has taken the back seat with telling consequences. This, set against well-known external factors, such as deteriorating terms of trade and the debt crisis, enhanced by the philosophies of ODA (Official Development Assistance) agencies, has led to the current socioeconomic abyss.

African economies are in deep crisis. The following selected 'litany' of African economic woes will tell the story:

- Out of 45 least-developed countries in the world (measured by GNP per capita), 29 are in Sub-Saharan Africa. So can these form a common market? (A pauper's club maybe?)
- Over the 1980s, Sub-Saharan African economies together grew at an average of –1.2 per cent per annum.
- Yet over the same period, the external debt grew at about 10 per cent per annum (on average) and now stands at around 300 billion US dollars (well over 100 per cent of the total GDP of the entire Sub-Saharan economic basin), while the Aid Retention Coefficient (ARC – funds retained as first economic effects) averages less than 10 per cent. This is a formula for economic slavery.
- Most African countries have been (or are, or are soon to be) under the IMF/World Bank-brokered Structural Adjustment Programme (SAP), under which, ironically, Africa is a net exporter of capital. Moreover, currently Africa employs over 100,000 expatriates from OECD countries as technical assistants (compared with about 40,000 thirty years ago at independence) while close to 100,000 high-quality African professional experts are employed in OECD countries and/or international organizations. With this seemingly massive flight of both financial and human capital, the historical pillage of the African continent continues. Certainly no meaningful development can take place.
- And as for the total Sub-Saharan GDP in question, this is less than that of Belgium (a country about the size of Buganda, the central region of Uganda!).
- This figure is confirmed by the fact that Africa's share of world trade is less than 2 per cent (although clearly the geographical, natural resource and population shares are much higher).

If the economic benefits indicated earlier can accrue from economic integration, then for Africans, this is not only an obligation but is long overdue. We must do it. And do it fast. Perhaps it is in recognition of the urgency that a statement of intent, in the form of the Abuja

Treaty to integrate African economies, was signed by African heads of state on 3 June 1991.

Strategies and programmes of action

The treaty establishing the African Economic Community: the Abuja Treaty

Economic cooperation is a complex and tortuous exercise typified by leaps and stops. One leap forward was made in 1991 at Abuja. The Abuja Treaty provides for a 6-phase programme, ultimately leading to the creation of a Pan African Economic Community (PAEC) over a period of 34 years (see Appendix 1) with effect from the date of ratification. This treaty was developed by the OAU and African governments over a period of 20 years (see, for example the African Declaration of Cooperation, Development and Economic Independence (1973); Kinshasa Declaration (1976) on Principles of the African Economic Community; Monrovia Declaration (1979); and Lagos Plan of Action (1980)). The Treaty puts emphasis on the following aspects:

- the need for *evolution*, rather than *revolution*, toward the creation of the African Common Market;
- hence the need for creation of strong 'building blocks' in the form of subregional common markets. This will call for internal cohesion of African states as the more basic building blocks, although the prospects of impending larger markets may also enhance internal integration of African states, arbitrarily drawn by colonial powers in the nineteenth century.
- Cooperation institutions for the Economic Community;
- trade and harmonization, consolidation and development;
- physical infrastructure development, and
- human and social affairs.

However, in my view, the Treaty does not go far enough on decision-making processes, which should be by majority or qualified majority for most decisions and not by unanimity which will only slow down the process. In addition, the Treaty does not address fully the problems of political, social, and economic *convergence*, and especially the role of the *private sector* (and more specifically as to whether PAEC is going to be a 'Union of African peoples' rather than a 'Union of Governments'). In the area of funding, the Secretariat is to be funded through members' contributions; this has consistently failed elsewhere, for example, the OAU. It ought to be reviewed in favour of some kind of retention scheme; for example, of common customs collection and/or other common market dues). Finally the Secretariat (especially in its role of common market enforcement) is rather weak. The OAU is supposed to assume this role. This would call for a drastic restructuring, transformation and empowerment of the OAU.

The Abuja Treaty is on the whole a very sound document. But we need a strategy and programmes for faster realization of sub-regional common markets and subsequently the African Common Market. My submission is that such a strategy should include:

- restructuring and empowerment of the OAU;
- strategies for consultative regional planning, and
- empowerment and involvement of the private sector, including all the African masses, in order to bring about a 'union of African peoples' (rather than merely governments).

Empowerment of the OAU

I believe that the process of creating an African Common Market ought to be driven by both *trade* and *development* as an overall strategy. It is currently estimated that if all non-tariff trade barriers in Africa were removed, inter-state trade could increase by 8 billion US dollars per annum. While this would be a sizeable increase, it may not offset the costs of liberalization (in all cases). Since most African economies are weak, governments would like to see positive prospects for faster development in economic integration. For development-driven economic integration to take place, a strong and independent implementation body is required.

Currently, the OAU is run as a supra-national bureaucracy without powers. It must have powers to enforce sanctions on members for non-compliance. For the OAU to be effective, a number of reforms are urgently needed. The Treaty should be revised to provide for a strong, independent, secretary-general, not one that will only 'follow up and implement decisions of the Assembly of Heads of State' but one that has powers to *originate* and *execute* certain aspects of the process of integration. This would call for the elevation of the post to some kind of 'prototype' African President. A respected ex-head of state would be a good candidate for such a post.

More generally, the provision regarding the Assembly, the Pan African Parliament, the Court of Justice, and the Secretariat ought to be reviewed to make each one of these important cooperation institutions relatively independent in content, powers and functions for effectiveness. (African governments cannot have their cake and eat it. The 'sovereignty' impediment to African progress should be recognized.)

Since the process of creating an African Common Market is going to take about thirty years, there is need for a smaller and faster-acting monitoring body than the Assembly of Heads of State. I therefore suggest the possibility of an African Regional Integration Commission (ARIC) on which there could be:

- a chairman (possibly Chairman of OAU)
- selected heads of state (say ten)
- some ministers (say ten)
- private-sector representatives, including manufacturers, investors, farmers, traders, bankers, trade unions and other popular forces
- institutional representatives (for example, PTA/COMESA, ECOWAS)
- representatives of Africans in the diaspora
- eminent Pan Africanists/professionals.

This would obviate the need for AEC business to be entangled with routine OAU affairs, which would introduce bureaucratic marking time in the integration process. Apart from monitoring, the Commission would advise on various aspects of the integration process and might ultimately be merged with the PAEC Secretariat as a powerful integrating organ. Funding could be from member-state contributions, contributions from friends of Africa and donors and possibly in the medium term, from market dues.

There is a need to review very critically not only the *processes*, but also the *institutions* that will deliver an African Common Market in the shortest time. And time is not on our side. Besides, a detailed implementation plan for the Abuja Treaty is urgently required.

Need for consultative regional planning

Partly because of historical colonial ties and the post-colonial management of aid-driven development, African countries tend to cluster around the world economic order as *individual* satellites without any significant economic linkages amongst themselves. For instance, the World Bank negotiates national programmes, including SAPs, with each state individually at a time. So do most donors, for example ADB, EEC, USAID. This tends to 'nationalize' development in Africa. Clearly, economic integration cannot take place in this setting. Regional SAPs are required for economic convergence and, in a larger setting, national plans that dovetail into each other to enhance overall regional master plans are a clear need in the process of integration for development.

For this reason, there is a need to enhance regionally-conscious national planning as well as regionally conscious official development assistance (ODA). For this to happen effectively, indicative sectoral (and subsectoral) regional master plans for the African Common Market will be needed. This could be one job for ARIC.

Private-sector empowerment

In a properly functioning common market, the public sector ought to be the *facilitator* while the private sector plays the central role of *main actor*. Cases where governments have attempted to play both roles, for example, East African Community, ECOWAS, PTA, have not worked well. For this purpose, deliberate and elaborate strategies and programmes for empowerment of the private sector will have to be part of this process since the private sector in Africa is generally weak.

The African peoples, as economic actors, are currently (and have been for the last century or so) characterized by technological displacement, making them ineffectual actors in their own economic destiny. The limited technology they knew and handled with confidence is no more. The imposed technology they handle only with diffidence and apparently without the right of initiative. This is a society in a semi-permanent state of *technological transition*. This development impasse has to be broken. The key to this is education, acquisition of knowledge, health, more attention to social issues. African populations have been increasing without improving. This is a good recipe for socioeconomic disaster.

I would like to propose specific programmes for enhancement of the formal private sector to include: constitutional/legal recognition of the role of regional chambers of commerce and/or manufacturers or similar associations; facilitation/regulation of this sector through appropriate investment laws, financial reforms, divestiture (in advance of regional corporations), etc., and transformation and development through specific programmes will be thought through and put in place.

My chief concern here is to do with the informal and subsistence sectors. These two currently dominate the African market. And unless they are enabled to perceive it and participate in it, the integration effort is doomed from the start. What is needed is an agenda for *economic liberation*, a *mass movement* for economic liberation of the African person just as was the case for political liberation. And because economic domination is more intricate and deeper than political domination, often being the *raison d'être* for the latter, this will be a much harder job. Where the economic Du Bois's, Padmores, Nkrumahs, Kenyattas, Sekou Toures, Nyereres, Mugabes, Machels, Sankaras, Musevenis, Mandelas will come from is the challenge of our age (in general) and of this 7th Pan African Congress (in particular). Just like the 5th PAC delivered the *political independence* movement in 1945, the 7th PAC must deliver an *economic liberation* movement.

Conclusion

Economics is to be the driving force of the Africa of the future. Good economics will deliver both good politics and equitable social systems. This discussion has omitted (knowingly or through ignorance) some aspects of common market formation, for example, external influences since other stronger markets are in the process of formulation or have been formed. Such omissions may possibly be judged by some as more important. This I accept and tender my apologies for my 'sins' in advance.

But, in mitigation, let me say that the subject covered was rather wide. However, I have emphasized that:

- the last 30–40 years of African independence have been an economic failure;
- Africans and their 'oppressors' are equally to blame;
- we Africans need to critically examine our failures and put them straight, and
- this must be done as part of the process/movement towards the formation of an African Common Market.

To paraphrase the motto of my high school (King's College Budo, near Kampala) *Gakyali Mabaga*: the economic struggle has just begun.

Bibliography

Abuja Treaty
COMESA Treaty
Mtei, Edwin; Maitha, K. Joe; Sebalu, Paulo and Tulya-Muhika, Sam, *Evidence for Disintegration of the East African Community*, (Manuscript in Press).
Museveni, K. Yoweri (1991). *Towards Closer Cooperation in Africa*, Paper, October.
Nkrumah, Kwame (1963). *Africa Must Unite*, London: Mercury Books; Heinemann.
Tinbergen, Jan (1964), *International Development: Growth and Change*, New York: McGraw Hill.

Further reading

African Alternative Framework to SAP for Socio-Economic Recovery and Transformation (UNECA, Addis Ababa).
Berg, Elliot J. (1993). *Re-thinking Technical Cooperation (Reforms for Capacity Building in Africa)*, Regional Bureau for Africa, UNDP.
Hancock, Graham (1991). *Lords of Poverty*, London: Mandarin.
Museveni, K. Yoweri (1992). *What is Africa's Problem*, Kampala: NRM Publications.
Mutharika, Bingu W.T. (1992). 'Regional Economic Integration in Africa: Rationale and perspectives' in Proceedings of an International Conference on Liberalisation and Regional Integration in Africa, Arusha, Tanzania: Friedrich-Naumann-Stiftung, 25–28 May.
Ndongko, W.A. (ed.) (1985). *Economic Cooperation and Integration in Africa*, Dakar: CODESRIA Book Series.
Tulya-Muhika, Sam (1991). 'A Global Overview of Economic Cooperation with Special Reference to Africa'; Paper written for a Symposium on Re-integration of East African Common Market within the PTA Framework (March 1991, pp. 1–164).
Tulya-Muhika, Sam (1993). 'Strategies for Regional Integration and Cooperation for Economic Growth and Development in Africa'; Paper presented at a Workshop on Democracy, Development and Growth in Africa: Lessons, Challenges, and Strategies, Goree Insitute, Dakar, Senegal, June 1993.
Tulya-Muhika, Sam (1993). 'Structural Adjustment Progammes: Causes, Purpose and Problems with Special Reference to Uganda

and other PTA Countries', International Seminar Paper, Kampala, September 1993.
UN Human Development Report: 1990, 1991, 1992, 1993.
World Bank Development Report: 1989 (Special Report on Sub-Saharan Africa) 1989, 1990, 1991, 1992, 1993.

Appendix 1
Evolutionary stages for implementation of the treaty for the African Economic Community

Stage	Duration in Years	Emphasis on
1st	5	Strengthening existing regional communities (RCs), and establishment of new ones where they do not exist.
2nd	8	Trade facilitation within RCs; sectoral integration (RC and continental levels).
3rd	10	Transformation of RCs into free trade area and customs unions
4th	2	Tariffs and non-tariff systems harmonization (intra-regional communities) and customs union (continental level)
5th	4	Completion of African Common Market
6th	5	Establishment of African Economic Community and monetary union
Total	34	

Appendix 2
Attempts at regional cooperation in Africa

1. East African Community (Defunct) (EAC)
2. East African Development Bank (EADB/CAE)
3. Economic Community of West African States (ECOWAS)
4. La Communate Economique de L'Afrique de L'Ouest (CEAO)
5. Union Dovaniere et Economique de l'Afrique Centrale (UDEAC)
6. Le Fonds D'entraide Et de Garantie Des Emprunts Du Conseil De l'Entente
7. Le Fonds De Solidarite Et d'intervention Pour Le Developpe-De La

8. Commonate economique De L'Afrique De L'ouest (FOSIDEC)
9. West African Development Bank (WADB/BOAD)
10. West African Economic Community 1962 (WAEC/UMOA)
11. West African Economic Community 1974(WAEC/CEAO)
12. Economic Community of Central African States (ECCAS/CEAS)
13. Bank of Central African States (BACAS/BEAC)
14. Lake Chad Basin Commission
15. Economic Community of the Great Lakes Countries (ECGLC/CEPGL)
16. The Mano River Union (MRU)
17. The Preferential Trade Area (PTA)
18. The Southern African Customs Union (SACU)
19. Southern African Development Co-ordination Conference (SADCC)
20. Arab Maghreb Union
21. Association of African Development Finance Institutions
22. African Development Fund (ADF)
23. African Development Bank (ADB)
24. African Economic Community (AEC)

Attempts at regional cooperation in Africa

	Institution	Date of Est.	Members	Purpose	Success rating
1.	East African Community (EAC)	1967	Uganda, Kenya, Tanzania	– Adapt a longstanding arrangement to meet the needs of independence – Share common services like railways and harbours, air transport, research and higher education – Customs union.	Successful until breakup in 1977
2.	East African Development Bank (EADB/CAE)	1967	Uganda, Kenya, Tanzania	– Provide financial assistance to national projects and complementing the efforts of national development finance institutions	Successful
3.	Economic Community of West African States (ECOWAS)	1975	Benin, Burkina Faso, Cape Verde, Cote d'Ivoire, Gambia, Ghana, Guinea-Bissau, Liberia, Mali, Mauritania, Togo, Niger, Senegal, Sierra Leone	– Promote balanced development – Finance fiscal losses arising from liberalized trade – External customs tariffs – Plagued by funding problems and multiplicity of such institutions in West Africa – Promotion of improvements in telecommunications and regional transport network	Not very successful

Institution	Date of Est.	Members	Purpose	Success rating
4. La Communate Economique De L'Afrique de l'Ouest (CEAO)	1959	Burkina Faso, Cote d'Ivoire, Mali, Niger, Senegal, Mauritania	– Operate a modest partial free-trade area for Industrial – Free trade in un processed agricultural products.	Partial Success
5. Union Dovaniere et Economique de l'Afrique Centrale (UDEAC)	1959	Cameroon, Chad, Congo, Central African Republic, Equatorial Guinea, Gabon	– Promoting industrial specialization – A comprehensive reform of grade and fiscal arrangements for an enlargement of economic cooperation in the Union	Not working very well
6. Le Fonds D'entraide Et De Garantie Des Emprunts Du Conseil De l'Entente	1959	Benin, Burkina Faso, Cote d'Ivoire, Niger, Togo	– Established vehicle for procuring external support – Gives funds for rural development – Promotion of political, social and economic coordination among the member states.	Not very effective
7. Le Fonds De Solidarite Et D'intervention Pour Le Developpe-De La	1978	Benin, Mali, Burkina Faso, Niger, Senegal	– Promote projects and feasibility studies and providing guarantees	Not very effective
8. Communate economique De L'Afrique De l'ouest (FOSIDEC)	–	Cote d'Ivoire, etc.	– To support economic development of member countries and contribute to regional equilibrium	Not very effective

Institution	Date of Est.	Members	Purpose	Success rating
9. West African Development Bank (WADB/BOAD)	1973	Benin, Burkina Faso, Cote d'Ivoire, Mali, Mauritania, Niger, and Senegal	– Promote balanced development of the Union and to achieve West African integration.	Reasonably Successful
10. West African Economic Community (WAEC/UMOA)	1962	Benin, Mali, Niger, Burkina Faso, Togo, Senegal, Cote d'Ivoire.	– Share a Common Central Bank which issues a common currency (the CFA France)	Effective and successful
11. West African Economic Community (WAEC/CEAO)	1974	Benin, Burkina Faso, Cote d'Ivoire, Mali, Mauritania, Niger and Senegal	– Promote the harmonized and balanced development Economic activities of of member states – To launch, at a regional level, an active policy of economic cooperation and integration with regard to the development of agriculture, fishing industry, etc.	Not very effective
12. Economic Community of Central African States (ECCAS/CEAS)	1983	Burundi, Cameroon, Central African Republic, Chad, Congo, Gabon, Rwanda and Zaire.	– Finance, fiscal losses arising from liberalized trade – Promote balanced development	Not yet very effective
13. Bank of Central African States (BACAS/BEAC)	1973	Cameroon, Chad, Central African Republic, Congo, Equatorial Guinea	– Provide members with a convertible currency – A coordination of the monetary policies of of their member states.	Some success
14. Lake Chad Basin Commission	–	Cameroon, Chad	– To regulate and control utilization of fresh water resources in the basin.	Some success

Institution	Date of Est.	Members	Purpose	Success rating
15. Economic Community of Great Lakes Countries (ECGLC/CEPGL)	1976	Burundi, Rwanda, and Zaire	– Promote regional economic integration among members – To pursue objectives consistent with the UN Charter and the Charter of OAU.	Some success
16. The Mano River Union (MRU)	1973	Guinea, Liberia, Sierra Leone	– Common external tariff – Liberalized trade in local products.	Not very successful
17. Preferential Trade Area (PTA)	1981	19 Eastern and Southern African States	– Intra-area trade – Promote cooperation and and development in all fields of economic activity, i.e. trade, customs, industry, etc.	– Beginning to take shape – Rather slow but sure and promises to be effective.
18. The Southern African Customs Union (SACU)		South Africa, Botswana, Lesotho, Swaziland, Namibia	– Monetary 'union' – Common external tariff (Customs Union) – Distribution of the revenue derived from the tariff – Protection of their infant industries against competition from more advanced patterns	Very effective

Institution	Date of Est.	Members	Purpose	Success rating
19. Southern African Development Coordination Conference (SADCC)	1980	Angola, Botswana, Lesotho, Malawi, Mozambique, Swaziland, Tanzania, Zambia	– Reduction of economic dependence on South Africa – Forging of units of a genuine and equitable regional integration – Mobilization of resources to promote the implementation of national, interstate and regional policies – Concerted action to secure international cooperation within the framework of the strategy for economic liberation	Reasonably successful, especially with reference to political liberation
20. Arab Maghreb Union	1980s	Mauritania, Morocco, Algeria, Egypt, Tunisia, Libya, Sudan, Polisario	– To study all problems facing economic cooperation in the Maghreb – To build up the Maghrebian Economic Community – To direct and coordinate their activities	Not yet very effective.
21. Association of African Development Finance Institutions	1975	94 ordinary members	– To stimulate cooperation for financing of economic and social development in Africa. – To establish among its members the machinery for systematic interchange of information – To accelerate the process of economic integration in the African region	Not so effective

Institution	Date of Est.	Members	Purpose	Success rating
22. African Development Fund (ADF)	1973	50 member countries	– Provides finance on concessional terms for the purpose of assisting the Bank's contribution to economic and social development of Bank members	Effective
23. African Development Bank (ADB)	1966	75 members – 50 African states and 25 non-regional	– To lend for national projects – To lend for multinational projects – To lend sub-regional development banks	Successful
24. African Economic Community (AEC)	Late 1991	All OAU member states	– Treaty signed on 3 June 1991 in Abuja, Nigeria. Planned to come about in six phases (including building and strengthening of regional blocks) over a period of 34 years. – To establish a Community (PAEC)	Ratification process rather slow

N.B. Other (smaller) institutions exist e.g.,
- Kagera Basin Organisation (KBO) for Rwanda, Burundi, Tanzania, Uganda
- Northern Corridor

6

Improving Access to Natural Resource Potentials and Regional Cooperation in Southern Africa

Sam Moyo

Introduction

An essential component of any envisioned regional cooperation in Southern Africa, let alone the promotion of economic integration within the framework of collective self-reliance and economic growth, is the rationalized distribution and utilization of natural resources. The literature on sustainable development and the environment abounds with crisis-based analyses of rapid resource degradation based on demographic growth considered by conventional scientists to be involuted. Explanations of resource degradation and human fertility, based on presumed cultural deficiencies and associated environmental programmes, have so far failed to deliver optimal resource use strategies. These are essential because cultural and behavioural environmental approaches neglect fundamental political and economic processes which influence resource access and use, and the lag in technological developments essential to improve human and resource productivity and efficiencies. A basic way forward is to define a demand-led strategy of resource and technology management based on the requirements of the majority of the region's population.

The purpose of this chapter is to develop a framework for improving the efficient use of natural resources in the Southern Africa region and improving access for the majority to those resources in order to improve their livelihoods and productivity. The nature of resources available is outlined; then I discuss their utilization, and the nature of poverty in the region.

Regional policy on natural resources is outlined as founded in Southern African Development Coordination (SADC) documents, and an alternative framework which sketches the conceptual basis for concrete actions is presented. The chapter is intended to contribute to the Pan African agenda of developing a people-oriented development strategy for the African continent.

The resource base

Human resources

Southern Africa has a rich human-resource base totalling close to 85 million people, with about 45 per cent of this population being below 15 years of age. Thus for every 1.5 adults of working age, there is one young or old dependent person. The population continues to grow at approximately 3.2 per cent per annum, with an average 70 per cent of this population residing in rural areas. A few countries (like Zambia and South Africa) have urbanization rates close to 50 per cent, while the majority of the countries have over 80 per cent of their populations living in rural areas. Therefore urbanization remains a slow process, due to the slow pace of industrialization as discussed below.

The Southern African area covers 5 million square kilometres or about 480 million hectares of land. The population is sparsely distributed, at about 15 persons per square kilometre. The bulk of the rural populations depends on a mixed farming system with a heavy dependence on livestock for traction energy, food and manure resources, as well as for trade. Staple foods vary but are predominantly based on coarse grains (maize, millet and sorghum), with an increasing role played by imported rice and other locally produced tubers in the region's diets.

The regional human-resource structure was heavily influenced by settler colonialism which ensured that, while less than 10 per cent of the present population are white, they are the dominant class. Thus, the white population consumes the bulk of the infrastructure, goods and services in value; controls or owns the commanding height of the economies and retains the highest proportions of incomes earned in each country. Land, water and other natural resources are predominantly controlled or owned by whites in South Africa, Zimbabwe and Namibia. The region is thus characterized by very skewed access to and control of natural resources, with landlessness growing to as high as 30 per cent in many of the countries.

The average per capita gross domestic product (GDP) of the region is 300 US dollars, with four of the largest countries having per capita GDPs of below 250 US dollars, while a few countries such as South Africa and Botswana have per capita GDPs of above 1500 US dollars. All the countries have highly skewed income distributions such that real per capita GDPs for the bulk (70 per cent) of the population are below 100 US dollars. Life expectancy is below 60 years in the region, while infant mortality is at 66 per 1000 births, and literacy rates average 65 per cent with over 80 per cent of the children enrolled in primary schools in most countries, except Malawi and Mozambique.

The gender-based dimension of natural-resource access and use is also a fundamental arena of distortions in terms of human productivity, labour repression, basic human rights of access, and resource use efficiency. Colonially induced labour-discriminatory urban home-ownership and residence policies, discriminatory technology and capital-resource allocations to agricultural and rural development, the exclusion of women from land-ownership rights and access to land in communal areas have accentuated the marginalization of women in the region. Women cultivate marginal and inadequate lands with the least access to technology and credit, perform the bulk of the farm labour and management work, and are responsible for the management of natural resources and their families. Under these conditions the prospects for improving both human and natural-resource productivity and sustainability are remote.

Essentially, wage-labourers and their dependents and peasant households run mainly by women survive on a restricted consumption base. Unfulfilled and ineffective demand and contained productivity are thus central to poverty in Southern Africa. Strategies are needed to address these constraints as they may also provide a basis for triggering-off broader economic developments, on the basis of industrial and agricultural strategies, which accord the regional domestic markets a crucial place.

Broadening the consumption base through promoting employment, productivity and income-diversification strategies requires extra-market interventions, which need not necessarily contradict macroeconomic balancing, the operation of markets and private-property relations. Greater research into these issues and related strategies, as well as into appropriate definition and target of demand expansion, within a 'social market' context, is well overdue.

The labour force of the region is predominantly agricultural, with 75 per cent of the populations engaged in farming and directly associated economic activities. A few of the countries including South Africa, Zimbabwe, Namibia and Zambia have industrial and mining sectors which occupy larger segments of the population. But an average of only 10 per cent of the labour force is engaged in industry while another 15 per cent is engaged in the services sector.

Yet while the bulk of the labour force are agricultural and agricultural exports dominate in about half of the region's economies, labour and land productivity tend to be low. In most small-holder farming enterprises of all the countries, the productivity of land and labour tend to be less than 40 per cent of the existing agronomic potentials for all of them. This is better illustrated by an examination of the natural resource use-patterns in the region.

Resource use-patterns

Natural resources in Southern Africa tend to be under-utilized or concentrated in the hands of ministries and land-owners of European descent, rather than farmers of African descent. While only about 6 per cent of the total 480 million hectares available in Southern Africa are arable, even this land potential is under-utilized. For instance, less than 25 per cent of the 40 million arable hectares found in the region are used for crops. Some countries such as Zimbabwe and Zambia with less than 15 per cent of high-potential arable land have their marginal grazing or pasture lands increasingly brought under cultivation by the poor peasantry. In most countries, pastures still occupy up to 45 per cent of the lands, while forests and woodlands occupy up to 33 per cent of the land. But both pasturelands and woodlands are increasingly diminishing due to the land pressures consequent upon inequitable ownership of arable technologies suitable for intensive high-productivity land uses. This means that the majority of Southern African rural dwellers continue to practise extensive mixed farming methods with low yields based on arduous labour systems. Women bear the major brunt of these marginal farming activities, and their incomes increasingly fail to cover basic costs of the reproductivity of their households.

The bulk of the region's prime lands are devoted to export crops of which cotton, sugar, tobacco, tea, beef and coffee are major land users. Most of the export earnings of the majority of the countries are highly dependent on these six agricultural commodities. About 25 per cent of the foreign currency earnings from export (forex) come from these, while gold and diamond mining play a key role in the earnings of at least six of the countries. Therefore the region's land-use systems tend to be heavily dependent on export agriculture and mining activities in the hands of minority white, elite, groups. This export-orientation, and skewed resource ownership and use-patterns, are also evident in the utilization and ownership structures of the forests, woodlands and natural resources of the region.

While the region has just under 160 million hectares of forests and woodlands, it is estimated that close to 669,000 hectares of forests and woodlands in the area are lost through deforestation each year. This annual loss of plant biodiversity has been proceeding at a rate of 0.5 per cent per annum, while the reforesting of the land in the region has proceeded rather slowly. Less than 27,000 hectares of land are planted with trees each year, leaving a net loss to deforestation of around 650,000 hectares per annum. While the bulk of the deforestation is accounted for by agricultural expansion into marginal lands, political pressures are also critical.

Seventy per cent of the forests and woodlands are found in Angola, Mozambique, Tanzania and Zambia. Two of these countries have suffered continued destabilization from South Africa and internal opponents, which has led to the rapid destruction of forests and woodlands there. Deforestation has taken away over 400,000 hectares of forests and woodlands in the four countries, due to war and the displacement of peoples and farming. These countries, which are really the largest and contain over 73 per cent of the region's population, have also experienced the greatest levels of growing poverty. These four countries account for less than 50 per cent of the regions' GDP in spite of their large populations. The economic and political pressures in these larger countries have been reflected in the relatively high rates of deforestation. The efficient and sustainable utilization of forest and woodland resources in these large natural resource-rich countries will require enduring peace.

Although not the key factor behind the deforestation of forests and woodlands, the dependence of over 80 per cent of the Southern African people on wood for fuel has taken its toll on natural resources. The inaccessibility of available electricity resources and technologies which depend on such energy has meant that most people depend on nature for basic cooking, heating, boiling and rudimentary manufacturing energy. The region's bulk of electricity resources from thermal and hydro sources have been concentrated towards urban centres, excluding the working classes. The latter have increasingly resorted to charcoal which consumes much wood in its production, and coal which is unsound for their health, leading to increasing land degradation and pollution. Therefore, the inadequacy and concentration of energy resources has forced the masses of the region to over-exploit wood resources.

Yet commercial and state-owned forest plantations and reserves tend to contain excess supplies of woodfuel, as do private farms and woodlands. These are inaccessible to the majority of the poor who instead are relying on increasingly distant sources of woodlands in local districts. These resource anomalies mean that communities – mostly women – expend greater human energy and time procuring woodfuels, to the detriment of other household and economic activities crucial for their survival.

Water resources are also controlled and utilized in the interests of minority segments of the population and are inaccessible to the majority in Southern Africa. For instance, the per capita availability of water resources was highest in Zambia, Angola and Swaziland, while their ability to harness these water resources was minimal. Most of the Southern African countries could harness less than two per cent of available water resources in their countries due to the low level of investment in water storage and distribution infrastructures.

On average most countries accessed less than 100m^3 per capita as a result. Zimbabwe and Swaziland withdrew about five per cent of the available resources leading to high per capita water resources availability at 130m^3 and 414m^3 each respectively. But in both these countries, large-scale commercial farmers, urban residents, and mining and industrial firms accounted for the bulk of the consumption of such resources. Equally, South Africa, which in the 1970s could withdraw 18 per cent of available resources, had the highest per capita consumption level, which in reality were directed at the white community and formal-sector enterprises.

Agriculture has tended to dominate water withdrawn for consumption at between 50 per cent and 80 per cent in most countries. Zambia has the least percentage (26 per cent) of water drawn for agriculture due to the high urban-based channelling of withdrawn water. Malawi also has proportionately high levels of water withdrawn for domestic and industrial purposes; however, this reflects the relatively under-developed use of irrigation in that country. Yet in countries such as Zimbabwe and South Africa with high water-withdrawal rates and large amounts of these withdrawals targeted at agriculture, less than 10 per cent of such irrigation as available are provided to small-holders of indigenous origin. The widespread under-development of water and irrigation infrastructures in the region explains the low levels of agricultural productivity and incomes, the poor quality of life facing many and the increasing degradation of natural resources consequent upon extensive farming livelihoods.

Both the water and electricity resources of Southern Africa are increasingly seen as key resources through which regional cooperation can be promoted to enhance the 'collective improvement of people's livelihoods'. The extension of water and electricity resources across borders, through equitable mechanisms managed by regional institutions is feasible and can set the basis for improving food security, natural resources management, land and labour productivity and value-adding activities in rural areas. These are critical steps in attaining sustainable natural resources management from a people's perspective. The optimal distribution of access to natural resources and their efficient utilization can only be guaranteed when the sustainability of human livelihoods is guaranteed. This requires poverty alleviation in the short term; the systematic development of the infrastructural substitutes of naturally procured energy, water, housing materials and yield-enhancing resources is essential. The structural basis of poverty in the region is thus critical in developing further the strategies required to enhance the effective use of natural resources by the majority in Southern Africa.

Poverty alleviation and development strategy

There is recognition that at least 50 million Southern Africans live in abject poverty and this requires specific explanation. Poverty here is based on 'dualistic' economic structures, whereby consumption in the broadest sense is restricted mostly to minority white 'classes' and, in some countries, super-elite black classes. Thus out of the total of over 80 million people in the region, the present patterns of incomes, markets and distribution systems mainly service the consumption preferences of approximately 15 million Southern African elites.

The economies provide these elites with the bulk of the resources (materials, finance and expertise) required for housing, education, services (water, electricity and so on), food and beverages and other consumer goods through capital-intensive and cheap labour-based production systems. The majority of the population provides its own meagre subsistence, through financially unremunerated labour, from restricted resource bases (land, finance and other inputs) and based on extremely low labour and land productivities. Low productivity and low-quality consumption patterns are the key elements of poverty. Yet official regional strategies for sustainable resource-use focus on the physical symptoms of natural resource degradations and their mitigation, neglecting the role of people's sustainable development in all this.

Official regional environmental strategy and major environmental concerns

The Southern African Development Co-ordination Conference (SADCC) policy stance on the environment, which has been gradually modified, remains an eclectic catalogue of project-derived areas of environmental problems to be addressed, rather than a systemic and people-centred strategy to enhance wider development as a guarantee for natural resource management efficiencies. For instance, the SADCC document 'Natural Resources and the Environment: Policing Development Strategy' approved by the SADCC Council of Ministers in October 1987 outlines the following as priority problems of the region:

- reduction in quality and quantity of agricultural and grasslands, accelerated soil erosion and land degradation;
- overgrazing;
- desertification, for example, the advancement of the Kalahari Desert;
- climatic variation and periodic drought;
- introduction of undesirable species and subspecies of plant and animal life;
- loss of the support systems of fisheries;
- inadequate monitoring, assessment and regulation of job stocks;
- deforestation, and inadequate afforestation and reforestation;
- inadequate control of bush and veld fires;
- inadequate environmental planning and inappropriate resources allocation;
- lack of information and awareness and lack of environmental education programmes for different target groups;
- lack of support for conservation and of conservation-based rural development;
- inadequate research on natural resources, for example, indigenous trees, vegetables, fruits and game, and
- operational mechanisms essential for land-use planning.

The official policy framework does not identify the uneven distribution or access to land, water, nature parks, forest and woodland resources and hydro or thermal electricity resources as fundamental causes of the environmental problems to be addressed by SADCC. Nor is the quest for improving land and labour productivity through improving access to appropriate technology and natural resources based on national policy and resource-allocation shifts even cited as a critical problem. This is why the official lists of environmental projects as an essentially pedagogic and ideological programme aiming to change the thinking and practices of ordinary peoples without any measures aimed at enhancing their material returns to natural resource use or their returns of labour applied to their survival and to market participation.

For this reason the official strategy for natural resource utilization does not contain concrete and sustainable action plans and an indication of how the framework would be operationalized. As a matter of fact, one would go so far as to suggest that SADCC does not have as yet an operational strategy on the environment, but has in its place a political statement of intent. Given the time and procedure undertaken to arrive at the policy framework, one can surmise that there has been some but not extensive internal regional debate on the issue of the environment. This may also be because of the fact that, even at national levels, there has not been a vigorous debate on the environment. The environment issue is usually an appendage in a discussion of other issues. The end result is that at the regional, SADCC, level, what comes out is a response to donor concerns or a Northern perspective of environmental problems.

Yet the SADCC plans to separate the management and policy process of critical sectors of water, energy, forests, agriculture and tourism. For instance the plan has a scattered format for the sectoral co-ordination of environmental responsibilities in the various SADCC countries as shown below:

Energy	Angola
Transport	Mozambique\Southern African Transport and Communication Coordination (SATCC)
Information and culture	Mozambique
Agriculture and food security	Zimbabwe
Agricultural research and training	Botswana
Livestock production and animal disease control	Botswana
Fisheries, forestry and wildlife	Malawi
Soil and water conservation and land utilization	Lesotho
Tourism	Lesotho
Industry and trade	Tanzania
Mining	Zambia
Manpower development	Swaziland
(To be decided)	Namibia

But as we have argued earlier, the rejuvenation of the people's livelihoods, which requires improved access to various natural resources, access to energy, water and technology and improved access to technology, in turn requires a more integrated identification and management of natural resource problems.

Sustainable development policy issues

The disjointed nature of official policy and action plans for environmental action demonstrates the environmental policy and strategy formulation which underlies the lack of clear political commitment towards resolving the key bottlenecks that confront the majority of people. Because of the vagueness of policy, its donor-driven eclecticism and the narrow project-planning logic underlying the plans, it is not possible to isolate the strategic basis for future natural resource-use optimization. Indeed this shows the poverty of environmental thinking and expertise even though some experts would like to argue that existing environmental research and documentation in SADCC is considered to be exemplary compared to that of most Sub-Saharan countries. In a related study we have explained the lack of prioritization, poor problem-identification and indeed the poor understanding of environmental issues in Southern Africa to be a product of the unresolved political and economic polarization of key classes, intellectuals and policy makers. This can be traced through the insufficient treatment and understanding of the nature and courses of differences in access to resources by different ethnic and social groups. This has influenced environmental and agricultural research and extension work as well as state and private environmental programmes of historical and apolitical approaches towards policy formulation based on physical processes of natural resources reproduction. This has led to the polarization of attitudes to natural resources between analysts with a narrow ecological perspective and others with a nationalistic, socioeconomic approach. A similar polarization of environmental concern between the general public and amongst those comfortably concerned with the environment is characteristically focusing on the survival of endangered species such as the black rhino. This has those in environmentally degraded areas struggling daily for survival without any role in defining the nature of the problems to be addressed and how to resolve them.

Such exclusive narrow and non-participatory planning systems as are found in the region explains the inadequacy of state policies to deal with the range of environmental issues and difficulties confronting the nations. The efforts by the state to mobilize consensus on basic environmental issues have failed in the face of daily efforts by people to 'illegally' access natural resources dominated by elites and the state, and as communities increasingly defy state-led environmental programmes. Coupling this trend with the underdevelopment of environmental management skills at all levels in the state, reflecting the absence of a generally accepted environmental management tradition or praxis, the majority of existing local environmentalists are uncritically receptive to externally imported ideas and agendas surrounding global environmental management concerns. For this reason global focuses on biodiversity forest management and climatic change override the survival issues of ordinary people in the environmental work of the region's governments and NGOs.

Instead, governments have adopted populist approaches to people's participation in the formulation and implementation of environmental policies which seem to be driven towards endorsing global agendas rather than addressing local concerns.

Therefore, the absence of autonomous programmes to address poverty alleviation, resource-distribution inequities and the unwillingness of governments to change the colonial laws that govern resource distribution, allocation, access and management, are the key problems which a people's programme for sustainable resource utilization will need to address. This will also require the commitment to develop local capacity to formulate policies and manage natural resources. Indeed the growing tendency for international agencies to introduce environmental policies conditionally into their aid programmes will require trained personnel which can promote alternatives in development planning, policy analysis and legislative reforms. Mobilization of indigenous expertise to provide intellectual and technical support to a people-oriented or demand-led environmental strategy is thus the key strategic basis for future Pan African initiatives.

Only when indigenous capacities exist to address the underlying environmental problems facing the majority, will incoherence of the existing environmental policies of the region, which conflate legal and institutional instruments into contradictory environmental programmes, be resolved. In turn, this will require research and policy-analysis activities which can show how national accounts can include environmental values such that SADC officials can begin to appreciate the true values of natural resources, the comparative costs of different methods of resource exploitation and the costs of neglecting the majority in access to natural resources. Policy should thus be based on understanding the relative merits of arable agriculture, animal husbandry and wildlife utilization by different classes in terms of the ecological, social and financial sustainability of existing resource uses and future development programmes aimed at satisfying the basic needs of the majority. Indeed such policies should be based on studies of the values that local communities place on natural resources and more acceptable ways of including communities in the growing tourist and recreation industry which the region is frantically promoting.

Conclusion

Any future strategy for effective natural resources use will thus have to be based on investing in technologies, infrastructures and natural resource exploitation which can improve the livelihood of the majority. Sustainability of development will require re-creation of a productive base that is sustainable both ecologically and socioeconomically.

Government and groups presently holding political and economic power will have to accept that there are real costs involved in the neglect or postponement of the survival problems of the poor in terms of environmental degradation. Such consequences will include declining yields, resource conflicts, increased demand for food relief and ultimately, social and political agitation. Therefore what is required is a more efficient allocation of investment resources to improve access for the poor in the following areas:

- water development for irrigation and health improvement to enhance the stability of food systems and improve human and agricultural productivity;
- the development and dissemination of technologies to improve agricultural, and natural, plant and animal productivity for the benefit of the majority;
- rural electrification for improved agricultural, domestic and industrial enterprise in rural areas based on local and regional large and small-scale projects;
- land redistribution within countries to enhance access to arable, grazing and woodland areas for the poor, and
- opening nature parks and the tourist and forest industries to the poor to enhance their non-farming economic benefits from natural resources.

The way forward is thus to broaden the participation of indigenous people of various classes, from various regions and resource systems, in the articulation of the specific nature of investments, into natural resources distribution and use and into the technologies and infrastructure required to enhance resource and labour productivity that they will support. Research evidence suggests that improving the material and productive conditions of the majority of people making a living from unmarginalized natural resources and whose reproductive capacities are rapidly degrading, is the central prerequisite for any sustainable development initiative. The Pan African agenda has to focus on promoting ways to achieve more equitable access to the use and benefits of nature, improving the productivity and livelihoods of the African people and invoking the participation of the majority of the region's poor people in an African strategy for sustainable development. This approach can lead to more effective institutionalization of regional cooperation strategies because their viability and sustainability will rest upon popular support, unlike current preoccupations aiming to physically engineer the connection of water, energy and nature reserves among countries. Infrastructural integration of the region which is based on the economic dominance of some countries and their elites in the control and access to the vast natural resources potential of Southern Africa, will only further marginalize the poor, increase natural resource degradation and invoke popular resistance in the future.

Further reading

African Development Bank (1993). *Economic Integration in Southern Africa*, vol. 3, Oxford: Oxford, Ltd.
Biodiversity in Sub-Saharan Africa and Its Islands (1990). IUCN Species Survival Commission No. 6.
Booth, A. *et al.* (1994). *State of the Environment in Southern Africa*, Harare: SARDC, IUCN and SADC.
Chabwora, H. (1991). *Wetlands: A Conservation Programme for Southern Africa*, Harare: IUCN and SADC.
FAO (1990). *Source Book for the Inland Fishery Resources of Africa*, Rome: FAO.
Funnel, D.C. (1988). 'Water Resources and the Political Geography of Southern Africa: The Case of Swaziland', *Ecoforum*, vol. 19.
Mackinnon, J. *et al.* (eds) (1986). *Managing Protected Areas in the Tropics*, Cambridge: Cambridge University Press.

Moyo, Sam *et al.* (1993). *The Southern African Environment: Profiles of the SADC Countries*, Earthscan Publications.
Report on the Symposium on Wildlife Management in sub-Saharan Africa (1987).
SADC Wildlife Sector (1989). *Report on the SADCC Workshop on Processing and Marketing of Wildlife Products in the Region*, Lilongwe, 13–21 November.
SADC – Environment and Land Management Sector Coordination Unit. *SADC Regional Policy for Environment and Sustainable Development: Equity-Led Growth and Sustainable Development in Southern Africa*, draft for discussion.
SADCC (1991). *Natural Resources and the Environment: Policies and Development Strategy*, Maseru: SADC/ELMS.
UNDP (1994). *Human Development Report 1994*, Delhi: Oxford University Press.
World Bank (1994). *World Development Report: Infrastructure for Development*, Washington, DC: Oxford University Press.
World Development Report (1992). *Development and the Environment*, Oxford University Press.
World Resources Institute (1994). *World Resource 1991–95: A Guide to the Global Environment*, New York: Oxford University Press.
World Resources Report (1994–95). *People and the Environment*, New York: World Resource Institute.

7

Towards a New Political Map of Africa

Arthur S. Gakwandi

During the early 1960s the African people achieved a short but concentrated period of self-realization. New national flags were raised everywhere, embassies were opened in the world's capitals, African Studies centres mushroomed across the globe to encourage favourable interpretations of African history, festivals celebrated black culture, new poems and novels announced the unique humanism and nobility of the black soul as pop music ran ecstatic commentaries on those exciting events of a new era. African economies were buoyant, culturally the continent was resurgent, politically it was self-assertive and socially it was optimistic. It was a period of pride, confidence and high aspiration as the African people showed their determination to take full advantage of the post-war political order, full advantage of the Cold War and full advantage of high-commodity prices in order to make their contribution to world history.

However, within three decades, an atmosphere of gloom had descended on the continent. Economies were in disarray, political crises and civil wars were widespread, skilled labour and capital were taking flight, newspaper reports about Africa were dominated by disasters and calamities and a new disease called *Afro-pessimism* had afflicted the continent.

As the twenty-first century looms on the horizon, African leaders and intellectuals are desperately groping for solutions that will arrest the current drift towards the outer margin of global currents and steer the continent towards the centre of world events. Seminars, workshops and conferences of political leaders, inter-governmental groups of experts, academicians as well as NGOs are all involved in this search which seems to be moving towards a consensus that economic restructuring is the answer. The rough-shod diplomacy of donor countries, the arm-twisting tactics of credit institutions, as well as Africa's own self-abandonment to trading paths that have led to other people's success, are all contributing to the building of this consensus.

This chapter will propose that *political restructuring* of the continent is a more important priority that needs to be addressed before economic restructuring can bring about the desired results. It argues that the main achievements of the African people in this century have been realized through political and cultural convergence and not through *laissez-faire* economic interaction. Finally it puts forward some bold recommendations for a new political framework through which economic and other aspirations of the African people can be realized.

A concerted revolt

When, in 1884, major European powers met in Berlin to parcel out Africa into territorial possessions, they had no idea that the patchwork divisions which they had hurriedly created would, within half a century, form a basis for the emergence of new nation-states. The pressing business of forestalling conflict among the powers themselves did not leave room for indulging in such long-term forecasts. Nor did it leave room for scruples about the likely consequences of such arbitrary demarcations upon the affected human communities. The main agenda, which was the allocation of sizeable estates for economic exploitation to the principal rivals in the scramble, was accomplished with remarkable speed and in an admirable spirit of give and take, thanks to the ample size of the estate that was being shared out.

The fact that within such a short period of time the arbitrary entities created at Berlin were to rebound with claims to the status of nationhood remains one of the amazing phenomena of modern history. By sustaining a claim based on arbitrary territorial frameworks, the African people had resourcefully improvised a weapon with which to assert their will for self-determination. Indisputably, these territorial entities on which the claims were based lacked the heritage of a common language, shared memories, pride in a unique history and other attributes conventionally regarded as prerequisites for the emergence of nation-states. It was therefore a major credit to those mid-century nationalists that they were able to forge expedient solidarity against foreign occupation. The inter-group rapport that went into building this solidarity on a national and international scale was not so much an assertion of common identity as it was an assertion of a desire to get rid of a common enemy.

Only the euphoria of success, however, could have sustained the presumption that the common solidarity forged in the struggle against colonialism had created indissoluble bonds between heterogeneous cultural and social groups. Although Africa's cultures and languages overlap and enjoy certain commonalities, especially at sub-regional level, the differences cannot be wished away or ignored. More than thirty years after independence, the primary consensus needed to provide anchorage for social and economic development remains as elusive as it has ever been. While early Pan Africanists had forged an ideology that played down these differences, second and third-generation African leaders indulged in policies that sharpened these differences. This had led to alarming developments on the continent. The breakdown of central authority in Somalia and Liberia, the destructive civil wars that have crippled Angola, Mozambique and Chad, the threats of secession in Sudan and Zaire as well as the ethnic tensions that abound in many states on the continent or the recent genocide in Rwanda (which actually unfolded as the 7th Pan African Congress was sitting) all call for a re-evaluation of the viability of post-colonial African states and the sanctity of their borders. That sanctity has already received a slap in the face from Eritrea which has shown that there is nothing sacrosanct about existing boundaries. The likelihood that this example will be emulated poses a major challenge to Africa.[1]

There is no better forum for addressing this challenge than in a meeting of the Pan African Congress. Regrettably, the Congress is no longer the influential body that it once was and it is largely the attenuation of its influence that has led to the current dearth of ideas and to recourse to the World Bank and IMF in the hope that they can chart a way out of the present predicament. The centre of the problem does not lie in economics but in politics. Africa's economic stagnation is a result of political instability and not the other way round. The political framework therefore has to be changed so that dynamic, confident and coherent politics are established before economic goals can be pursued meaningfully.

The majority of African states are small, poor, characterized by ethnic conflicts and incapacitated by a host of contradictions that have their origin in the very fact of their arbitrary creation. Their shapes, their sizes and their whimsical boundaries reflect the interests of those who created them. Ten states have each a population of less than one million people. Twelve of them are landlocked. Thirty of them have per capita GDP of less than 500 US dollars. Fifteen of the states can be destabilized by an armed gang of 100 foreign mercenaries, or by a sharp drop in the price of a single commodity on the world market, or by an externally imposed programme of structural reform. There is therefore an urgent need to build strength from a wider solidarity than can be mobilized within the polities as they exist today.

The role of the OAU

The first summit of the Organization of African Unity in 1963 decided not only to legitimize the preposterous colonial boundaries but went even further by declaring them to be inviolable. It is tempting to blame this first generation of African leaders for acquiescing in such an obvious travesty of all known laws of social and political evolution. But we need to recognize that there were no tenable options at that moment. Twenty-two African countries were still under colonial rule and their claim to independence was based on the UN's recently declared principle that each people had a right to self-determination. Any suggestion that the populations of African colonial states were divisible into separate peoples or that the various groups within each state could separately determine their own political destiny would have challenged the very basis on which the claim for African independence was based. Moreover, although the colonial governments were ready to abandon direct control, they each hoped to keep former colonies within their own sphere of influence. It would be naive to imagine that the imperial power would have given their consent to new territorial arrangements in which their interests were not firmly entrenched. Add to this the unfortunate personality factors which had come into play within the leadership of the Pan African Movement between 1958 and 1963 which had created a baleful undercurrent of rivalry and suspicions that could not be resolved quickly, especially in the absence of an institutionalized mechanism for dialogue and compromise. Colonial boundaries therefore had to stay.

Decolonization agenda

For the next quarter-century, decolonization was to remain the dominant issue on the agenda of the Organization of African Unity, overshadowing everything else; and therefore the agreed framework of cooperation could not be tampered with. But now that the task of decolonization is virtually completed, African states can afford to give due attention to other important issues. This does not mean that Pan Africanism should put its programme into the hands of the Organization of African Unity. The agenda of the OAU has never been the same as the agenda of the Pan African Movement. The OAU was a brainchild of Pan Africanism but the former was much more oriented towards addressing the practical problems of inter-state cooperation and less towards rallying the African people around well-defined ideals. Pan Africanism started essentially as a movement of intellectuals: writers, political thinkers, trade unionists and journalists. It became the well-spring of political activism, literary renaissance, industrial action, cultural nationalism and other manifestations of a well-orchestrated rebellion against foreign domination. But the vigour of Pan Africanism's assault on oppression and privilege became vitiated by the palliative of flag independence in many African states; thus giving way to divergence in the pursuit of Pan African goals. The turning point was 1961. Since that time, Pan Africanism has been on two, sometimes parallel, sometimes divergent tracks: the one pursued by African governments which takes the form of official cooperation, the other pursued by free thinkers which since the 1960s has had no well-defined agenda.

The boundary issue

One issue on which divergence is very clear is the issue of boundaries. Throughout the 1950s, Pan Africanism denounced colonial boundaries and called for their dissolution to facilitate unity among African people. Nowhere is this denunciation more explicit than in the final resolutions of the All African People's Conference, in Accra, in 1958. The Conference made the following declaration on frontiers and boundaries:

> Whereas the great mass of African peoples are animated by a desire for unity;
> Whereas the unity of Africa will be vital to the independence of its component units and essential to the security and general well being of the African peoples;
> Whereas the existence of separate states in Africa is fraught with the dangers of exposure to imperialist intrigues and of resurgence of colonialism even after their attainment of independence, unless there is unity among them;
> And whereas the ultimate objective of African nations is a Commonwealth of Free African States; Be it resolved and it is hereby resolved by the All-African Peoples Conference that the Conference;
>
> (a) endorses Pan Africanism and the desire for unity among African peoples;
> (b) declares that its ultimate objective is the evolution of a Commonwealth of Free African States;

(c) calls upon the Independent States of Africa to lead the peoples of Africa towards the attainment of this objective; and
(d) expresses the hope that the day will dawn when the first loyalty of African States will be to an African Commonwealth.[2]

As more and more states gained independence there was a shift of emphasis from unity to cooperation. Pan Africanism was now dominated by diplomats and politicians whose careers and status depended on the existence of independent sovereignty of their states. The All African People's Conference in Tunis in 1960 was not so vociferous on the issue of unity. Instead, it passed a long list of resolutions recommending that independent African states cooperate in a wide range of spheres. In the same forum at Cairo in 1961 the idea of unity was generally played down and replaced with words like cooperation and solidarity in a few narrowly defined spheres. Thus, in the few years between 1958 and 1963 the long-standing Pan African drive for unity had been overturned. No wonder that the Organization of African Unity was established in 1963 after ruling out unity within its charter. Three years after Tunis, the OAU Charter made a 180-degree turn on the issue of boundaries from the position upheld by the Pan African meetings that preceded it. In Article III Part 3, the charter not only upholds the sovereignty and territorial integrity of African states but declares their right to independent existence to be *inalienable*.[3] In other words, the OAU charter calls off the search for political unity.

We have already made an apology for the authors of the OAU charter. But circumstances have now changed and Africa can afford to revisit the whole issue of boundaries.

One of the most compelling reasons for restructuring the geographical boundaries of African states is the urgent need to end the distress of the communities which have been divided by these boundaries. In his *Partitioned Africans*,[4] Professor A.I. Asiwaju has documented the psychological torture and social hardship which the divided nationalities of the continent have had to cope with in response to their forced separation. The best known among such groups are the Somalis who live in Somalia, Ethiopia, Kenya and Djibouti; the Bakongo who are divided between Gabon, Congo, Zaire and Angola; the Masai divided between Kenya and Tanzania, and the Yoruba divided between Nigeria, Benin and Togo. There are numerous other groups mercilessly chopped up in a similar manner. Professor Asiwaju counts no less than 103 cases of nationalities and communities which have been sliced into pieces and scattered across artificial international borders.

Obviously, the answer does not lie in going back to the nineteenth-century political divisions. The answer lies in consolidating existing states into larger, more viable units that will bring each severed community inside one national border. The All African People's Conference sitting in Accra in 1958 took the following stand on this issue. The Conference:

(a) denounces artificial frontiers drawn by imperialist powers to divide the peoples of Africa, particularly those which cut across ethnic groups and divide people of the same stock;
(b) calls for the abolition or adjustment of such frontiers at an early date;
(c) calls upon the independent states of Africa to support a permanent solution to this problem founded upon the true wishes of the people.

Unfinished business

Pan Africanism therefore has an unfinished business with our arbitrary borders which must be addressed. What is being proposed here is one way of tackling this unfinished business. The approach is based on the observation that Africa's cultural boundaries tend to run along lines of latitude rather than those of longitude. This means that there is a broad coincidence between climatic and cultural zones. It is along these imaginary lines of broad cultural differentiation that we have drawn the demarcations of the proposed new states. The Horn of Africa is an exception that could not be fitted into this pattern. For centuries, this region has had close contact with the cultures of the Gulf and the Middle East. This sets it apart from other regions of Sub-Saharan Africa. A separate state has therefore been proposed in the region of the Horn.

The new demarcations proposed in the attached map would achieve the following objectives:

- They would banish the phenomenon of landlocked countries from the continent and thus ease the flow of commercial goods and services between Africa and the rest of the world.
- They would eliminate all existing border disputes by including the disputed areas and the disputant states in one country.
- All divided nationalities would come together once again under one state. The actual demarcation lines would be negotiated to

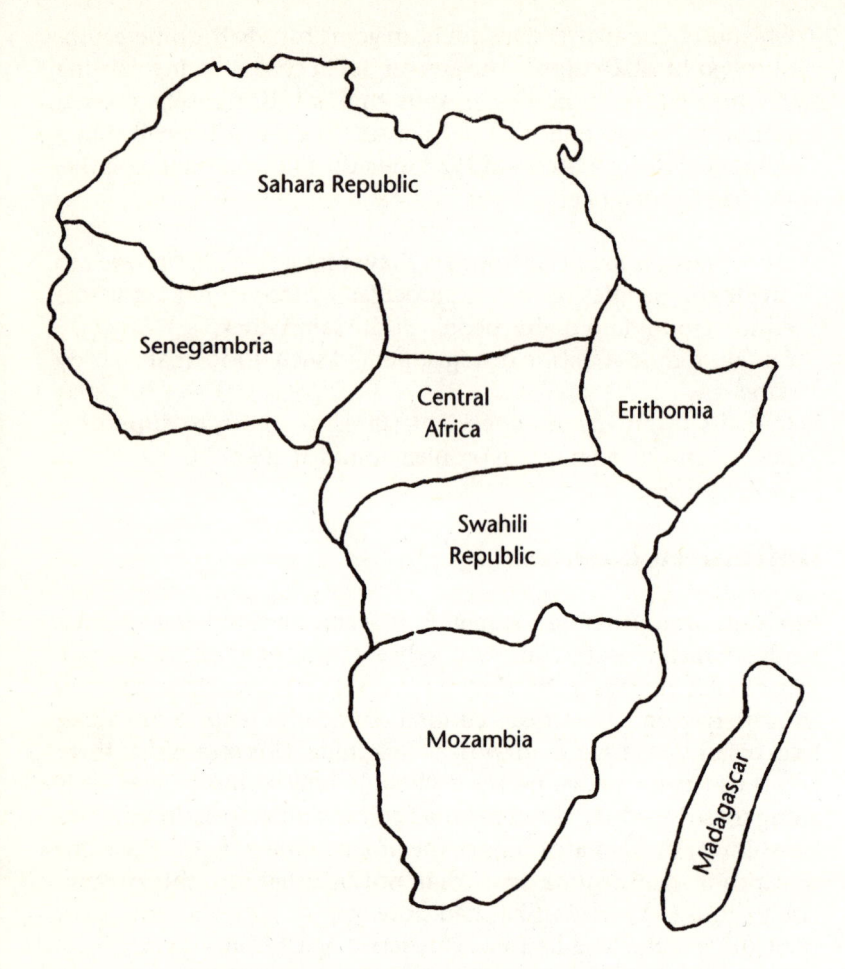

Map 7.1 Proposed New Political Map of Africa

ensure the removal of this piece of human cruelty. Special cases of nomadic groups such as the Tuaregs which could still defy the new borders would be addressed in a special conference.
- All the new states would have an adequate resource base and critical masses of population that would form a solid basis for development.
- Ethnic tensions now existing within states would be eased considerably as threats of domination by some small groups over some still smaller groups would disappear. The conditions for the survival of warlords and tyrants would also disappear as the

ethnic base of such power monopolies would no longer be tenable. Democracy would thus have a better chance to grow and flourish as the new complexity would give greater latitude for cultural fusion.
- The newly consolidated states would be able to command greater power and respect in the world than the existing states are able to do. This would create a new climate of confidence in Africa and dispel the self-doubt that has lingered among African communities since the advent of colonialism. The quest for self-reliant and self-sustaining development would gain a fresh momentum.
- The reduction of inter-ethnic tensions would considerably reduce the crying shame of some twelve million refugees who would now find accommodation.

The OAU's basic strategy for pursuing unity remains different from that originally advocated by the Pan African Movement. The OAU has adopted the model which holds that market forces can bring about political unity. It is thus envisaged that free movement of labour, capital and services will create a merger of markets which will in turn foster a common social and political outlook. This paradigm may well work where there is a solid political foundation on which economic integration is built step by step. But economic integration cannot be promoted in an area where the units are in a state of political disintegration. There is therefore a need to tackle the unity agenda from both the political and economic perspectives. What is needed is a political manifesto that is equivalent to the Lagos Plan of Action. Such a manifesto would set the pace to which economic cooperation could be marched.

The countries of Western Europe had to adopt the paradigm of market forces because of the fierce exclusionist ethos on which the nation-states of the West were built. Such exclusionist attitudes do not exist in Africa except perhaps along the Mediterranean coast. But even along the Mediterranean coast the common Arab culture renders national differences less important. Africans are accustomed to living with neighbours who believe in different gods and who speak different languages. Political allegiance is something that has historically been negotiable. There would therefore be no hostility to the idea of merging existing African states for the purpose of making them politically and economically stronger.

Notes

1. See Ali Mazrui, 'The Bondage of Boundaries' in *The Economist*, 24 September 1993.
2. 'The OAU Charter' (OAU Information Department).
3. Colin Legum (1965). *Pan Africanism*, New York: Frederick Praeger.
4. A.I. Asiwaju (1985). *Partitioned Africans*, University of Lagos Press.

Part IV

Facing the Future

8

Science and Technology as a Solution to Africa's Underdevelopment

Yoweri K. Museveni

The major developments in science and technology have taken place in the last five hundred years. This period, unfortunately for the Africans, coincided with their enslavement and transportation to the New World followed by the colonization of Africa in the nineteenth century. The slave trade robbed us of most of our active population and colonialism subordinated us physically, structurally and mentally to our colonizers.

It is due to these circumstances that Africa missed the boat of science and technology. To make it even worse, the science and technology we had developed before these misfortunes overtook us was abandoned and we became dependent on the manufactures of our enslavers and colonizers.

Our ancestors made their own tools, weapons and clothing; they grew enough food to feed themselves; they had their own medicines; they were, therefore, self-sufficient communities, albeit at a low technological level. Today, Africans depend on others for their tools, weapons, medicines, clothing and increasingly, food. What claim can we make to be really independent or even viable in these circumstances?

One of the major contradictions is that a continent that is so generously endowed with natural resources is so poor and backward. We sing songs of praise for these endowments of ours and those who have mastered science and technology come to Africa with their knowledge and take our resources away for a song; for a song, because we are unable to add value to our raw materials. These same materials are sold back to us at great cost because the products of today are knowledge-intensive and it is because we lack that knowledge that we pay so dearly for goods whose original source is Africa.

Societies that do not master science and technology will either be slaves, surviving at the mercy and sufferance of others, or will perish altogether. Indeed, a futurist cartographer's map of the world of 2025 AD recently appeared in *The Economist*; in that map, only bits of Northern and Southern Africa appeared on that map. In only a short 31 years, most of Africa will economically disappear. The only way we can prevent this tragedy is to begin our scientific and technological revolution now and in an organized and systematic manner.

Some of our leaders have already recognized the need first to incorporate the development of science and technology in their national development plans and secondly, the need for collaboration between African countries in research and development as well as in the commercialization of the results of research.

The Presidential Forum on Science and Technology

In November 1993, President Masire of Botswana hosted the first Presidential Forum on the Management of Science and Technology for Development in Africa, in Gaborone. In July 1994, President Chissano of Mozambique hosted the second Presidential Forum in Maputo.

These fora of the top leadership in Africa are a clear demonstration of their commitment to play their role in the stewardship of science and technology in Africa to effect social and economic development.

Amongst other things, at the Gaborone Presidential Forum, we agreed to establish an autonomous, continent-wide African Foundation for Research and Development (AFRAND) in order to provide an enduring resource base for sustaining development-oriented research in Africa. I sincerely hope that all African leaders will give this institution in the making, all the support they are capable of, so that Africa can move into the scientific and technological age.

Education

In order to build communities responsive and capable of internalizing science, we must concentrate on the conquest of illiteracy. Literacy is the key to the creation of a scientifically and technologically conscious population. Our friends in South-east Asia have made tremendous strides in the direction of literacy and have consequently managed to create this consciousness and to master science. The way forward, therefore, is to concentrate on primary education and we, in Uganda, are aiming at the establishment of universal and compulsory primary education for all by the year 2003. The programme itself will start but our scientists and engineers, who are not few and some of whom are very highly trained, lack the confidence and the will to carry out the scientific and technological revolution on our continent. In many cases, they have not been motivated and facilitated enough to be of use to this continent. Something must be done and done quickly to put our skilled human resources to work. I do not think that the UK had more scientists than Uganda presently has, when Stevenson invented the steam-engine. I do not think France had more scientists than Uganda has today when de Lesseps built the Suez Canal; or that the United States had more scientists than Uganda has today when the African labour of the diaspora built the Panama Canal. It is just a question of organization and confidence.

It is true that scientists and engineers cannot do their work unless there is stability, peace and tranquillity. It is true that most African countries have gone through a period of turbulence these last thirty years. However, it is also true that many discoveries, especially in the military field, are made during periods of turbulence and war. So our skilled people cannot continuously cry wolf and stay away from their continent on account of instability, but instead they must combat it. At the same time the instability should stimulate them to invent or learn techniques that can help their communities during that time and afterwards.

I understand there are around 100,000 highly trained African scientists, engineers, doctors and managers outside Africa, mainly in Europe and North America. I am also informed that a similar number of expatriate 'experts' are working in Africa, courtesy of technical assistance programmes. Africa spends about four billion US dollars of the money we borrow and the grants we get, annually, to maintain these expatriates in Africa. If we were to get our own people back, even if they cost us four billion US dollars annually, at least there are many patriots among them who would invest the money here on this continent.

Africa should undertake a major repatriation exercise of our skilled labour especially in the critical areas of science, technology and management. I have heard of several initiatives such as the Distressed and Expatriate Scientists and Scholars from Africa (DESSA) and the African Capability Building Foundation (ACBF) to reclaim these people; but I do not know how much they have achieved to date.

Of course, getting these people back and paying them the salaries they are accustomed to can keep them here; but we cannot get any results if we do not give our scientists and technologists the facilities to carry out research and development.

At the moment, Africa spends 0.4 per cent of gross national product (GNP) on research and development. This amount represents about a tenth of what the already scientifically and technologically developed countries spend on research and development. In actual fact, we should be spending a bigger proportion of our GNP on research and development than those developed countries in order to eventually catch up with them. The UN recently recommended that in order for the developing countries to realize any results from research and development, they must spend, at least, 2 per cent of their GNP on research. What we are now doing is underdosing the patient. This cannot cure the patient; it merely prolongs misery. It is therefore crucial that in our national budgets, we reconsider the importance of research and development in our future struggle for emancipation from our socioeconomic backwardness.

Our research must be problem solving-oriented; it must be relevant to our needs and not esoteric, merely satisfying the intellectual curiosities of our scientists. Both governments and industries which consume the research results must chip in to support research and development. The manufacturers must, to some extent, dictate the kind of research done because we shall rely on them to transform research into products that our people can readily use.

Technological transfers cannot take place between governments for the simple reason that most of the technology available in the developed countries is in private hands. The big concerns have their own research and development departments and this is where most of the action is. The private firms cannot give away their technology or discoveries freely because they are in business and not charity. Under these circumstances, technological transfers are not easy. We must, therefore, endeavour to create our own research capacity in Africa.

We do not have enough material and human resources in our individual countries to make much headway in research and development. Yet if we were to pool our regional resources and cooperate in research we can achieve something. For this, we need the political will and I am confident that the commitment which some of us undertook at the Gaborone Forum will be adopted on a continent-wide scale.

Promoting African products

In some respects, we Africans, are our own enemies. We easily make pious declarations of intent but that is where we normally stop. In my view scientific and technological research cooperation can precede regional political integration. It seems to me that scientists can work together better than the politicians can. We, the leaders, should facilitate them to get on with their work.

In October 1993, I passed through the city of Calcutta, India, on my way to Japan. I was being driven in an Indian car with the ambassador, moving around the city. All the cars I saw were of the same make and all of them white. These cars may not be the best cars on the world markets; but they are capable of moving people around. The Indians quite deliberately make and use their own products before they look for markets elsewhere. In Africa, there is a tendency to shun home-made goods in preference to those made outside. It is true that we are all running liberal economies; we are all free marketeers and the best goods capture the market. However, certain allowances should be made to give room to our manufacturers in Africa to come up with their products on the market and sell them. This will be the basis for the improvement of their products. Our people should be educated about the need to support their own scientific and technological revolution through the consumption of goods that are a product of home-grown research. Our friends outside the continent who wish us to develop have to be flexible in order to encourage African industrial products to come to the market.

Science and technology are not mysterious. The laws of nature are already in place. We Africans are also made in the image of God, the top scientist. Our young people should be introduced to science and technology in a way they can comprehend so that they do not give up and grow to consider them mysterious. Science and technology should be domesticated and internalized. If other human beings have succeeded in doing so and if we had succeeded before 1500, we can do it again. Science is nothing but understanding our environment and ourselves. At Gaborone, I pointed out that new scientific knowledge is not inventions but mere discoveries. The real scientist is God. He is the one responsible for bonding of atoms and molecules to compounds and elements respectively. The developed societies are those that are enterprising enough to know these gifts of God and use them to solve their problems. The under-developed societies are those that do not know about the gifts of God and suffer in deprivation in complete ignorance of these natural supports to life.

Amongst Africans of the diaspora, we have some concentrated skills and exposure to science and technology in the developed countries of the world, especially in Europe and North America. I call upon our brothers and sisters of the diaspora who possess these skills to organize themselves, even as individuals, to assist us in research and development in our scientific and technological revolution.

9

Pan Africanism, Democracy, Social Movements and Mass Struggles

Ernest Wamba-dia-Wamba

The place of Pan Africanism in world history

> ... the evil system of colonialism and imperialism arose and throve with the enslavement of Negroes and the trade in Negroes, and it will surely come to its end with the complete emancipation of the Black people.
>
> Mao Ze-dong.

We are in the epoch of so-called 'rapid globalization'. It took about 500 years to come to maturation: from the world-wide primitive accumulation which led to the rise of capitalism in Europe to the extension of capitalism to the most remote corners of our planet.[1] Resistances to this accumulation of wealth and extension of capitalism had to be destroyed through wars of conquest, genocides, enslavement, colonizations, enclosures, looting, deporting, murdering, 'low-intensity warfare', violent destruction of self-sustaining survival systems, violence against women (mass rapes, slave breeding farms, forced sterilization, sex tourism), 'imperial diseases' and so on. Still resistances continue. African people, black people,[2] despite their crucial founding contribution as slaves, as gifts to capital, as colonial and neocolonial forced labourers, have lived this period principally as victims and subordinates, that is, as a legitimate prey: from non-people (speaking machines-cum-commodities) to sub-people (that is, a third of a person in the first US constitution) to dominated people.

Indeed, the attempts to justify the resulting unequal system gave rise to the idea of classifying people of the world by race and then setting them in a social hierarchy. The white supremacist doctrine of civilisation was built on it. For a long time, Black people were confronted with a 'common' fate (first racism, then colonialism) which forced them to accept a 'common identity'[3] – of which the negritude movement, for example, sang.

The cost of resisting such an imposed fate was heavy. Some mothers prefered to kill their children than to see them sold; some refused to bear children for sale. *Lemba Kangaism*[4] – doctrine and practices for protecting the community – for example, arose in the area of Kongo society devastated by slave trading. Escaped slaves, here and there in the Americas, staged maroonian revolts.[5] These profiles of courage are often left in historical silences. The first successful slave revolutionary victory, under the leadership of Toussaint L'Ouverture, took inspiration from *Lemba Kangaism* in its first anthem: *Kanga Bafioti, Kanga Mindele* – Protect the weak and tie up (arrest) the white! Abolitionist historical self-celebrations have been marginalized in written histories.[6]

Ultimately, Pan Africanism, as a form of global consciousness – the realization that no black person will be free until all black people are free – emerged precisely to confront the old race-based global consciousness which underlined capitalist expansionism. It aimed at defending human equality, human rights against racial discrimination and at organizing the process of liberation of black people from subordination world-wide. Any thought or doctrine is always determined by that against which it arises and thus it is also limited by it.

The horizon of Pan Africanism, was to develop into a form of internationalism and emancipatory politics. The latter starts from the conviction that things are not to remain so because they are so; people may live differently than they presently live. It is rooted in a break from submissive consciousness in favour of a political consciousness which is an active, prescriptive attitude to reality, that is, politics as a prescriptive invention.[7]

Since about 1989, a world-wide consensus seems to exist, especially around social movements, on the need to expand democratic rights and extend to all people all the human rights. A new global consciousness is rising, one which discredits the old one built on racial, religious, gender or cultural discriminations. This is a significant development,[8] though doubts still prevail. The ancestors to this modern global consciousness have not always been consistent in upholding human equality and rejecting the subordination of black people. The secular traditions of the French and American revolutions did not necessarily recognize the major contribution by Toussaint L'Ouverture in the struggle for human liberty. The Enlightenment philosophies, for example, could not have seen him as an associate. The much acclaimed Condorcet and Diderot, for example, did not favour rapid transition to the end of slavery.[9] The visions of the global class unity of the socialist and communist movements often failed to 'deminoritize' black labourers. Even communist parties held the view that colonialism was a 'short-cut for the development of productive forces'. Consequently Pan Africanists such as Aime Cesaire[10] and George Padmore[11] had to resign from those types of parties. The world community of believers in Christianity and Islam did not consistently fight against the race-based social hierarchy, despite protesting voices such as that of Las Casas. 'Humanist' priests in Kongo kingdom demanded only that slaves be baptized before boarding the slaving ships – one of these was even named *Jesus*! Placed at the bottom of social hierarchy (some theologians even speculated that blacks had no soul), black people were denied civilization, culture and history.[12] Their experiences were said to have no educational value, no truth value and no knowledge value. It is principally to provoke the break with submissive consciousness, on the part of some Africans believing in their being useless to 'humanity', that people like Cheikh Anta Diop worked so hard to set the record of African civilizations straight.[13]

The notion of a racial hierarchy in intelligence and creativity became most influential when European empires were at their greatest expansion (1890–1940). Of course, the fact that imperial museums were filled with African artefacts and that acclaimed European artists such as Picasso copied some Congolose art forms, for example, did not stop the imperialist apologists from proclaiming the African artistically inferior. The brutal colonial expropriation of land and labour was justified on the basis of the hierarchy. Western powers portrayed themselves as the purveyors of 'civilization' and thus the territorial occupation of Africa was done in the name of 'bringing civilization to Dark Africa'.

It was during this period also that concrete organizational forms of Pan Africanism (for example, the Pan African Conference/Congresses) took shape. Despite colonial conditions in Africa, Africans participated actively. Panda's party, Union Congolaise (1919–30), for example, participated in the 3rd Pan African Congress which took place in Brussels in 1921.[14] Two other Congolese, from the Belgian Congo, went to Jamaica, in 1928, to meet with Marcus Garvey. A small Pan Africanist movement, led by Jackson, organized an anti-colonial struggle in the Belgian Congo. The maroons' struggles and successful resistances, slave victories, anti-slavery movements and struggles, the abolition of slavery itself, and so on were not successful in abolishing white supremacist ideology and practices highly supported by European imperialism. The complete freeing of Africa became viewed as the condition for the abolition of the black person's bondage.

Certainly, anti-colonial national liberation movements gave tremendous impetus to the vision of racial equality. Through its 5th Congress (1945), Pan Africanism made important contributions in advancing the victory of those movements in Africa. The establishment of a global system of nations – including African ones – all with equal legal standing (ending the second-class world citizenship); the expansion of literacy and national systems of education; formal renunciation, in many national and international declarations, of discrimination by race, ethnicity, religion or gender and an extension of principles of non-discrimination into many new areas; the changing social conditions of women and the rise of feminist critiques of society giving rise to a range of debates not only about gender discrimination but about the nature of human interdependence generally, leading to new claims of human rights; technical advances of modern telecommunications[15] and the end of Cold War: all these things have considerably undermined the race-based global consciousness. Pan Africanist struggles and cultural (arts, music, dance, etc.) and scientific productions have had an impact as well.

Having been obtained on the basis of 'defeat through victory',[16] political independence in Africa was a limited victory. It reproduced, with minor changes, the colonial partition of Africa and the imperial restructuring of Africa's economy. However, the burial of apartheid brings to an end the struggle for formal political independence in Africa. Until recently, apartheid, a system exclusively based on the 'minoritization' of blacks, echoing the race-based global consciousness, was seemingly undefeatable. At the height of the struggles US imperial democrats and most of its Western allies refused to endorse the UN condemnation of apartheid as 'a crime against humanity', settling for the weak 'gross violation of human rights'. Indeed, the general reluctance to view the transatlantic slave trade as a human holocaust and the continued resistance against the demands for reparations for both the transatlantic slave trade and colonialism (based on unjust wars of conquest and thus having no moral or legal justification), means that the 'minoritization' of black people on the basis of race remains active in the global consciousness. The recent retreat in the pursuit of racial equality in the imperial democratic US is well-known:

> Despite pervasive litanies about Latin America's *colour blind racial democracy*, blatant discrimination continues to plague descendants of the ten millions African slaves who were brought to toil on the plantations and mines of the New World. Such a discrimination

is compounded by a nearly universal denial of black heritage and identity, even countries with large black populations, have effectively rendered blacks invisible.[17]

While still being squeezed through structural adjustment programmes and debt-servicing, Africa, especially Sub-Saharan Africa, is increasingly marginalized and sinking into absolute poverty as it continues to transfer capital abroad.[18] This state of affairs calls for revitalization of the historical role of Pan Africanism.

World context of democratization

Democratization or re-democratization has to be conceptualized at the level of the whole planet Earth. It involves global relations of power and not just those inside a specific territory. It is good to have full democracy in a reservation; the most crucial thing is to abolish democratically the reservation itself. Democracy has to be grasped from the point of view of its entire history. The experiences of a great part of humanity have been bypassed in systematizing the theory of democracy. When the majority of the world's people were reduced to colonized and neocolonized sub-humans, initiative and creativity in relation to democracy were made an affair of the few. Imperial democrats have been responsible, in many ways, for growth, development and maintenance of authoritarianism in many parts of the world – often in the name of protecting 'the free world'.

A democracy erected on the basis of colonial conquests, that confines the indigenous people (such as the Aborigines in Australia or the indigenous Indians in the Americas) in reservations, must be criticized from the point of view of those victims. People without rights in those democracies constitute a radical witness of those democracies' limitations. In my opinion, the ancient Greek democracy – *agora* democracy – is comparable to the *Mbongi* (fireplace) palaver;[19] though the *agora* excluded women. You cannot label as 'uncivilized' those people whose way of life contains elements recognized as civilized in your own culture. National conferences, at least in some African Francophone countries, did take inspiration from experiences of African palaver.

Social movements (old and new), including pro-democracy movements around the world, are demanding for consistent democracy, a democracy-from-below. Imperial democrats act democratically in some parts of the world and at the same time support all kinds of authoritarianism elsewhere. The Haiti 1990 election, for example, is a radical witness: a broad mass democracy-from-below movement led to the election of Father Jean-Bertrand Aristide (1990). The US imperial democrats, eager to see liberal democracy in Cuba, were reluctant to give unqualified support to President Aristide and the Haitian democratic forces until it became impossible for Haiti's tyrannical generals to continue to hold on to power.

As a rule of the people by the people for the people, historical experiences of democracy have often been based on a concept of people which excluded some other people. The challenge for world social movements is to see that all of humanity is constituted as one community of people. Global democratization must aim at eradicating situations of 'minoritization' of parts of humanity. Its aims must include the creation of a political space of general equality around which multiple and diverse individuals, peoples, groups, races, classes, gender and so on, may contend in the pursuit of their respective interests. The extension and the centrality of human rights in this challenge, has led people in a wide range of countries to feel free to criticize the state, the principal force, which tampers with various human rights rather than protecting them.[20]

There will not be a meaningful democracy in one corner of the world when the whole world is fundamentally undemocratic. Imperial democrats, now regrouped in the gang of the G7, and other Northern democracies, consume more than two-thirds of the world resources. No normative imperative is rising in those countries to democratize the situation, that is, to shift power relations in favour of the redistribution of world wealth at all levels. Some level of material empowerment is necessary to compete democratically and effectively. Schemes being put in place: from structural adjustment programmes (welfarist aid rather than productive or strategical one),[21] to GATT decisions or the World Trade Organisation still aim at squeezing the remaining one-third of the world's resources out of the poor. Africa is now sending more capital to the centres of global capitalism than the aid it is receiving, intensifying its decline into absolute poverty. The UN system, as organized for the world conjuncture of post-1945 – already obsolete – is tending towards becoming a machinery for the New World (Dis)Order.

Rethinking democracy

Democratization is creativity itself and not just a model to be applied to a territory. The imperialism of dominant paradigms, concerning democracy as well as development, must be challenged. Western democracies (imperial democracies) should not be allowed to have a monopoly on democracy. The entire range of historical experiences of peoples, movements and groups who have fought for democracy and peace must be taken into account. Imperial powers are now portraying themselves as the guardians of world peace and democracy and as the best promoters and defenders of democracy and human rights. The starting point of emancipatory politics is that all people think (every person thinks). Dominant paradigms imply that few people have the right to ask questions for themselves while the others (often Africa, Latin America and South Asia) must disarm themselves of the right to ask those questions for themselves.[22] The dominated person is the one on whom and at the expense of whom, dominant paradigms exercise effect, blocking his/her right of creativity and innovation. Each time, by whom, for whom, how and for what purpose are questions which must be asked about any paradigm. The instruments of democracy (scope, forms of representations, types of elections, form/regime of state, and so on) must be subordinated to the fact that the human rights of every person and peoples must be upheld.

The history of democracy is *precarious*. Advances and deepening of democratization may be followed by retreats. There are signs of retreat in Western democracies. While their countries have become internationalized or multinationalized, through immigration laws they are practising a form of national cleansing. Increasingly they are unable to deal democratically with 'minorities'. Blinded by capitalist triumphalism, lessons from the collapse of socialist states as far as democracy is concerned (namely consistent recognition, tolerance for and respect of multiple differences), are not learnt. Western values are presented as uniquely universal and so-called particularist values are fought against.[23] The development of techno-bureaucracy has brought a rule by experts in all domains, restricting political discussions and decisions.[24] A gap is growing between hyper-specialized and esoteric techno-science on the one hand and citizen's knowledge on the other. Knowledgeable people have more rights than ignorant citizens. Yet there is a frightening retreat from any desire and need to democratize knowledge. If the community is unable to control its knowledge, as it is said in Kongo society, the community is at the mercy of the few 'sorcerers'.

With the protracted character of the world economic crisis, a tendency has developed to reduce politics to economics; democracy is reduced to market economy and the economy becomes the sole permanent political problem. This is the other side of developmentalism in countries of the South. Society is increasingly divided on an unequal basis: the haves and have-nots, those who have the right to live and those who live by dying little by little.

Talks of the 'end of history' are an indication of the collapse of great aspirations for the future. There is a profound crisis in the revolutionary project which is expressing itself in a real intellectual abasement and powerlessness in conceiving great ideas. The healthy conflict of ideas is being reduced to conflict of interests or racial ethnocentrism. Democratic institutions (parties, pressure groups, etc.) are already showing signs of decay. Great problems of civilizations, including the threat to the life process *per se*, posed by industrial civilization are not seen as priority problems for public debates.

The military and civil society

With reference to Cheikh Anta Diop's typology of states[25] in world history, the existing system of states was born out of conquest. The political independence movements in colonial states born out of conquest did not completely transform these. The articulation between military and civilian power has always favoured the military one. This factor has profound implications for democratization. How can the articulation be reversed in favour of civilian power? The defeated states, in 1945, which were forbidden to arm themselves are now rearming themselves. While it is true that liberalization (marketism) is not the answer to all problems of human rights (as the Ejercito Zapatista de Liberation Nacional (EZLN) in Peru shows), armed struggles have not necessarily led to consistent democracy.

The Cold War ended, which was a good thing for democratization. Nevertheless, it remains to be seen how we can effectively deal with its legacy, that is, its extensive machinery and militants – the Mobutus, the Eyademas and other dictators and warlords in Africa. This challenge is analogous to the situation in South Africa: the apartheid legacy will be a major challenge for democratic struggles.

The status quo and democracy

The world is in real motion. Forces of consistent democracy and those of the status quo are contending. A new global consciousness, favouring the first camp, is rising. It stands against racial discrimination: the success of post-apartheid non-racial democracy in South Africa and that of resolving the Chiapas question based on the discrimination of Maya native population will be positive developments. It stands against religious discrimination: democracy will be challenged by the outcome of the struggle against fundamentalism (in Algeria, ex-Yugoslavia, and so on). It stands against ethnic discrimination: whether in Rwanda, Burundi or elsewhere; the challenge is to democratically build a multi-ethnic state. It stands against gender discrimination: the democratic challenge here may be to come up with a new theory/conception/practice of love with dignity and equal respect as the basis of the best interdependent relationship between man and woman at all levels.

The de-minoritization of peoples, groups and the recognition of full individual rights is ultimately a form of emancipatory politics against the submissive consciousness of accommodation to the violation of human rights world-wide. Pan Africanism must internalize these gains to be able to become a truly emancipatory political movement.

Africa: democracy and second independence

For the last five hundred years which it has taken for the present planetarian epoch to come to maturation, Africa has been under siege. Centuries of international slave trade were followed by economies of predation and formal colonization. For a long time, most (if not all) of the people of Africa were not people at all; they were commodities often obtained by storming villages. African 'mercantilists' who emerged through the process did not feel the labour hunger European mercantilists felt.[26] They were selling abroad the strategic elements of the production process in exchange for commodities which were essentially irrelevant for the local development of production. Their counterpart European mercantilists were putting African slaves into the production process in the so-called New World.[27] In this atmosphere, it was difficult for the remaining Africans to relate freely among themselves.

Institutions of survival which developed under those circumstances, from the *Mbongi* palaver to the *Lemba Kangaism*, in the Kongo area for example, are not well known. Histories produced on the basis of paradigmatic silence – the notion that uncivilized people know nothing or only Europeans 'discover' things – don't give any account of those experiences. They are only available in rapidly diminishing oral traditions.

Colonial rules, imposed by force, were based on the cultural justification that Africans were not full human beings. Their institutions were defamed and studied only to enhance the colonial grip on the African people ('indirect rule' which was in fact very direct). The colonial partition of Africa blocked the process of *Africanization* (various people increasingly coming into contact, and relating to each other) of African peoples which was developing. In this regard, by reproducing, with minor changes, the colonial partition of Africa, the OAU is a continuation of the Berlin conference.

With the gradual (though sometimes sudden) break of social ties provoked by the capitalist privatization of property, many people have lost the secure sources of their means of life, no matter how insufficient these were, and have become reduced to lives of unspeakable poverty and misery. Until very recently, in countries of Africa, community ties (kinship, collective and so on) were the main form of social security for most people. The privatization of clan land through enclosures without compensation introduced by colonial economies of predation accelerated the breaking of those ties. The most enduring social tie now under extreme pressure of being broken is the family itself (the community family or 'extended family' as well as the nuclear one). Its material basis is increasingly destroyed, throwing children on to the street which has become their only 'social security'.

Even after political independence, African economies continued to be based on forced labour (labour-power paid below its value) making it necessary to reproduce or create new forms of bondage (clientelism, etc.) as sources of people's means of life. The process of individualization tends, thus, to be limited. Demands for liberal democracy remained limited to urban environments and limited social categories. Mass struggles tended to be based on common identity and demands for group interests and rights rather than individual rights.

Models of democracies, proposed by the departing decolonizing colonial states, failed to take root. Dominant myths serving as paradigms of acts which emerged through the mass struggles for national independence and self-determination were all based on and emphasized common identity, interests, rights *vis-à-vis* the permanent threat of an outside enemy. These included: the West as an enemy and as a model to aspire to; cultural identity to be reasserted under permanent siege; independence not as a project of continuous struggle but as a time of victorious celebration; development as a pretext for mass political demobilization and aspiration to consumerism rather than a vision for mass political remobilization; liberation as a symbolic call rather than a construction of a rational conception and reasonable vision of the world. Democracy as political pluralism appeared as a threatening anarchy. Cold War polarizations reinforced this global consciousness. The break with early postcolonial experiences of multi-partyism was thus seen as an advance – where this happened more or less freely.

In some cases such as Congo-Zaire, the possibility of a people's sovereignty appeared threatening to the Western Cold War powers. Lumumba and other militants who stood firm in favour of people's controlled national sovereignty had to be eliminated.[28] The Congolese became unable to relate to themselves freely and practice democracy. Through Western power- inspired (the US especially) assassinations, Western powers instigated secessions and coups d'état; the people's sovereignty was assassinated and state power was entrusted in the hands of pro-Western Cold War militants (Mobutu and his Binza group). They 'abused the Congolese-Zairean state sovereignty to meet the demands of foreigners morbidly obsessed with the threat of communism'[29] in Congo-Zaire. Mass struggles developed and were focused around the demand for a Second Independence, that is, the resurrection, as it were, of the people's sovereignty. Mass armed insurrections by the supporters of Pierre Mulele, protracted students' movement struggles (through marches, riots, and so on), workers' strikes (often illegal), in the circumstances of the Cold War, made the state even more repressive: repression became the very core of government's policy. Freedom and human rights of the dissenters and critics were grossly abused with impunity. A single party state/regime became, ultimately, the institutional framework for repression as state policy.

Various types of social movements came to the fore after the end of the Cold War and the formal acceptance, by the regime in place, of multi-partyism. These included: veterans of the struggles against state interference in music and other art forms; forces against misuses/abuses of the Bible to justify gender oppression – specifically led by the Female Protestant Theologians' Association; struggles against arbitrary taxes at the market led by market women's associations; struggles against bureaucrats' land enclosures led by *la solidarite paysanne*; religious struggles for independent churches against state-coopted ones; struggles for independent student associations against one-party youth sections; struggles against one-party women sections; struggles for a second-party movement; struggles for a free press and mass media; struggles for the autonomy of magistrates led by the advocate association, and more. All these struggles and movements aim at the reconstruction of society on the basis of a profound transformation of the state in favour of one which respects the proper articulation between the common interest (public) and the proper (private) interest.[30] To achieve this, it became clear that the various protagonists had to come together in a national conference to first empower themselves as a people capable of exercising national sovereignty while drawing the contours of a new state and a new society. However the local, still existing, Cold War machinery and its militants have almost blocked the advance of the democratization process in Zaire.

In a number of countries of Africa, democracy has been reduced to multi-partyism. When elections did take place, on that basis, they brought minor reforms in the functioning of the state. A vibrant civil society is needed for a real political pluralism to take place.

Africa is experiencing almost all the problems confronted by world democracy movements: violation of individual human rights, religious fundamentalist exclusivism, ethnic discrimination/oppression (even genocide as in Rwanda), threat of military coups d'état, racial discrimination/domination, loss, erosion, or usurpation of national sovereignty, gender discrimination/oppression, economic exploitation, foreign domination, civil wars, state terrorism, state non-accountability, intolerance, negative values, and so on. There is no real forum in which African people involved in the struggles to confront these problems can exchange their experiences. That is why Pan African structures of democratic empowerment and independence of states must be worked out. They are important for the deepening of the democratization process, the democratization of Pan Africanism itself and the process of unification of Africa. Post-colonial states have continued to make it very difficult for African people to constantly interact and relate with each other. Pan Africanism must bring together those forces, inside each country of Africa, which is active in making political pluralism a reality. It will be one way of contending with the pro-imperialist NGOs aiming at dominating civil society in African countries.

Conclusion

The world is in a rising motion: no clarity of a single vision is emerging after the dissolution of socialism. Democratization and re-democratization are about the need to recognize and respect the multiple differences which characterize our humanity. The unity of humanity must be achieved under the banner of multiplicity and avoidance of one-sidedness. The deepening of democratization in each country in Africa and the democratic opening of African countries' 'borderlines' (through various ways, including telecommunications) will allow African people to interact and democratically relate to themselves. This process will allow African people not only to achieve and control national sovereignty but to be able to control the continent and its resources. Pan Africanism must root itself in that process so that its vision can become enriched and popular.

Notes

1. The issue is well examined by Edgar Morin and A.B. Kern, *Terre-Patrie* (Paris: Editions du Soleil, 1993).
2. 'African People, Black People', expression inspired by Mongo Beti's review: *Peuples Noirs – Peuples Africains*.
3. Theme developed by Patrick Manning in his *Songs of Democracy: the World from 1989 to 1991*, forthcoming.
4. John M. Janzen, *Lemba, 1650–1930*, New York and London: Garland Publishing, Inc., 1982.
5. C.L.R. James, *A History of Pan African Revolt*, Washington, DC: Drum and Spear Press, 1969.
6. This important theme of paradigmatic silence in historiography is being thoroughly investigated by Jacques Depelchin.
7. For details on emancipatory politics, see E. Wamba-dia-Wamba 'Democracy, Multipartyism and Emancipative Politics in Africa: The Case of Zaire' in *Africa Development*, vol. XVIII, no. 4 (1993), pp. 95–118.
8. For details, see Manning, *Songs of Democracy*.
9. According to a book, *Les Miseres des Lumieres* by Louis Salamolins, brought to my attention by Jacques Depelchin (personal correspondence).
10. See his *Lettre a Maurice Thorez* (Paris: Presence Africaine, 1956).
11. George Padmore, *Pan Africanism or Communism?*, London: Dennis Dobson, 1956.
12. G.W.F. Hegel, *Lectures on the Philosophy of World History: Introduction*, Cambridge: Cambridge University Press, 1975.
13. See his work of synthesis, *Civilization or Barbarism* (New York: Lawrence Hill Books, 1991).
14. Kalubi M'Kola, *De Paul Panda a Simon Kimbangu* (Kinshasa: Editions Betras, 1982).
15. Details in Manning, *Songs of Democracy*.
16. Irungu Houghton, *Defeat through Victory: Two Case Studies of African Nationalist Movements: Kenya 1940s to 1969 and Zimbambwe 1960s to 1988* (Dar-es-Salaam: MA Dissertation in History, UDSM, 1991).

17. 'The Black Americas: 1492–1992', special issue of *Report on the Americas*, vol. XXV, no. 4 (February 1992), p. 15.
18. Mary Chinery-Hesse, 'Poverty Alleviation in Developing Countries, with particular reference to Africa'; a keynote address made at the Conference on Social (In) Security and Poverty as Global Issues, Maastricht, 5 March 1994.
19. E. Wamba-dia-Wamba, 'Experiences of Democracy in Africa: Reflections on the Practices of Communalist Palaver as a Method of Resolving Contradictions Among the People', *Philosophy and Social Action*, vol. XII, no. 2 (April–June 1986), pp. 19–29.
20. Again, for details, see Manning, *Songs of Democracy*.
21. The Marshall Plan for post-1945 Europe and aid given to defeated Japan, after 1945, constitute cases of strategical types of aid.
22. Mamousse Diagne, 'Contribution a'une critique du principe des paradigmes dominants' in Joseph Ki-Zerbo (ed.), *La Natte des Autres: Pour un Developpement Endogne en Afrique*, Dakar: CODESRIA, 1992, pp. 109–19.
23. Jeremy Seabrook, 'On the Dangers of Western Fundamentalism', *Philosophy and Social Action*, 18 March 1992, pp. 27–31.
24. Edgar Morin and A.B. Kern, *Terre-Patrie*, Paris: Editions du Soleil, 1993.
25. Cheikh Anta Diop, *Civilization or Barbarism* (New York: Lawrence Hill Books), Chap. 8.
26. William A. Darity, Jr, 'Mercantilism, Slavery and the Industrial Revolution', *Research in Political Economy*, vol. 5, JAI Press, Inc., 1982, pp. 1–21.
27. Today, members of the African ruling classes keep resources in their accounts abroad rather than invest them at home. Their counterparts in the West put their resources through the World Bank structures to get more money through schemes of debt-servicing of developing countries.
28. Madeleine G. Kalb, *The Congo Cables: The Cold War in Africa – From Eisenhower to Kennedy*, New York: Macmillan Publishing Co., Inc., 1982.
29. E. Wamba-dia-Wamba, 'National Reconciliation in Zaire: Reasons for the Impasse', *CODESRIA Bulletin*, no. 2, 1993, pp. 10–13.
30. This articulation has been at the core of democratic thought since Pericles, according to Jacques Ranciere, *Aux Bords du Politique*, Paris: Editions Osiris, 1990.

10

Pan Africanism in the Twenty-First Century

Horace Campbell

Introduction

The thrust of this contribution is to reflect on how the spirit of redemption and emancipation can be harnessed to make a decisive impact on humanity in the twenty-first century. The victories of the African peoples in rolling back the frontiers of colonial domination must be tempered by the realities of the conditions of the African at home and abroad. The elections and transition process in South Africa in 1994 encapsulated the strengths and weaknesses of the liberation process of this century. It is because of the changed political conditions for the African in the context of reorganized imperialism that the question of liberation needs to be reconceptualized.

In the call for the 7th Pan African Congress that was held in Kampala, Uganda, 3–8 April 1994, the International Preparatory Committee hoped to maintain the old spirit of the broad nature of the Pan African Movement of the past century. This meeting, the third of its kind to be held since the All African People's Conference in 1957, was open to all shades of opinion, groups and individuals in the Pan African world. The broad theme of the Congress was Pan Africanism: Facing the Future in Unity, Social Progress and Democracy. The conference organizers had to find ways to harmonize the direction of the 7th Pan African Congress with the Congresses which are going on in the streets, valleys, villages and communities all across the Pan African world.

The broad themes set by the conveners of the 7th Pan African Congress had to reflect and to confront the reality of the basic differences of Pan Africanism from above and Pan Africanism from below. Pan Africanism developed from among the slaves who created a vision of the unity of the struggles of the African peoples at home and abroad. It was the totality of the system of oppression which forced the African to create a vision of the world which was larger than the nation or ethnic group from which the slave was captured.

The aspirations of the slave were larger than the plantation and the vision of the slave holders. African women were at the forefront of the resistance to slavery by teaching the principal lessons of resistance and dignity.

From the period of slavery there have been field slaves and house slaves, those who want to overturn the oppression of Africans and those who want to find ways to live with that oppression. This division of Pan Africanism from above and below is now manifest in the distinctions between the African leaders (at home and abroad) and the broad masses of sufferers. As such, it is now impossible for Pan Africanism to have the same nationalist appeal embracing all classes and strata as did the appeals made in the period of constitutional decolonization and armed struggles. The anti-colonial appeal were the calls of the 5th and 6th Pan African Congresses.

The Pan African movement is faced with a number of responsibilities. The conference organizers spelt out the usual catastrophes of debt, war, food crisis, refugees, structural adjustment, the rise of racism internationally, with the question of recolonization figuring prominently. In this contribution one would want to point to three of the tasks of the Pan African Movement. The first task is to make an impact on the African people in the process of transforming the nationalist consciousness of the twentieth century. Second, we must make a decisive impact on world opinion with respect to Africans at home and abroad. And third, we want to be able to realize the spirit of dignity for the renewal of the human spirit. Western European narratives of both the modern and postmodern variants devalued the spiritual dimension of humanity with an artificial distinction between thought and matter, between the material and the spiritual. One of the principal challenges of the Pan African Movement is 'to offer spiritual leadership to a world corrupted by worship of market forces'.[1]

In essence, the spiritual renewal and revival which is at the core of the movement is part of the attempt to break with the crude philosophical traditions of materialism of Europe. This conception of materialism encouraged greed, corruption and the worse forms of individualism. At the philosophical level, this individualism promoted leaderism in the Pan African Movement. Pan Africanism must inspire the spirit of collective efforts over individualism, and plenty rather than poverty. The concept of scientific progress and capitalist development can now be critiqued clearly in the face of the way capitalism promotes death tendencies. The death tendencies are manifest in wars, poverty, AIDS, racism, destruction of the environment and the devaluation of the lives of women and deforming the lives of the youth. The objective of this period is to be able to discourage and isolate death tendencies and encourage life tendencies.

This Congress met at a time when death tendencies are on the ascendancy. The urgency of the tasks as they face the African whether in South Africa, Angola, Burundi, Rwanda, Sudan, Somalia, Liberia, Zaire, Haiti or even Brazil, presented the movement with the challenge to respond concretely to the demands of the poor and powerless for a new vision beyond the old rhetorical approaches to Pan Africanism. The very traditions of mobilization of the past meetings and strategies contained the seeds of demobilization. Pan African Congresses in the past were important historical interventions, but the very nature of the organization created the breeding ground for elite politics.

There are those who believed that the primary aim of the Congress was to debate who is an African. However, this debate must be undertaken in a spirit of democratic give and take and should reflect the kind of tolerance which would distinguish this movement from those who exploit and manipulate differences of opinions. Most Africans live in multi-ethnic and multiracial societies. In this instance, the supreme task is to struggle against racism globally while ensuring that we do not internalize the ideas of the oppressors. Because victimization of people developed in racist cultures, sometimes one enters into the thought pattern of struggling with those that we are struggling against. One of the major challenges of the Pan African Movement is to become self-reliant in the realm of ideas. The Pan African Movement must develop a strong critique of racism and must propose constructive alternatives with an agenda of how to pool together to fight it.

New forms of mobilization

Democratic decision making and new forms of political mobilization in this period are required to place the movement on a new path from the nationalist leaders who demobilized the producers once they occupied the institutions of colonial governance. Democracy includes the freedom of speech, freedom of movement, freedom of expression and the right to participate in elections and the freedom to be creative. The Congress was itself part of the transition and the transformation of the forms of political intervention. One clear demand which is echoed from every corner is that Pan Africanism must be part of the transformation of gender relations internationally.

We have to reconceptualize the tasks of emancipation for the Pan African Movement in the context of the reorganization of imperialism

(General Agreement on Tariffs and Trade (GATT), North American Free Trade Agreement (NAFTA), the expanded European Community, the new World Trade Organisation, the Pacific Rim, a resuscitated NATO and its expansion under the guise of a New World Order). Conferences represent one of the many fora where the African peoples are discussing how to respond to the new internationalization of capital. At the forefront of these discussions are African women, who are discussing the principal weakness of the movement in the past. African feminists are exploring ways of dealing with the myriad forms of subjugation of the African woman. These progressive Africans seek the full emancipation of women and the consequent humanization of the male. They want a Pan African Movement vibrant with social truth and activated by free women.[2]

The present struggles for self-determination and transformation of gender relations lay at the centre of the wider struggle to liberate humanity from those forms of economic and social organization that are antithetical to our realization of our full capacities as human beings.

The reconceptualization of African liberation

The Pan African Movement has historically been one of the principal currents of political change and a force against racism on both sides of the Atlantic. In the twentieth century, Pan Africanism accepted the task of rolling back the frontiers of colonialism in Africa. This task assumed that the content and meaning of political independence would advance the dignity of the African. This position had been underlined by Kwame Nkrumah who had urged: 'Seek Ye first the Political Kingdom and all will be added to thee.' The intellectual and organizational tasks necessary for the conquest of political independence were undertaken by the Pan African intelligentsia. The victorys over colonialism has been the high point of this century. In April 1994, 20 years after the fall of Portuguese colonialism, the victory of an ANC government in South Africa was an historic turning-point in achieving the goals of the twentieth century. Yet, while it is important that the Pan African Movement celebrate the liberation of colonial entities, there are still the colonies of Puerto Rico, Martinique, Cayenne, Guadeloupe, Aruba and over a dozen colonies in the Caribbean. The movement must demand that Britain, France, the Netherlands and the United States end the outmoded principle of colonial possession.

The call for solidarity with those struggling against colonialism will be a concrete step in bringing back the values and ideals of African liberation from the leadership who have delegitimized the ideas of African liberation. The fact is that in the discourse today the dominant literature on the so-called civil wars and conflict resolution seeks to silence the history of African liberation. This has reached the point where, instead of liberation and self-determination being a source of inspiration to bring about a brighter future, the present process is seen as a never-ending nightmare of death and destruction.

Many of the leaders of the past Pan African Movement and the African liberation struggle have contributed to this sense of nightmare. These leaders can be found in Haiti, Angola, the Ivory Coast, Kenya and Malawi, amongst us at home and in the diaspora. Movements in struggle and parties in governments began to clarify very early the difference between Pan Africanism from above and Pan Africanism from below. From the very beginning of the mass mobilizations against external rule, some of the most articulate spokepersons of the Pan African/Negritude Movement reneged on one of the cardinal principles of Pan Africanism: 'that the people of one part of Africa are responsible for the freedom and liberation of their brothers and sisters in other parts of Africa; and indeed black people everywhere were to accept the same responsibility'.[3]

This principle is at the heart of the conceptualization of Pan Africanism in the face of leaders who foment ethnic, regional, religious and gender inequalities. The social composition of the OAU along with its inability to intervene in areas of dispute such as Rwanda, Liberia, Sudan, Somalia and Angola condemns the present leaders of the OAU as stumbling blocks to peace and renewal.

During the period of the liberation struggles, Africans waging war on the continent called for international solidarity in the struggles against colonialism. This call was important and in this period we must respond to the call of the people of Haiti who need Pan African intervention to rise above the dictatorship and the recent history of the manipulation of the symbols of racial consciousness. The same solidarity is in the short run demanded by the Cuban people. Cuba responded with a major sacrifice to assist the African people to defeat the South African army at Cuito Cuanavale in Angola. At present the people of Cuba are being punished for daring to conceptualize a different way of organizing society. The economic embargo against Cuba must be opposed by Pan Africanists everywhere, but especially by Pan Africanists in the Americas.

These short-term tasks of social reconstruction will be deepened by the long-term struggles against racism in Europe, North America and Brazil.

The reconceptualization of the tasks of liberation must also seek to define the purpose of the movement. From the time of the David Walker appeal in the early nineteenth century, in the United States, the struggle of the movement has been internationalist. Walker defined the tasks of Pan Africanism by declaring that

> ... it was an unshakable fact and forever immovable fact that your full glory and happiness, as well as that of all other colored people under heaven, shall never be consummated without the entire emancipation of your enslaved brethren all over the world.

This call for global redefinition of Pan Africanism has been carried forward by every generation since David Walker. Unfortunately, the movement has so far responded to the written records and not to the oral traditions. In this way the voices of women have been silenced in the call for the reconceptualization of Pan Africanism. Eusi Kwayana, one of the contemporary activists of the movement stated in his personal call to African males, that the

> ... cultural constitution of Africa in relation to women and in relation to youth is in need of revision. And this must not be done behind the backs of women and the youth. Pan Africanism will have validity only if it seeks to solve the fundamental problems of social injustice among Africans and supports every human community in its efforts for justice, freedom and development. [All quotes from Kwayana in this chapter are from an unpublished lecture given in 1993.]

What is Pan Africanism?

Kwayana's invitation above seems to be basic and simple and summarizes the issues which confront the movement as we approach the end of this century of depression, fascism, war, revolution and African independence. It is this challenge that is necessary to reassess the conception of how to define Pan Africanism. Prior to the 6th Pan African Congress, Walter Rodney had declared that Pan Africanism was an exercise in self-definition. In his words, inevitably this exercise in self-definition 'is undertaken by a specific social group or social class which speaks on behalf of the population as a whole'. African women have been able to develop on this position by saying that in the past the self-definition was simply in relation to the difference between Europeans and Africans. African women are at the forefront of developing a new self-definition of the movement. At all meetings since the 6th Pan African Congress the principal criticism has been that the movement has been male-centred and that the very forces who were speaking of liberation on the continent and in political parties were carrying out domestic exploitation.[4]

The question which can be posed with respect to the organizers of the 7th PAC is: which class is leading the present definition of the movement? What steps are being taken to end the historic silencing of women in the ranks of the Pan African Movement? What steps are being taken to end the demobilization and depoliticization of the youth? How capable are the leading forces in carrying out the present tasks of resisting and rolling back the looming recolonization? Which are the silent classes on whose behalf the calls for continental unity are being made?

The exercise in making the claim of which class is leading the call for social emancipation has been made easier by the experience of the independent governments of Africa and the Caribbean over the past thirty years. The assumption of power by the nationalist leaders in Africa, black mayors, senators and generals in the USA and black elected officials and parliamentarians in Europe, has not changed the quality of life of the broad masses. If anything in the era of the transition from Fordism (mass automated modes of capitalist production) to just-in-time production (the application of the most advanced forms of technology, computerization and robotics to production) has meant the further impoverishment of the African people. The conditions of the black working class have deteriorated considerably in the period since the civil rights gains of the 1960s. This deterioration mirrors the oppression meted out under the name of 'structural adjustment' in Africa.

The fact that the Pan African leadership of yesterday now constitutes the problems and obstacles of today helps us to sharpen our understanding of Pan Africanism. Kwayana gives this working definition of Pan Africanism. Underlining the Rodneyite conception of the self-emancipation of the working people, Kwayana developed a working definition which sees Pan Africanism:

> ... as a body of thought and action, shared but not uniform or dogmatic. A dynamic movement continually transforming itself and gaining new ideological perspectives in light of changing circumstance. Enriching itself through its own experience. Flowing

from masses, groups and occasionally leaders of governments. Tending to the goal of the restoration of freedom and dignity for *Africans at home and abroad*.

This definition underlines the transformation of ideas which have gone on in the Pan African Movement since the first conference was called in 1900. The dynamism of the movement is now apparent with those who are not satisfied with the present content and direction of the movement. The formation of the OAU in 1963 was the culmination of the asserted goals of self-determination. In the context of the twenty-first century, Pan Africanism will continue to mean the struggle for emancipation through diverse means; seeking unity and expressing the common purpose of fighting white domination and restoring African community. Undertaken by any group with the above purposes, both with and without international focus the struggles for freedom continue on a day-to-day basis. The goals of Pan Africanism include: finding techniques of governing that build self-reliance and community, identifying and rejecting the values of white domination and consumerism, and holding that those educated in every tradition or discipline should put that education to work to serve the working people.

African women and the redefinition of the Pan African struggle

All of the issues of the emancipation of the African people in the twenty-first century converge on the principal question of the transformation of gender relations. All parties in the movement and in governments will agree that the African woman is the most oppressed member of the African people. Governments and official organizations for women will recite the statistics of the oppression and how the reorganization of capitalism has impacted on African women. The indices of public exploitation are present but the issues of the relations between the public and the private sphere remains one area where many parties are conniving to silence African women.

This new form of silencing African women is present in the plethora of women's groups and non-governmental organizations (NGOs) which seek to promote a particular form of association among women. The leading culprits in this regard are those who seek to deepen capitalism in the rural areas of Africa by speaking of 'women in development', of 'empowering' women, yet shackle them with the onerous burden of structural adjustment and devaluation. The most odious in this enterprise are those who speak of women in development yet support the economic measures which cut back on water supplies, health care, education subsidies, electricity, food and those elements of the social wage which was developing in Africa, the Caribbean and in the social democratic areas of capitalism.

The conspiracy to silence women is well-developed in the international arena where the centrality of the African women in the African liberation struggle was well-known. This silencing has been taken over by the state-sponsored women's organization syndrome. This is manifest all over the continent with women's organizations led by corrupt party functionaries or the first ladies or the wives of top government officials. Invariably, these organizations are in the forefront of the exploitation of women by calling on women to observe specific 'traditions' and support degenerate leaders. These organizations assist in devaluing the lives of African peoples in general and African women in particular. Some of these organizations in supporting so-called traditions extol the physical abuse of African women.

This form of the state-centred organization of African women can be seen even in those organizations which were at the forefront of the African liberation struggle. From Mozambique to South Africa and from Namibia to Zimbabwe, it is now clear that the slogans of the emancipation of women which were proclaimed in the liberation movements did not take concrete manifestation in the course of developing new institutions. Mozambique, which was the most advanced of the liberation movements, in its declarations and state policies went only so far as to develop welfarist policies. These were positive in legislating equality with respect to employment, wages, health care and access to social services. The balance of the experience is that legislation is important but cannot deal with the fundamental oppression which is justified in the name of tradition.

All over the Pan African world, many of these oppressions in relation to sexuality, conceptions of motherhood, nurturing, sexual oppression and harassment, genital mutilation, incest, rape and child abuse take place in the spheres outside of the public sphere and are not open to political discussion.

The experience of Mozambique has been that though the elementary steps were taken for the 'equality of women', the conception of equality is itself problematic. Elementary steps are being made by women's movements in the Pan African world to develop autonomous organizations to forward the struggle of women. Often, there is the mistaken belief that if Pan Africanism was associated with great men, then to repair this historic imbalance, it is necessary to bring to the fore all the great women from Queen Nzinga to Harriet Tubman to Winnie Mandela who have been at the forefront of the African struggle.

While the conception of Pan Africanism from below must celebrate the contributions of these women, this celebration is not enough to bring to the fore the issues of the reconstruction of the African society away from the capitalist values of individualism, patriarchy and private ownership. Women as property in Africa and in the diaspora touches on deep cultural values and beliefs. The reconstruction of gender relations is tied to the search for spiritual renewal, in the transformation of cultural values. The emancipation of the continent and of all peoples require the fundamental restructuring of gender relations in the society.

The experience of UNITA in Angola is a supreme example of an organization which manipulates all of the symbols of Pan Africanism for the most obscene oppression of Africans. It is not accidental that it was from the ranks of the 6th Pan African Congress that UNITA sought to mobilize African-Americans against the so-called whites, mezticos and communists. The weapon of a women's organization against the interests of women can be seen in the organization of LIMA (League of the Independent Women of Angola), the women's arm of UNITA.[5]

The women in the areas controlled by UNITA were especially exploited since the ideas of military communism of UNITA precluded any form of independent thinking by women. In late 1987, women soldiers were integrated into the official fighting force of UNITA's army and there were seven who were even commissioned as officers. The organizational arm of UNITA which represented women was a vehicle to sing praises to the supreme leader of the organization, Dr Jonas Savimbi, and women had no control over their lives.

Sexual abuse and violence was the norm in the military camps of UNITA where women, especially the younger ones, had to be made available to the commanders. The leader of UNITA established a tradition where, as the maximum leader, it was possible for the political leadership to arrange marriages. The traditional reproductive roles of women in these areas are seen as an extension of the war effort since women produce the human labour necessary for UNITA to continue fighting. Their roles as mothers are seen as essential in providing the next generation of fighters. UNITA recruits youths at six years old for military training. Women also act as porters carrying weapons for the South African-supported forces of UNITA.

UNITA as an organization represents the most vulgar form of the manipulation of the symbols of African liberation and the promotion of death tendencies. This Pan Africanism of UNITA seeks to mobilize on the narrow issues of race, ethnicity and regionalism to foster the ambition of those who seek to reduce Africa to war and destabilization.

Mobilization and demobilization

One of the ironies of the present attempt to organize for the twenty-first century is the ways in which the organizational forms of the twentieth century have crippled imagination and creativity. African males inherited European forms of expression and communication. One of the principal weaknesses of this form of communication has been the importance of the speaker and organizer and the passive participation of the listener. This took the form of the mass political rally. These traditions were to have a major impact on the post-colonial era when the very forces who called on the people used the same vehicles of communication for demobilization.

This situation is present all over the continent and among Africans in the diaspora, where there is an intolerance for diverse views. This intolerance has led to the maximization of differences and to wars of ethnic, regional and religious forms. The ways of processing and accessing knowledge in the West are fundamentally undemocratic. Pan Africanism must develop a new pedagogy, in essence a new way for the reproduction, transference and use of knowledge. This new democratization of knowledge must draw from oral transmission so that one does not privilege any one form of processing and reproducing knowledge.

Participating in the oral traditions has been one of the sources of the strength and the creativity of the African people. These traditions are harnessed and preserved in song, poetry, dance, music and in other cultural forms. The vividness of oral communication has been reduced in the political movement by the emphasis on the idea of the great leader. Leaderism suppresses the creative instincts and this can be seen in the ways in which public forms of entertainment in Africa are oppressive. In the state media and television, the dependence of the leaders on the West is manifest in the promotion of ignorance among the people. This ignorance ensures that the young have to find out for themselves many of the forms of the continuity in the struggles from the period of slavery to the present. The reconstruction of cultural values will be one of the ways in which African peoples will make a statement to the world in the twenty-first century.

Pan Africanism in multi-ethnic and multiracial societies

It is now clear that one of the demobilizing factors of the twentieth century has been the elaboration of racism and racist values. In the current reorganization of imperialism, racist ideas and racist cultural instincts are on the rise. One of the ways some Pan Africanists have responded to this globalization of the ideas of apartheid is to deepen the concept of race consciousness. This is especially the case in the Caribbean, North America, South America and Western Europe.

The resistance against racism took many forms, from the mass organization of Garveyites and the Civil Rights movement, to the armed struggles against apartheid and settler colonialism. Among some Africans, the opposition to racism took the form of the glorification of the African past. This was a liberating experience under colonialism and helped to mobilize the people. Unfortunately, the unscientific ideas about racial inferiority and superiority were internalized to divide the working peoples. The experience of Guyana and Trinidad in the past thirty years has demonstrated that it is not possible to struggle against racism without developing an alternative interpretation of the world, other than that of the racists.

The present international situation demands that Pan Africanists become more self-reliant in the realm of ideas to be able to fight racism. Pan Africanists cannot seek to dominate or discriminate against others. It is very important to learn from the experiences of Walter Rodney and the Working Peoples Alliance (WPA) in Guyana. First, Africans were taken to Guyana where the indigenous peoples – the Amerindians – were nearly wiped out. Second, there were indentured workers taken from India to break the industrial muscle of the African workers and small farmers. European colonialists manipulated the differences between the Amerindians, the Indians and other ethnic groups. Third, a so-called Pan African leader in Guyana sought to develop these traditions to the point of assassinating one of the foremost spokespersons of the working people and of African liberation, Walter Rodney.

Eusi Kwayana, who is of the same political and ideological persuasion as Rodney, underlined the fact that Walter Rodney appreciated from the beginning,

> that human development would not take place to its full potential outside a harmonious ethnic environment. Such an environment takes for granted the prior resolution of ethnic rivalries, indignities

and oppression, a law that appears even more fundamental than normal class contradictions.

The alternative chosen by the WPA, yet to be emulated by any other party in the Caribbean so far, is to subject everything else to the creation of a politics based on ethnic reconciliation. The party affirmed that it would rather not go forward than to go forward with one race. The question is that in a multi-ethnic situation any sense of progress on the basis of one race is a mere illusion of progress.

This concept of rising above the nationalism of Western Europe is a fundamental requirement of the Pan African Movement in the twenty-first century. It is very simple and easy to point to imperialist domination but less easy to see the ways in which undemocratic resolution of racial and ethnic differences weaken the African everywhere. This question of a multi-ethnic society is especially true for Africans in the diaspora: 'Pan Africanism must recognize first and foremost the remaining minorities of the great nations almost made extinct in several countries by the genocidal traditions of Europe.'

Democratic approaches to dealing with ethnic and racial differences will distinguish democracy in the Pan African world from the elementary forms of democracy in Europe. The ethnic diversity of the African continent is a source of great wealth and great strength. Popular democratic interventions beyond the politics of leaders and manipulations are required for the peoples of the world to move forward. Kwayana who has formulated the concept of Pan African humanism has called on the movement to insist on conditions of empowerment and equal opportunity for the oppressed of all ethnic groups. This will be a lasting contribution to the anti-racist struggle internationally.

The drive for spiritual renewal in the Pan African world

All of the indices of the destructive nature of capitalism are present before humanity. The ecological disasters, wars, AIDS, drugs, exploitation and plunder are all hallmarks of the present era. The plans for the organization of imperialism in the transition to just-in-time production seeks to completely marginalize the African at home and abroad. Cultural and ideological oppression are manifestations of the drive for the recolonization of the African continent.

The crisis of capitalism points to the crude materialism and values of the West. The so-called myths of progress, science and technology have been exposed in many ways. The crisis in this form of materialism can be seen in the collapse of the planned economies and the inability of the twentieth-century concept of socialism to rise above the European conception of liberation. The fall of socialism and the retreat of many progressive forces has led to despair. In some parts of the world the opposition to the culture of capital seeks forms of religious fundamentalism. The rise of fundamentalism in the Pan African world in many forms is an attempt by peoples to develop new cultural and spiritual values. Unfortunately, in the attempt to develop spiritual reference points, there are some zealots who develop religions and religious expressions that may dominate and exploit the spiritual values of the African peoples. These extreme forms of bigotry, ironically develop in the process of opposing racism and cultural oppression, and only further deepen the divisions in the Pan African world.

Spirituality is an area which encompasses our total being. When African peoples were oppressed and the oppression was extended to the spiritual realm by the church and schools of Europe, a gut reaction to domination emerged through spiritual expression. The self-definition of the African people through spiritual and religious realms became central to political struggle. There are numerous examples of this in the anti-colonial period. Spirituality offered an emotional outlet to the masses and religion developed out of this. African religion became a popular form of relating to Pan Africanism, because Western philosophy demonized African philosophy.

In the era of the consumer culture of the West and the debased values of greed and corruption, African religious forms and other forms of spirituality are now important forms of Pan African expression. Africans and other oppressed peoples want to identify with spiritual values which can provide a base for emancipation and redemption. African customs, values and traditions are being interpreted in a way which could oppose the cultural domination. However, in many cases, there are those who exploit these spiritual values to promote organized forms of religious expressions which are also oppressive.

The presence of religious fundamentalism in many forms (both Christian and Islamic), exploiting the spiritual values of the poor, shows that the Pan African Movement is in need of spiritual renewal. Eusi Kwayana who understood the importance of class struggle and the appreciation of some aspects of historical materialism was also aware of the necessity to develop a political philosophy which can be built upon the positive spiritual attributes of the African peoples. The spiritual values of self-reliance, love, redemption and deliverance are values which can unleash the creativity of the African to develop new forms of organizing and conceptualizing society. The task is to find new ways to harmonize the relations between human beings and between humans and nature. Africa is a rich continent. Thus far, the conception of the Pan African leaders has been to mobilize resources and raw materials based on the vision and demands of Europe.

The Pan African Movement must move in a new direction and at the core of this direction is the spiritual and cultural renewal of the African peoples. Spirituality means different things to different peoples, but in this presentation we want to draw from the insights of Kwayana:

> Spirituality speaks about a strength which cannot be assimilated, assassinated or eliminated by other means. It is the reservoir closest to the mind, interflowing with it, gaining and receiving. In domestic, political and social life, it is the extent to which a community and individual sustain an option for virtue rather than vice, for justice rather than injustice, freedom rather than oppression, purity rather than perversion, plenty over poverty and the future of universal love rather than universal greed.

The Pan African struggle

At every stage in the past two centuries, the spiritual values of love and the collective good of humans has been at the base of the Pan African Movement. Pan Africanism is about the dignity of the African person and it is now clear that this dignity cannot be quantified in material terms. During the twentieth century the demands for self-respect and freedom were articulated as the demand for political independence and an end to apartheid. The leaders and the intellectuals articulated the concept of African unity as one of the principal elements of freedom. With the defeat of apartheid, the major stumbling block to African political unity and social development will be removed. Popular participation, the transformation of gender relations, cultural freedom and the development of new forms of social existence remain part of the task to place Africa on the road to alternative forms of economic organization. The political unity of Africa is an elementary precondition for the task of economic change so that the African peoples everywhere can draw strength from the spiritual and cultural strength of Africa.

This task is also sharpened by the economic and social marginalization of the African peoples in South America. The cultural resistance of the African peoples in Brazil, Cuba, Haiti and the rest of the region provide a fertile base for real multiracial democracy in this region. Thus far however, even those social movements aspiring to democracy continue to predicate development on catching up with Europe and America. The models of consumption of the culture of capitalism reserve this mode of consumption for a small minority of humanity in Europe, North America and Japan.

Pan African liberation in the twenty-first century is thus inscribed in the struggle beyond the culture of capital and the effort to lobotomize humanity into mindless consumers. The liberation of the African peoples is linked to the liberation of other oppressed peoples and sharpens the elements of Pan African humanism. Pan Africanism which seeks to reproduce the chauvinism of the European categorization of race has been unable to inspire the kind of humanism necessary to emancipate human beings from the European classification of races. The battle against racism cannot continue to accept the unscientific category of race. The struggle for democracy includes the ability to benefit from the cultural and ethnic diversity of Africans. This challenge is clearest in the field of developing Pan African educational institutions.

Pan African liberation is not only linked to the quest for a new social system, but also one in which the development of the productive forces is not simply linked to the production of goods but also the creation of new human beings. This perspective of the transformation of gender relations, free men, women and children, of cultural freedom, of harnessing the positive knowledge of the African past now forms part of the conception of the struggle for Pan African liberation in the twenty-first century.

The tasks of emancipation are formidable and require a new theory of social reality. Small steps are being made with the social commitment of those in the movement who see liberation not as the work of individual leaders or intellectuals but as part of the process of self-mobilization and self-organization of the African peoples.

Notes

1. Eusi Kwayana, 'Pan Africanism in the Caribbean', *Southern Africa Political Economy Monthly*, Harare, December 1993.

2. Bonita Harris, 'Combatting Women's Over Representation Among the Poor in the Caribbean', *Southern Africa Political Economy Monthly*, Harare, December 1993.
3. Walter Rodney, 'Towards the 6th Pan African Congress: Aspects of the International Class Struggle in Africa, America and the Caribbean' in Horace Campbell (ed.), *Pan Africanism: Documents of the Sixth Pan African Congress* (Toronto: 1975).
4. This has been brought about in the book *In Search of Mr McKenzie* by Isha Mackenzie-Mavinga and Selma Perkins, London: Women's Press, 1991.
5. For an elaboration of this argument, see Horace Campbell, 'African Women and the Electoral Process in Angola', *Africa Development*, vol. XVIII, no. 2, 1993, pp. 23–63.

11

The OAU and the Future

Salim A. Salim

The Organization of African Unity, which I have had the honour to serve for the past few years, owes its birth to the ideals of Pan Africanism. In the days when Africa was viewed not in its own right, but as an extension of Metropolitan Europe, the activities of Pan African giants from the diaspora such as William Du Bois, Marcus Garvey and George Padmore as well as those from the Continent such as Kwame Nkrumah and Jomo Kenyatta, put Africa on the world agenda. The dignity of the African was then and continues to be even today, a matter of grave concern. Liberty and freedom became the battle cry for liberation.

The history of the OAU, its purposes and principles of its *modus operandi* are well-known. Its formation was in response to a desire; a desire that our shared historical experience made necessary, a desire that the political and geographic configuration as well as the economic viability of the continent have made necessary, a desire to give Africa the appropriate hearing it deserves in the councils of the world and a desire that had been bequeathed to Africa by the Pan African Movement. The founding fathers recognized then, as we recognize more vividly today, that the salvation of Africa, does not lie in individualized action but on a collective approach at the continental level. Consequently, the search for unity has continued to be a guiding philosophy and an ideal whose achievement the OAU has dedicated itself.

The struggle against apartheid

Foremost item on its agenda was the question of the total liberation of Africa upon which the dignity of Africa rested. For three decades and more, the OAU waged an unremitting and relentless struggle for freedom. Armed struggle and diplomatic action became the dual strategy adopted by the OAU in support of the prosecution of the liberation struggle. With the independence of Namibia in 1990, Africa technically closed the chapter on decolonization, even though apartheid still remained an agenda issue. The first democratic elections of 27 April 1994 and the inauguration of the first democratic and non-racial government on 11 May 1994, in South Africa effectively closed the chapter on decolonization. The OAU, rightly, attached so much importance to the political process in South Africa and did whatever it could within its means to assist in the process of political transition in that country. It had an Observer Mission based in Johannesburg, both to monitor violence and to help in the process of transition generally. The OAU presence there and that of other International Observers, not only had a moderating effect on the level of violence but had, most importantly, demonstrated Africa's attachment to the struggle to put an end to the last vestiges of colonialism and institutionalized racism on the continent.

Africa has invested a lot of effort and resources and, above all, hope in the process in South Africa. The situation in the country gives great promise and serious challenge. The promise is that by holding its first democratic elections, South Africa has emerged from the oppression of racism and begun the engaging process of national reconciliation. The promise is equally that a free South Africa at peace with itself and its neighbours will be an important addition to the ranks of the African community world-wide. Freedom in South Africa enlarges the freedom of Africans everywhere. It is their freedom, it is our freedom which we all celebrated, after the elections.

The challenge before the elections was to ensure that at that critical juncture, the process of transition was sustained up to the election day and beyond. The forces of the status quo were still strong and doing everything to undermine the transition. We played our part in not allowing them to succeed. I believed then and now that the people of South Africa need the solidarity and full support of the Pan African Movement.

The OAU has also made an important and at times crucial contribution to all those territories that have become independent since 1964. By all accounts, it is a monumental achievement of which the OAU is justifiably proud. Yes, there might have been difficulties but these cannot in any way diminish the magnitude of that achievement. And during this period of struggle, we enjoyed the full support of the states in the Caribbean as well as the support and solidarity of the brothers and sisters in the United States and the diaspora as a whole. And for this I want to thank them for recognizing that the struggle on the continent was equally their own. Africa's freedom enlarges that of Africans everywhere.

New frontiers for the OAU

With the successful completion of the liberation struggle, a second window has already been opened for the OAU. The dawn of a new era signalling the emergence of new challenges and opportunities. In other words, the end of the liberation struggle, the economic crisis and the developments in the world have made it necessary for the OAU to revise its priorities in a world order marked by increasing complexities and uncertainties.

In 1980, the heads of state and government addressed the economic and developmental issues affecting the continent at the Extraordinary Session of the Assembly of Heads of State and Governments in Lagos, Nigeria. It was at this session that the historic document 'The Lagos Plan of Action' and 'The Final Act of Lagos' were adopted as the economic blueprint for Africa. It was initiated, designed and tailored by Africans for Africa. The principles of collective self-reliance and self-sustained development were its bedrock.

By the 1990s, with the end of the Cold War, the agreement on the Single Market in Western Europe and the expansion into Central and Eastern Europe, the efforts at economic arrangements in the Pacific Rim as well as in North America, all made it absolutely urgent for Africa to re-evaluate its options and to act with speed. In 1990, as in 1980, the Assembly, in a historic session, took stock of all these developments and in particular of the increasing poverty of Africa and among many other issues decided to revisit the main tenets of the Lagos Plan of Action. Second, it resolved to play a leading role in finding solutions to the conflicts, including internal conflicts, that hitherto had been recognized, as a 'no-go area' or a taboo, because of among other reasons, the principle of non-interference. The heads of state and government committed themselves to pursue the 'further democratization of our societies'. The burning issue of human rights was also recognized and the Assembly resolved to work for greater respect of these rights in our continent. In sum, these are the main tasks the Assembly set for itself in the declaration it adopted on the political and socioeconomic situation in Africa and the fundamental changes taking place in the world.

These tasks then have become the main priorities of the OAU since 1990. Translated into action programmes, they have come to mean the following for the next decade and beyond.

The commitment to the establishment of an African Economic Community

This is not just a desire to follow what is happening elsewhere in the world, but is an imperative, emanating from a deep-seated conviction that the welfare and prosperity of the African peoples could better be enhanced through the integration of the economies of Africa. By these means the OAU has clearly opted for a functional approach to integration which, with time, will extend to other important domains. It must be pointed out that this commitment had been on the drawing board since the 1980 Economic Summit in Lagos. The 1990 Summit gave the necessary fillip and impetus to the establishment of the Community. In 1991, in Abuja, the Treaty establishing the Economic Community for Africa was signed. The ratification process has taken a bit of time but it is expected that the Treaty will come into force very soon. Following its coming into force, the African Economic Community (AEC) will become fully established over a period of time.

The AEC is by far the single most important project for Africa. Through it, the OAU hopes not only to bring prosperity to Africa, but also to bring the people of Africa together in a larger unity transcending ethnic and national boundaries. That would be in fulfilment of a major objective of the OAU. Progress and prosperity in Africa will be a beacon to all her sons and daughters in the diaspora and a source of pride to them all. The challenge to Africa is to translate what we have designed into reality.

Resolution of conflicts and the creation of the OAU mechanism for conflict prevention, management and resolution

Development can only take place in an atmosphere of peace, security and stability. The OAU has been increasingly involved in the continent's search for solutions to the many conflicts which now afflict the continent. In a radical departure from past restrictive practices, the member states now not only concede a role to the OAU in helping them resolve conflicts, they are more and more requesting and expecting the organization to be involved actively. As a result of this new perspective on how member states view the role of the OAU, we are now actively engaged in a number of countries. The OAU is in Liberia, Rwanda, Burundi, to some extent in Mozambique, Somalia, Congo and in South Africa lending its hand in the internal efforts to resolve the conflicts.

Within the context of bringing greater political and operational consistency in the way Africa wants to deal with these conflicts, OAU leaders at the July 1993 Summit Meeting in Cairo, Egypt, established within the organization a mechanism for conflict prevention, management and resolution. This mechanism, which will operate with the Bureau of the Assembly of Heads of State and Government as its political organ, will have the Secretary-General and the Secretariat as the Operational Arm as well as a Peace Fund to provide resources for its operations. The mechanism is already functioning and it has met several times at ambassadorial level and once each at ministerial and summit level to consider the conflicts that are now raging on in the continent.

The genesis of the decision to establish this mechanism was the determination by the member states that the time has come for Africa to regain the initiative and provide leadership in all attempts at finding solutions to the continent's conflicts. The founding of the mechanism was historic, coming as it did, with Africa's mounting concerted efforts at economic development. Our continent needs peace and stability if the efforts at economic development and further democratization are to achieve their desired objectives. We cannot serve the cause of unity, of economic integration or that of human rights without finding durable solutions to the conflicts in the continent. In empowering itself through this mechanism, Africa is saying *enough is enough* and that we are determined to grasp the nettle and put our house in order – even if we shall continue to need international solidarity and support.

Democratization
From 1986, Africa has continued to witness its second wind of change, involving a transformation to a multi-party system of government. The OAU has welcomed the transition to democracy on the understanding that the transition is in accord with the socio-cultural values of each of the member states. The transition process is fraught with many pitfalls, but the process has continued. The Secretariat has been encouraged to monitor and to assist, whenever possible, the democratic process. Monitoring of elections has now become a regular activity of the Secretariat. Most recently, the OAU has taken part fully in the observations of elections held in Uganda (1994), South Africa (1994) and Tanzania (1995). The Secretariat will continue to play this role until the transition period is fully completed and democratic culture is everywhere implanted.

Apart from these top priority concerns, the OAU will continue with its other activities especially in the socio-cultural domain. It is also envisaged that the OAU will give a lot more attention to those areas that had received less attention, such as protection of the environment, health and nutrition, labour, education and human resources development. Matters affecting women and children would no doubt be placed on a Certificate of Urgency.

For the OAU, the future is a life-and-death struggle. It is evident that if Africa should continue to operate the way it has been doing for three decades, it would no more be a question of marginalization, but whether Africa would be able to play a meaningful part at all in the affairs of the world. But there is hope and that hope is the immediate and speedy implementation of the provisions of the Treaty for African Economic Community. The biggest challenge is for Africa to appreciate the magnitude of the tasks facing Africa and move as fast as the circumstances demand. To do that, a new African, freed from the limiting interpretation of sovereignty and non-interference and imbued with a new sense of mission and purpose that transcends ethnic and national irredentism, would be required. This is why the 7th Pan African Congress was timely and opportune in the hope that it would help revive those ideals that hold the only hope for the advancement and progress of the Africans and their brothers and sisters in the diaspora.

Like the struggle for the freedom of our continent from colonial bondage which galvanized the African community world-wide, the future should be our utmost concern. The movement for the development of the African, for our dignity and larger freedom is one. The suffering of the African whether on the continent or elsewhere in the world affects us collectively as a people. This is why we ought to think together, to cooperate and to work together.

Within the continent, the OAU is exerting all efforts against many odds, not least those of lack of adequate resources. But we are not resigned to these constraints. Instead, we have sought to see how we can expand our resource base through mobilizing support from both within and outside Africa. And the response has been encouraging. We need more support and we see in the Pan African Movement a ready partner in this task. We need to work within this movement to mobilize for the welfare of the continent, for its development and for peace in it. Considerable resources exist within Africa and in the diaspora which, if fully accessible and creatively used, could make a major difference in terms of the capacity of the OAU to function effectively.

Beyond the task of mobilizing resources, we need political support. In this movement the OAU finds common identity, destiny and purpose with Africans world-wide. We equally must find solidarity to sustain our unity and enhance the cause of Pan Africanism and the belief that actions of those of us in the continent and those in the diaspora must be mutually supportive and reinforcing. A strong Africa and an efficient OAU will be able to address the many ills and problems which make the continent under-developed and in conflict. Conversely, a strong, prosperous and peaceful Africa will embolden the cause of Pan Africanism and the pride of every African everywhere.

Investment in Africa can be mobilized from elsewhere within the African communities. African businesses in the United States, the Caribbean, South Asia, Europe and the Pacific should be welcomed and encouraged to invest and trade in Africa. Tourism must be encouraged and promoted both as business and a means of building the bridges of contacts and interaction.

The 1990s are different from the 1940s, 1950s and even the 1960s. In the 1940s, the movement's battle cry for freedom acted like a magnet in its attraction of adherents. After independence, the attraction of the ideals of Pan Africanism seemed to have waned somewhat. In fact another source of attraction took its place. The sudden emergence on the continent of what has come to be known as 'sovereignty' and the raw political power that flowed from it became too great to be resisted or to be sacrificed in favour of a continental political union. So it was reasoned that the founding fathers at that early stage could not surrender even a part of that newly-won sovereignty. We have lived through a period during which many changes in leadership have taken place, from constitutionally elected governments to military governments, and from a one-party system to multi-party political systems. The situation has however remained the same, in some instances the attachment to sovereignty has grown stronger.

I say this in order to situate the magnitude of the problem. There must be no illusions; the task is formidable. But that is precisely why we must begin now. The more we wait and hesitate, the harder the task becomes. Our commitment to unity is not the product of a sentimental design. It is the product of the objective conditions of the time which Africa cannot afford to ignore.

Therefore from this rostrum let the word go forth to all corners of our world, the world of Pan Africanism, of our determination and resolve to revive and keep aloft the ideals of Pan Africanism. From Kampala let us give hope and confidence that through our united and collective efforts, we can build a secure and prosperous home for our children. Let us rededicate ourselves to the second stage of our struggle for socioeconomic salvation through continental unity and to strive relentlessly for the speedy realization of this cardinal objective.

I would like to conclude by addressing an issue which I know remains one of concern to many of you. I know that there are indeed millions of Africans both on the continent and in the diaspora who feel that the OAU has not done enough. Some may even feel that the Organization is sometimes irrelevant to the real needs and expectations of the African people. Most would want to see a more dynamic Organization in the interest of Africans and in particular in confronting the many ills and problems that confront our continent.

I share some of these concerns though I clearly disagree with the cynics. For the Organization to meet the enormous challenges that confront our continent and our peoples, it requires the commitment not only of governments but above all, of the African peoples, both on the continent and in the diaspora who clearly wish to see a better and more prosperous Africa. And this can be done more effectively by giving support to the Organization.

Earlier I referred to the historic commitments made by African leaders in their summit in Addis Ababa in 1990, towards democratization, greater respect of human rights, conflict resolution and economic progress of our continent. It is my contention that the African peoples must take these commitments seriously and strive to ensure that all our governments live up to them. The African people must, through their mobilization, demand that our continental Organization live up to these commitments. The value of grass-roots involvement and support is self-evident. This Congress and its follow-up mechanism must make these a part of its continuing agenda. Africans should stop treating the OAU as some distant body located in Addis Ababa where heads of state, ministers, ambassadors and officials frequently meet to deliberate on the destiny of our continent. Instead, the Organization should properly be viewed as our own Pan African organization and indeed, where necessary, even pressured to live up to the aspirations and expectations of our peoples in all domains. We must endeavour to strengthen it. Indeed, it should be made efficient and effective. It must therefore be the constant concern and commitment of all Africans to contribute towards making the OAU more and more relevant to our needs. If we do so, the OAU will emerge as a dynamic instrument in forging Africa's present part of the challenge of the 7th Pan African Congress. I equally believe that it should constitute a challenge for all Africans both on the continent and in the diaspora. It can and should be done.

12

Building a Pan African Women's Movement

Fatima B. Mahmoud

Introduction

> As African women, we share a common history. We have similar challenges to face and a better future to look forward to. On this basis, it is important to stress our similarities rather than differences, if we are to achieve any meaningful change.
>
> Fatima B. Mahmoud, Speaking at the Pre-Congress Meeting of Women at the 7th Pan African Congress, Kampala, 2 April 1994

The Pan African Women's Liberation Organization (PAWLO)[1] has as its main task the serious need to draw African women on the continent and in the diaspora together to be united in their liberation struggles against all forms of oppression. Our movement is a liberation movement and not a feminist movement; not because we do not like the term feminism but because while such a term often refers to the history of our sisters in the West, it does not tell our story.

As Pan African women, seeking to organize ourselves in a liberation movement, we need to begin by stressing our commonalities. This will help us to address our common problems and think about our future in light of the changing realities of today's social and economic order. There is now a serious need for a Pan African women's organization to address these commonalities. This organization should be based on a movement that is democratic and liberating; critical and constructive; autonomous but sensitive to all social issues and part of the wider social and political movement for change; independent from other international women's organizations yet cooperating with them and exercising mutual solidarity across all diversities and barriers; striving towards establishing very close contacts and cooperation with similar organizations in Asia and Latin America; and above all, committed to African women's problems and their immediate and long-term solutions and hopes.

This movement should be rooted in the history of struggle by African women on the continent and in the diaspora. Much of this history has yet to be written and made widely accessible. Revisiting our history is not a longing for the past; rather it is a call for self-empowerment as we look at the past in order to embrace the future creatively and persistently. We need to rewrite the history of our women ancestors, to shed light on their powerfulness, their prominent role in the history of Africa and the diaspora, and their ability, knowledge and wisdom in resource utilization, in religion, arts and all aspects of culture and life.

Some of these women include:

- The women Candace (rulers) of Meroe (Sudan): at least seven women ruled Sudan between 284 BC – AD 115.
- The Kahina of the Maghreb, a famous Berber prophetess who succeeded in temporarily holding back the Arab invasion of Africa in the eighteenth century.
- Helena and Sabla Wangel of Ethiopia: During the sixteenth century, a time of crisis in Ethiopian history, due to the resourcefulness and courage of the Empress Helena and her successor Sabla Wangel, the country survived near-destruction.
- Dona Beatrice of the Congo, who lived between 1682–1706, was believed to be a spirit medium. She was feared by the king and his foreign advisers because of the message she received from God that 'Congo should be reborn, free from the Europeans whose slave trade had reduced it to misery.'
- Nehanda of Zimbabwe (1863–1898) was one of the major leaders of the African resistance to white rule. She was persistent in her fight against those who enslaved her people and looted their resources. In 1897, the two male leaders surrendered but Nehanda struggled on until it became clear to her that her followers would be killed if she was not finally captured. She therefore allowed herself to be taken rather than cause any deaths amongst her people; she was executed by hanging.

These women represent but a very small part of the thus-far revealed history of how some African women leaders exercised power and resisted subjugation. There are a host of other valient African women from the continent and the diaspora whose history must be uncovered. They include: Nefertiti and Hatshepsut of Egypt, Anne Nzinga of Angola, Muthoni wa Kirima of Kenya, Harriet Tubman, Sojourner Truth, and Jane Lewis of the United States, Queen of Zaria and Moremi of Ife, both in Nigeria, Mary Prince and Mary Seacole of the Caribbean. From these women, we not only inherit and share our theoretical/conceptual tools of analysis but the ways in which we use these tools to achieve the total liberation of women.

The history that African women share and the present they are to challenge is that of slavery, colonialism, neocolonialism, issues of development and aid syndrome and the threat of recolonization. There is also the crisis brought to the African people and women in particular as a result of structural adjustment programmes of the international financial institutions, mainly the IMF and the World Bank, government dictatorships, and the dangers arising from the wave of Islamic fundamentalism in Africa.

The colonial period

The colonial system used a variety of forms to utilize African resources. These included destruction of some existing structures, maintenance of some of them and utilization of some of them. All of these forms were used to achieve the colonial objective of having the maximum access to Africa's human and material resources. The process affected all Africans adversely, but in particular, colonialism adversely affected African women.

Colonialism used the existing dominant culture to encourage women's invisibility and seclusion. For example, in the Sudan, where Islam predominates as a religion or culture or both, it was used to justify oppression and discrimination against women. Second, the maximization of the production of raw materials marginalized women farmers through alien and coercive forms of sexual division of labour; imported goods arrested and destroyed indigenous handicrafts of which women's share was considerable.

Third, colonialism introduced an educational policy that discriminated against women in both content and quality and destroyed women's informal knowledge, while adopting a double standard towards the education of women. While they allowed women's rights' organizations in the centres of colonization, they banned African women's organizations in the colonized countries.

It was out of such oppression that the women's movement emerged, as part of the general political movement of parties, trade unions or student and youth movements who were struggling to rid Africa of colonial domination. These movements were united across classes, religion, regional divisions, ethnicity and, to some degree, gender. However, the way they perceived of the process of liberation differed from one organization to another, including the women's organizations.

Because, during this time, women treated themselves as an anti-colonial force, specific women's issues featured rarely in women organizations and even less in political parties and other unions. The student movement was however more advanced in addressing specific women's issues, partly because of its nature and the educational system and partly because of the prominent role of the women students within it. Some of the issues around which discussion centred were:

- that political independence was only the first step in ridding the country of economic and cultural imperialism;
- the way in which different parties conceived of post-colonial development path, that is, as socialist, capitalist or mixed;
- in the recognition of women's rights, emphasis was on political rights, for example, women's rights to voting and election, and
- economic rights, that is, the right to an equal wage for equal work in the formal sector. The movement was divided as far as this issue was concerned, with the left-wing parties adopting the socialist path and the traditional or right-wing parties refraining from it. The Left endorsed socialism as a prerequisite for women's rights and liberation. The women's movement divided not only on political lines but some women's organizations did not accept the recognition of women's political and economic rights.

After political independence, women's issues were shelved as a less important agenda item in most states, who claimed that economic stability, development and nation-building were the immediate tasks. It was not even clear whether total liberation of women from all forms of oppression, exploitation and subjection was acceptable, or whether women would be granted their legal rights, especially in the case of Islamic fundamentalists who were opposed to a women's movement altogether.

The post-colonial period

The nature of the post-colonial systems of government only complicated the situation. They were characterized by military dictatorships and single-party rule which adversely affected the women's movement. These governments banned all the previous organizations and formed their own. There emerged pro-government organizations, organizations around presidents' wives or what is called the country's 'First Lady', charity organizations, organizations around specific issues and NGO organizations mainly associated with the programmes of foreign funding agencies.

The neocolonial period

The late 1960s and 1970s marked an important stage in forms adopted by international capital to integrate and dominate African countries. These included aid and development programmes, the expansion of capital in the form of multinational corporations and structural adjustment programmes (SAPs) of the IMF and the World Bank. The policies religiously implemented under these programmes have only brought a negative impact upon the African peoples. For instance, they generally marginalized women, especially those in rural areas; introduced schemes that degraded the environment; caused severe regional disparities; resulted in massive rural–urban migration, and led to the migration of men to join these schemes.

For women in particular they meant an inflated and unplanned informal sector under which women faced a host of problems: harassment by governments, life in an alien new environment, destruction of traditional child care systems, the rising phenomena of female-headed households and increased poverty economically, socially and culturally. Women became objects of study in programmes of integration of women in the process of development – new systems of production based on sexual division of labour to the detriment of women's property, credit marketing rights and their rights to technology and the produce.

However, these are only some of the issues that affect African women. There are many others: female circumcision, child marriage, teenage pregnancy, arranged marriage, aspects of culture and/or religion that justify women's economic, social and political inequalities, polygamy, violence and sexual harassment, women's displacement as a result of war and degradation of the environment, to name a few.

The Pan African Women's Liberation Organization can assist us in addressing these issues. The term 'liberation' appropriately refers to total freedom from all forms of subjugation, exploitation and inequality. In an effort to be practical, the following agenda should be adopted. The Pan African Women's Liberation Organization should:

- bring together all African women with the objective of liberation in a common programme and sustained action to work for improving the situation of African women;

- intervene to solve Africa's problems emanating from the heritage of colonialism, neocolonialism and the present socioeconomic and political order in so far as they adversely affect African people and women, in particular;
- rewrite African women's history with the emphasis on women as agents rather than victims of history;
- address issues of dictatorship;
- address the alarming issue of religious fundamentalism and its impact on women's lives, livelihood and status;
- organize courses, studies and/or seminars to raise the consciousness of women and to encourage them in participating in a liberating Pan African women's movement;
- publish a journal of African women that addresses African women's history, past and present, in order to change their situation, and, finally
- create a centre for providing training and basic education for African women to enable them address their present problems and future challenges.

In conclusion, what we have spelt out above are the minimum commonalities of African women's history, the shared perception of liberation, the challenges we face and the common agenda we share in order to change African women's situation. Enemies and friends have been identified in the face of the ongoing struggle of African women for liberation. It is for us to create a universal African women's liberation movement. We know our problems, programme tasks and future challenges. This is the time to act, in unity, for total liberation and the development of African women and Africa.

Note

1. The Pan African Women's Liberation Organization (PAWLO) was established to help implement the Pan African Women's Plan of Action, following the 7th Pan African Congress, held in Kampala, Uganda 3–8 April 1994. This historic Congress brought together African women from the continent and in the diaspora in a forum of their own, for the first time in the history of the Pan African Congresses. A two-day Pre-Congress Meeting for Women was held. High on the agenda was the challenge to address how participants of the Congress could utilize this unique gathering to act on specific needs of African women. PAWLO elected its leadership with regional coordinators from both Africa and without. The author is the current Chairperson of PAWLO.

Index

Note: Page numbers in bold refer to Tables etc.

Abdul-Raheem, Tajudeen, General Secretary of IPC, 10, 26n
Abdulai, Napoleon, and 7th PAC, 26n
Abiola, Chief M.K.O., 126, 127–8, 137
Abrahams, Peter, at 5th PAC, 4
Abuja Treaty for Establishment of PAEC (1991), 146, 149, 152–3, 232
  implementation of, 155, 234
  see also African Economic Community
ADB *see* African Development Bank
Addis Ababa, OAU Summit (1990), 231, 236
Adjei, Ako, at 5th PAC, 4
affirmative action
  and reparations, 138
  on women's equality, 75, 84
African Alternative Framework to Structural Adjustment Programme, 121
African Capability Building Foundation (ACBF) (Harare), 21, 195
African Declaration of Cooperation, Development and Economic Independence (1973), 146, 153
African Development Bank (ADB), 146, 156, **166**
African Development Fund, **166**
African Economic Community, 151, **166**
  Abuja proposals for, 153–4
  OAU commitment to, 232
  political institutions for, 154–5
African Foundation for Research and Development (AFRAND), 194
African Priority Programme for Economic Recovery, 121
African Regional Integration Commission, proposed, 155
Africanness, 7th PAC definition of, 11, 214
Afro-pessimism, 181, 213–14
agriculture
  as basis for industrialization, 101–2, 105–6, 111
  cash crops for export, 105, 108–9, 110, 170
  and famine, 52
  food crisis, 82, 91
  food grain production, 102, 105
  modernization strategy, 110
  Southern Africa, 168, 169–70
  and use of resources, 170–3
  women's role in, 76–7
  see also resources, natural
aid
  as means of neocolonial rule, 35, 49–50, 62, 203
  see also structural adjustment programmes
Akbar, Mohammed, IPC of 7th PAC, 29n
Algeria, French war in, 132
Alkalimat, Abdul, 27n, 28n

243

All African People's Conferences
  (1958 Accra), 5, 7, 185–6, 187
  (1960 Tunis), 186
  (1962 Cairo), 6, 34–5, 62
Angola, 124, 183
  Anne Nzinga of, 238
  natural resources, 171, 172
  UNITA's treatment of women, 221–2
  war with Portugal, 132–3
apartheid, end of, 201, 229–30
Arab Maghreb Union, **165**
art, African, 200
Association of African Development Finance Institutions, **165**
Awolowo, Obafemi, at 5th PAC, 4, 5
Azikiwe, Nnamdi, at 5th PAC, 4

Babangida, Ibrahim, President of Nigeria, 126, 137
Babu, Abdul Rahman, and 7th PAC, 27n, 28n
Back to Africa movement, 1–2
Bakongo peoples, 186
Banda, Hastings, at 5th PAC, 4, 5
Bandung Declaration (1955), 151
Bank of Central African States (BACAS/BEAC), **163**
Bankie, Bankie Foster, IPC of 7th PAC, 28n
Belgian Congo *see* Congo; Zaire
Berlin Conference (1884), 182
B'Itek, Okot, *Song of Ocol*, 68
borders, and proposed cultural demarcations, 187–9, **188**
borders, state, 19–20, 182, 187
  and ancient cultures, 126–7, 182–3, 187
  and economic cooperation, 149, 151
  and ethnic groupings, 186
Botswana, GDP statistics, 168
bourgeoisie, neocolonial African, 53–4, 55–6
Bretton Woods system, 13, 20, 117, 118–19
  and democracy, 203
  effect on economic development, 107–8
  and power transfer in Africa, 129
  see also IMF; World Bank
Brown, William Wells, abolitionist, 125
Bukharin, N.I., 103–4
bureaucracy, neocolonial, 53–4

Campbell, Horace
  and 6th PAC, 8
  IPC of 7th PAC, 28–9n
capital
  primitive accumulation of, 103, 106, 108
  speculative, 99–100, 101
  strategy for initial accumulation of, 108–11
capitalism
  and democratization, 93–4
  destructiveness of, 224–5, 227
  effect on African women, 219–20
Caribbean
  continuing colonialism in, 215
  education rates for women, 73, 74
  Pan Africanism in, 7, 8, 223–4
  women activists of, 238–9
  see also West Indies
Carmichael, Stokeley *see* Ture, Kwame
causality, calculus of, 129–33
Central African Airways, 146
Cesaire, Aime, Pan Africanist, 200
Chad, 20, 183
Child, Lydia Maria, abolitionist, 125
China
  economic development model, 104–5, 116
  economic experience of, 100
  Japanese annexation of, 103
Chissano, President, of Mozambique, 194
civil rights movement, US, 134, 223

class
    in New Democratic principles, 95
    and Pan Africanism, 218
Cocoyoc Declaration, on development, 41–2
Cold War
    and black advancement, 135
    end of, 205
    and liberation struggles, 208
    see also post-Cold War order
colonialism
    and anti-colonial wars, 132–3
    British model, 135
    culture under, 37–8
    development policies of, 48–9
    economic exploitation of Africa, 46–9
    French model, 135–6
    legacies of, 124, 206–7
    and origins of economic development, 101–2, 106
    women under, 239–40
    see also independence; neocolonialism
COMECON (Communist bloc economic association), 147
common market
    attempts at, 146
    definition of, 149–50
    need for in Africa, 150–3
    see also European Community
commonwealth, proposed African, 185–6
Commonwealth Conference (1971), effect of economic growth, 51
Communate Economique de l'Afrique de l'ouest (FOSIDEC), **162**
communism, and Pan Africanism, 199–200
comparative advantage, and free trade, 119–20
conditionality, effect on poverty, 51, 118–19
confederation, attempts at, 147
conflict resolution, OAU commitment to, 232–3

Congo, Dona Beatrice of the, 238
Congo, Belgian
    and Pan Africanism, 200
    struggles for sovereignty, 208
    see also Zaire
conservatism
    of black US officials, 59
    of educated Africans, 58–9
Conyers, John, US congressman, 134
corruption, 54–5
    and debt contracts, 109–10
crime
    against women, 82
    increasing rate of, 52–3
Crucifixion, The, 131–2
Cuba, and Pan African solidarity, 216
culture
    decline under neocolonialism, 53
    and oral communication, 222
    under colonialism, 37–8
    see also ethnic groupings
currencies
    French franc, 92
    US dollar, 92–3
customs unions, 147

debt
    crisis, 118–19, 122, 152
    renegotiation of, 99, 110
    renunciation of, 109–10
    service payments, 50–1, 82, 107–8
decolonization *see* independence
defence pacts, 146
democracy, 214
    and armed struggle, 205
    lack of, 151
    limitations of colonialist, 202–3, 207–8
    multipartyism, 208–9
    rethinking, 203–5
    see also democratization
democratization, 22, 127, 209–10
    history of, 204
    and market capitalism, 93–4
    OAU commitment to, 233–6

world context of, 202–3
see also New Democracy
desertification, 91
Deve, Thomas, and 7th PAC, 26n, 29n
development
  basis of common market, 154
  Cocoyoc Declaration on, 41–2
  concepts of, 38–9, 40–1
  imperialist view of, 41–5
  as liberation, 56–8
  and poverty, 45, 46–50, 114
  see also economic development; economy
development, sustainable
  policy issues, 176–8
  see also resources
Diallo, Falilou, IPC of 7th PAC, 28n
Diaspora, African
  and Back to Africa movement, 1–2, 5
  and origins of reparationist movement, 123, 125, 138n
  and Pan African Movement, 7, 224
  and post-Cold War order, 89
  scientific skills among, 197
  women in, 15
Diop, Cheikh Anta, 62–3, 200, 205
Distressed and Expatriate Scientists and Scholars from Africa (DESSA), 21, 195
Douglass, Fredrick, black abolitionist, 125
Du Bois, David, IPC of 7th PAC, 28–9n
Du Bois, W.E.B., 2, 11
  and Pan African Congress (1919), 1, 3
Dunen, Jose Van, IPC of 7th PAC, 29n

East Africa, customs and monetary union, 147
East African Community (EAC), 20, 146, 147, 148, 156, **161**
East African Development Bank (EADB/CAE), 146, **161**
East African High Commission (1948-61), defence pact, 146
Economic Community of Central African States (ECCAS/CEAS), **163**
Economic Community of Great Lakes Countries (ECGLC/CEPGL), **164**
Economic Community of West African States (ECOWAS), 20, 151, 156, **161**
economic cooperation, 145
  African common market proposed, 150–3
  alternative approaches to, 147–8
  history of, 146–7
  see also African Economic Community; economic development; economy
economic development
  alternative strategies, 120–1
  Chinese model, 104–5, 116
  economic imperative approach, 113, 114
  expansion strategy, 100–1
  investment for, 235
  Japanese model, 102–3
  New Democratic strategy for, 97–9, 113–15
  reduction of expenditure, 111
  Soviet model, 103–4, 116
  strategy for capital accumulation, 108–11
  US model, 101–2
  see also African Economic Community; economic cooperation; economy
Economic Recovery Programmes (ERP), 63
economy
  Africa's place in world, 115–19
  centrality of, 16, 18, 112, 157, 181–2
  effects of inflation, 82
  extent of crisis, 152, 181

foreign control of, 46–9, 50–1, 64
internal causes of crisis, 119–21, 122
and national currencies, 92
neocolonialist exploitation, 50–1, 90–1
origins of African weakness, 90–1, 97
scientific management of, 112
statistics, 51, 152, 168–9
see also economic cooperation; economic development; industrialization; resources
education, 53, 151, 156
expectations of independence, 38, 40
objectives of, 59–60
and oral tradition of communication, 222
for scientific development, 194–6
statistics, 169
of women, 73–5, **73**, **74**, **75**, 77, 242
Egypt
colonization of, 33
early women rulers, 238
elites
investments by, 211n
and poverty in Southern Africa, 173
embassies, expenditure cuts on, 111
employment, of women, 77–8, **78**
empowerment
democratic, 209
of OAU, 154–5
of private sector, 156–7
and reparations, 127, 128–9
of women, 238
environment, Southern African regional strategy, 173–6
Essack, Karrim, IPC of 7th PAC, 29n
Ethiopia
early empire, 145
empresses of, 238

ethnic groupings, 186
democratization and, 206
and proposed new demarcations, 187–9
and tribal disunity, 60–1
Europe
and economic development of Africa, 44
economic development model, 102
European Community (EC), 62, 145, 156, 215
market approach of, 147–8

famine *see* food crisis
Fanon, Frantz (1925-61), writer, 131, 132
Farrakhan, Louis, US reparations crusader, 134
federations, Central African, 147
Fieldhouse, Professor D.K., 34, 47–9
finance, international, 117–19
financial policies, to control speculative capital, 99–100
food crisis, 91
effect on women, 82
famine, 52
see also agriculture
foreign exchange, savings in, 112
forests and woodlands, in Southern Africa, 171–2
France
colonial policy, 34, 39, 40, 135–6
war in Algeria, 132
free trade
areas, 147
and comparative advantage, 119–20
fuel
electricity, 171, 172–3, 178
wood, 171–2

G7 countries, 203
Gaborone Forum, 21
Garrison, William Lloyd, abolitionist, 125
Garvey, Marcus, 3, 200, 223

GATT (General Agreement on Tariffs and Trade), 117, 203, 215
Germany, economic experience of, 100, 101, 120
Ghana, 145
  and 7th PAC, 10
  independence (1957), 5, 62
globalization, 198
  and consistent democracy, 205–6
Goldsmith, Oliver (1730-74), poet, 131, 132, 133, 138–9n
governments
  and consultative regional planning, 155–6
  and environmental policies, 176–7, 178
  and Pan Africanism, 12, 29n
  role in economic cooperation, 156
  role as facilitators, 197
Guinea-Bissau, war with Portugal, 132
Guyana, WPA in, 223–4

Haiti, 202–3
health services, 156
  cost-sharing schemes, 53, 79
  for women, 70, 78–80, **79**
Horn of Africa, exceptionalism of, 187
Houphouet-Boigny, Felix, of Cote d'Ivoire, 135
human rights
  abuse of, 52, 55, 209
  and democracy, 205

Ibn Battuta, Moroccan traveller, 35–6
Ibrahim, Gora, Azania delegate, 11
IMF
  advantage of free trade, 120
  economic control by, 50
  effect of fiscal policies, 100
  role of, 118–19
  see also Structural Adjustment Policies

independence
  and decolonization, 6, 62, 229–30
  expectations of, 37–9, 55, 201, 215
  struggle for, 33–8, 215
  and struggle for Second Liberation, 55–6, 207
India, domestic industry, 197
industrialization
  from agricultural base, 101–2, 105–6, 111
  Chinese model, 104–5
  and domestic markets, 197
  limits imposed on, 43–4
  in Southern Africa, 169–70
  Soviet model, 104
  strategy for, 98–9
International Women's Year (1975), 70
  Mexico World Conference, 71–2
IPC (International Preparatory Committee) for 7th PAC, 9, 10, 13, 26–7n, 28–9nn, 212
Ivory Coast (Cote d'Ivoire), 114, 135

James, C.L.R., 8, 9, 11, 27n
Japan
  and African industrialization, 44
  economic experience of, 101
  model of economic development, 102–3
Johnson, Lyndon B., US President, 135
Johnson, Wallace, at 5th PAC, 4

Kampala Group of 7th PAC, 9
Kamunanwire, Perezi, IPC of 7th PAC, 29n
Kenya
  economy, 114
  free trade area with Uganda, 147
  independent churches in, 37
  Muthoni wa Kirima of, 238
  post-colonial elite in, 41

Kenyatta, Jomo
  at 5th PAC, 4, 6, 151
  land policy, 39
King, Dr Yvonne, IPC of 7th PAC, 29n
Kinshasa Declaration (1976), 146, 153
Kongo society, 200, 203
  Lemba Kangaism in, 199
Korea, North, 116
Kwayana, Eusi
  IPC of 7th PAC, 28–9n
  and need for sprituality, 225–6
  on Pan Africanism, 217, 218–19, 223–4
Kzibwe, Dr Specioza Wandire, Ugandan Vice President, 80

La Communate Economique de l'Afrique de l'ouest (CEAO), **162**
labour, use of social labour time, 105, 108–9
Lagos Group of 7th PAC, 9, 10, 11–12
Lagos Plan of Action and Final Act (1980), 146, 153, 231
  strategy for economic development, 121
Lake Chad Basin Commission, **163**
land
  and access to resources, 37, 168, 178
  neocolonialist policies on, 39–40
languages, independence and, 38, 40
Latin America, education rates for women, 73, 74
law, and justice for women, 80
Le Fonds de Solidarite et d'Intervention pour le Developpe, **162**
Le Fonds d'Entraide et de Garantie des Emprunts du Conseil de l'Entente, **162**
leadership
  corrupt, 54–5, 109–10, 216
  economic, 157
  judging, 127
  leaderism, 222
  political accountability of, 151
  radical, 95–6, 97
  weaknesses of, 63, 90, 112
Lemba Kangaism, doctrine of, 199, 206
liberalism, and abolition of slavery, 124
liberation
  intellectual, 58–60
  movements, 7, 8
  of women, 241–2
  see also independence; Second Liberation
Liberia, 20, 124, 183
Libyan Group of 7th PAC, 9–10
Lincoln, Abraham, as abolitionist, 125
L'Ouverture, Toussaint, 199
L'Union Dovaniere et Economique de l'Afrique Centrale (UDEAC), **162**
Lwanga, Serwanga, Publicity Secretary of IPC, 10, 27n

Maghreb, Kahina of the, Berber prophetess, 238
Makerere University (Uganda), places for women, 75, 84
Malawi
  education rates, 169
  water resources, 172
Mali, early empire, 145
management
  economic, 112
  regional strategies, 173–6
Mano River Union (MRU), **164**
Mao Zedong, economic policies, 104–5
Marshall Plan (1948-52), 128
Masai people, 186
Masire, President, of Botswana, 194
Matembe, Miriam, Deputy General Secretary of IPC, 10
Mayombo, Noble, and 7th PAC, 26n, 27n

M'ba, President of Gabon, 39
m'Bow, Professor Mohtar, 137
Middle Passage Plan, for Africa, 128–9
mining, 169, 170
monetary union, regional, 147
Monrovia Strategy for Economic Development (1979), 146, 153
Mozambique, 183
   education rates, 169
   forests, 171
   war with Portugal, 132, 133
   women in, 220–1
Mugabe, Robert, President of Zimbabwe, 30n
Mulele, Pierre, Congolese militant, 208
Museveni, Yoweri, President of Uganda, 27, 81

NAFTA (North American Free Trade Agreement), 145, 215
Nairobi Conference, strategies for advancement of women, 70–1
Namibia
   access to resources, 168
   independence, 229
nationalism
   and African tradition, 189
   and consultative regional planning, 156
   and Pan Africanism, 224
   progressive nature of, 97
   used to fight colonialism, 182, 184
   see also neocolonialism
nationalist movements, 201
   at All African People's conferences, 6
NATO (North Atlantic Treaty Organization), 62, 215
neocolonialism, 34–5
   anti-development nature of, 49–50, 56–8
   and concept of development, 38–9, 40–1
   continued economic exploitation under, 50–1
   of international institutions, 214–15
   within United States, 136
   women under, 241–2
neofascism, 89
New Democracy
   economic development strategy, 97–9
   political organization for, 96–7
   principles of, 94–6
NGOs (non-governmental organizations), 12, 62–3
   and environmental issues, 177
   Pan Africanism and, 209
   for regional cooperation, 147
Nigeria
   and 7th PAC, 12, 30n
   Chief Abiola and, 127–8
   women leaders in, 238
Njem, Jean-Claude, IPC of 7th PAC, 29n
Nkrumah, Dr Kwame, 5, 11, 150
   Declaration to Colonial Peoples at 5th PAC, 4–5, 215
   on lack of democracy, 151
Nkrumah, Gorkeh, IPC of 7th PAC, 28n
non-alignment, 116
Nuba, early empire, 145
Nyerere, Julius
   and 6th PAC, 7–8
   and *Ujamaa* experiment, 57

OAU (Organization of African Unity), 6, 151, 189, 219, 229
   empowerment of, 154–5
   legitimization of borders, 184, 186
   limitations of, 6–7, 184, 207, 236
   and reparationist movement, 126, 137
   role for, 23–4, 231, 235–6
   struggle against apartheid, 229–30
   support for Pan Africanism, 234–5

Ocan, Akidi, 28n
ODA (Official Development Assistance) agencies, 152, 156
Ondoga ori Amaza, Deputy Publicity Secretary of IPC, 10, 26n
Osahon, Brother Naiwu, Lagos Group, 9, 27n, 30n
Otafiire, Col. Kahinda, Ugandan NRA/M, 10, 28n

Padmore, George, 11, 200
PAEC *see* African Economic Community
Pan African Congresses
  (1900 London), 1, 2
  1st (1919 Paris), 1, 3, 150, 151
  2nd (1921 Brussels), 3, 200
  3rd (1923 London & Lisbon), 3
  4th (1927 New York), 3
  5th (1945 Manchester), 4–5, 61, 151, 201
  6th (1974 Dar-es-Salaam), 5–8, 218, 221
  7th (1994 Kampala), 1, 8–25, 26–7n, 183, 212
  see also All African People's conferences; IPC; Pan African movement
Pan African movement, 184–5, 212–14
  commitment to, 11–13
  and definition of Pan Africanism, 217–19
  and democratization, 22–3
  economic proposals, 92–4
  leadership problems, 184, 216
  in multiracial societies, 223–4
  need for spiritual renewal, 213–14, 224–5
  permanent secretariat for, 23
  place in world history, 198–202
  and political borders, 183, 186, 187, 189
  reconceptualization of, 215–17
  revival of, 6–8, 64, 213–14, 226–7, 235
  and role of women, 220–2
  and the Second Liberation, 60–3, 64, 206–9
Pan African Women's Liberation Organization (PAWLO), 23, 25, 237–8, 241–2, 242n
peace, women's contribution to, 81–2
Peru, EZLN in, 205
political accountability, of leaders, 151
political restructuring, proposed, 181–9
politics *see* democratization; government; New Democracy
population, Southern Africa, 168, 169
Portugal, anti-colonial wars, 132–3
post-Cold War order, African crisis in, 89–90, 122, 181
poverty
  and development, 45, 46–50
  increasing, 51, 52–5
  and resource utilization, 178–9
  Southern Africa, 173
Powell, General Colin, US army chief, 135
Preferential Trade Area (PTA), 146, 156, **164**
Presidential Forum on Science and Technology, 21, 194
private sector
  empowerment of, 156–7
  role in African Economic Community, 153
  and technology transfer, 196

racism, 89, 137, 198
  racial hierarchy, 200
  struggle against, 214, 217, 223
  in United States, 124, 135
radicalism, role for, 94–7
regional cooperation
  attempts at, **159–60**, **161–6**
  consultative, 155–6
  problems of, 147–8
  on resources, 172–3
  Southern Africa, 167–8

regionalism, 18–19
  new regions proposed, 20–1
religion
  independent churches, 37
  missionaries, 37–8
  and need for renewed spirituality, 224–6
religious fundamentalism, 225
  democracy and, 206
  Islamic, 240
reparationist movement, 124–6
reparations (for slavery), 16–17, 137–8
  calculus of causality, 129–33
  cost-benefit analysis, 133–6
  cultural origins of, 136
  empowerment of states, 127, 128–9
  empowerment within states (democracy), 127
  Middle Passage Plan, 128–9, 134
  role of the West in, 127–9
research and development, need for increased, 196
resources, human, 152, 177, 179
  and education for science, 195
  Southern Africa, 168–70
  see also education; science; technology
resources, natural
  in proposed new demarcations, 188
  regional management strategies, 173–6
  and sustainable development, 176–8, 179, 234
  use patterns in Southern Africa, 170–3
  water, 172–3
  woodfuel, 171–2
Rhodesia and Nyasaland, Central African Federation of, 147
Rodney, Walter
  and 6th PAC, 8, 11, 27n, 63
  and Guyanan experience, 223–4
  on Pan Africanism, 217
Rwanda, 124, 183

Sabelo-Phama, Victor, IPC of 7th PAC, 29n
Savimbi, Jonas, of UNITA, 221
science
  development of, 21–2, 193
  need to repatriate trained African scientists, 195
  research and development, 194
  see also education; technology
Second Liberation
  demand for, 55–6, 63–4
  Pan Africanism and, 60–3, 64, 206–9, 226–7
self-determination, 182, 184
self-sufficiency, 102, 105, 193
Sene-Gambia defence pact, 146
Senegal, as French colony, 135
Senghor, Leopold Sedar, of Senegal, 135, 136
Shamuyarira, Dr Nathan, Zimbabwe foreign minister, 30n
slavery
  abolitionist movement, 123–4
  Arab, 11, 16
  effect on African society, 206–7
  effect on technological development, 193
  and emancipation, 133–4
  indigenous, 123
  and origins of economic development, 101–2, 105, 106
  and origins of Pan Africanism, 198–9, 200, 206–7, 212–14
  phases of benefits of, 131
  transatlantic, 11, 17, 123, 201
  see also Diaspora; reparations
Slovo, Joe, 11
social conditions
  and concept of development, 56–8
  decline of, 151, 207
  effect of neocolonialism on, 51–3
  in New Democracy, 95
  potential for conflict, 54–5
  and underdevelopment, 45–6
social movements, 208

socialism
    African versions of, 116
    Ujamaa experiment, 57
    world movement, 115–16
Somali peoples, 186
Somalia, 20, 124, 183
Songhai, early empire, 145
South Africa
    democratization of, 201, 205, 212, 215, 230, 233
    GDP statistics, 168
    urbanization in, 168
    water resources, 172
Southeast Asia
    economic development models, 103
    education in, 194
Southern Africa
    education rates for women, 73, 74
    regional cooperation, 167–8
    resource use strategies, 167
Southern African Customs Union (SACU), 147, **164**
Southern African Development Coordination (SADC), 167 Conference (SADCC), **165**, 173–6
Soviet Union, economic development model, 103–4
Stowe, Harriet Beecher, 125
Structural Adjustment Policies (IMF/World Bank), 14, 45, 51–2, 62–3, 92–3, 152
    need for regional, 156
Sub-Saharan Africa
    education of women, 73, 74
    see also Southern Africa
Sudan, 183
    and 7th PAC, 10, 29n
    women rulers of, 238
Sutherland, Bill, Coordinator 6th PAC, 26n
Swaziland, water resources, 172

Tanzania
    elections, 233
    forests, 171
    host to 6th PAC, 7–8

technology
    development of, 21
    importance of, 193–4
    old and new, 111, 156
    and resource utilization, 174–5, 178
Thomas, Clarence, US Supreme Court judge, 136
Thompson, Dudley, Jamaican diplomat, 137
TNCs (transnational corporations)
    African executives of, 41
    economic control of, 50, 90–1
towns *see* urbanization
trade
    adverse terms of, 50, 108
    African share of world, 152
    basis of common market, 154
    basis of European economic development, 102
    and colonization, 106
    free, 119–20, 147
    and protectionism, 120
    and Rules of Origin, 149
    treaties, 146
trade unions, under neocolonialism, 52
transport, public, 111
Trinidad, 223
Tuareg nomads, 188
Ture, Kwame (Stokely Carmichael), IPC of 7th PAC, 29n

Uganda
    Asians in, 48
    copper processing, 43
    education programme, 194–5
    education of women, 73–5, **73**, **74**, **75**
    elections, 233
    employment of women, 77–8, **78**
    free trade area with Kenya, 147
    host to 7th PAC, 10–11, 13, 27n
    origins of anti-colonialism in, 36, 39–40

role of women in agriculture, 76–7
status of women, 72–3
women in public life, 80–1
women's health, 79–80, **79**
Union Congolaise (1919-30), 200
United Kingdom
   and decolonization, 34
   opposition to Uganda, 13
United Nations, 203
   and African Priority Programme for Economic Recovery, 121
   Economic Commission for Africa (UNECA), 121
   influence of Africa in, 128, 129, 137–8
   and rights of women, 70
   statistical indicators for women, 71–2
United States
   civil rights movement, 134, 223
   Congressional Black Caucus, 125
   decline of hegemony, 118
   and economic development of Africa, 43–4
   emancipation of slaves, 134
   legacy of slavery in, 130–1
   model of economic development, 101–2
   and Pan African solidarity, 217
   racism in, 124, 135, 201–2
   women activists of, 238
urbanization
   effect on women, 78, 82
   and increased poverty, 52, 107
   Southern Africa, 168
USAID, 156

Wachuku, Jaja, at 5th PAC, 4, 5
Walker, David, Pan Africanist, 217
Wangel, Empresses Helena and Sabla, of Ethiopia, 238
water resources, 172–3, 178
West African Development Bank (WADB/BOAD), **163**
West African Economic Community (WAEC/UMOA/CEAO) (1962 and 1974), **163**
West African Students Union (WASU), at 5th PAC, 4
West Indies (British), compensation to slave-owners, 133–4
Wilberforce, William, abolitionist, 124, 125
wildlife, as resource, 111, 174, 175, 176, 178–9
Williams, Henry Sylvester, Pan African Congress (1900), 1, 2, 26n
women
   ancestral models for, 238–9
   contribution to peace, 81–2
   earliest role of, 69
   employment, 77–8, **78**
   health services for, 78–80, **79**
   and justice, 80
   marginalization of, 14–15, 67–8, 169
   milestones towards equality, 69–71
   organizations, 208, 219, 220, 237, 239, 240
   and Pan Africanism, 214, 215, 218, 219–22
   policies for equality, 83–5
   policy gaps on, 77–8
   in post-colonial period, 240–1
   and poverty, 82
   in public life, 80–1
   role in agriculture, 76–7
   role in resistance, 213, 239–40
   traditional perception of, 68–9, 72–3
   under colonialism, 239–40
   under neocolonialism, 241–2
   and urbanization, 82
   see also Pan African Women's Liberation Organization (PAWLO)
World Bank (IBRD)
   advantage of free trade, 120

development model, 41
economic control by, 50
opposition to industrialization, 43
see also Structural Adjustment Policies
World Health Organization (WHO), and women's issues, 70–1
World Trade Organization, 203, 215

Yoruba peoples, 186
and reparationist movement, 126

Zaire, 183
colonial exploitation of, 47
liberation struggles, 208–9
Zambia
agriculture, 170
natural resources, 171, 172
urbanization in, 168
Zanzibar, 111
Zimbabwe
agriculture, 170
early empire, 145
natural resources, 168, 172
Nehanda of (1863-98), 238
Zulu, early empire, 145

Index by Auriol Griffith-Jones